Everyman, I will go with thee,
and be thy guide

THE EVERYMAN
LIBRARY

The Everyman Library was founded by J. M. Dent in 1906. He chose the name Everyman because he wanted to make available the best books ever written in every field to the greatest number of people at the cheapest possible price. He began with Boswell's 'Life of Johnson'; his one-thousandth title was Aristotle's 'Metaphysics', by which time sales exceeded forty million.

Today Everyman paperbacks remain true to J. M. Dent's aims and high standards, with a wide range of titles at affordable prices in editions which address the needs of today's readers. Each new text is reset to give a clear, elegant page and to incorporate the latest thinking and scholarship. Each book carries the pilgrim logo, the character in 'Everyman', a medieval mystery play, a proud link between Everyman past and present.

William Shakespeare

KING LEAR

Edited by
JOHN F. ANDREWS

Foreword by
HAL HOLBROOK

EVERYMAN
J. M. DENT · LONDON
CHARLES E. TUTTLE
VERMONT

First published in Everyman by J. M. Dent 1993
Published by permission of GuildAmerica Books, an imprint of Doubleday Book and Music Clubs, Inc.

Reprinted 1993, 1998, 2000 (twice)

Photoset by Deltatype Ltd, Birkenhead, Merseyside
Printed in Great Britain by
The Guernsey Press Co. Ltd, Guernsey, C.I.
for
J. M. Dent
Orion Publishing Group
Orion House
5 Upper St Martin's Lane
London WC2H 9EA
and
Tuttle Publishing
Airport Industrial Park, 364 Innovation Drive
North Clarendon, VT 05759-9436, USA

British Library Cataloguing-in-Publication Data is available upon request.

ISBN 0 460 87333 4

CONTENTS

NOTE ON AUTHOR AND EDITOR

William Shakespeare is held to have been born on St George's Day, 23 April 1564. The eldest son of a prosperous glove-maker in Stratford-upon-Avon, he was probably educated at the town's grammar school.

Tradition holds that between 1585 and 1592, Shakespeare first became a schoolteacher and then set off for London. By 1595 he was a leading member of the Lord Chamberlain's Men, helping to direct their business affairs, as well as being a playwright and actor. In 1598 he became a part-owner of the company, which was the most distinguished of its age. However, he maintained his contacts with Stratford, and his family seem to have remained there.

From about 1610 he seems to have grown increasingly involved in the town's affairs, suggesting a withdrawal from London. He died on 23 April 1616, in his 53rd year, and was buried at Holy Trinity two days later.

John F. Andrews has recently completed a 19-volume edition, *The Guild Shakespeare*, for the Doubleday Book and Music Clubs. He is also the editor of a 3-volume reference set, *William Shakespeare: His World, His Work, His Influence*, and the former editor (1974–85) of the journal *Shakespeare Quarterly*. From 1974 to 1984, he was director of Academic Programs at the Folger Shakespeare Library in Washington and Chairman of the Folger Institute.

CHRONOLOGY OF SHAKESPEARE'S LIFE

Year[1]	*Age*	*Life*
1564		Shakespeare baptized 26 April at Stratford-upon-Avon
1582	18	Marries Anne Hathaway
1583	19	Daughter, Susanna, born
1585	21	Twin son and daughter, Hamnet and Judith, born
1590–1	26	*The Two Gentlemen of Verona* & *The Taming of the Shrew*
1591	27	*2 & 3 Henry VI*
1592	28	*Titus Andronicus* & *1 Henry VI*
1592–3		*Richard III*
1593	29	*Venus and Adonis* published
1594	30	*The Comedy of Errors. The Rape of Lucrece* published
1594–5		*Love's Labour's Lost*
1595	31	*A Midsummer Night's Dream*, *Romeo and Juliet*, & *Richard II*. An established member of Lord Chamberlain's Men
1596	32	*King John*. Hamnet dies
1596–7		*The Merchant of Venice* & *1 Henry IV*
1597	33	Buys New Place in Stratford The Lord Chamberlain's Men's lease to play at the Theatre expires; until 1599 they play mainly at the Curtain

1 It is rarely possible to be certain about the dates at which plays of this period were written. For Shakespeare's plays, this chronology follows the dates preferred by Wells and Taylor, the editors of the Oxford Shakespeare. Publication dates are given for poetry and books.

CHRONOLOGY OF HIS TIMES

Year	*Literary Context*	*Historical Events*
1565–7	Golding, Ovid's *Metamorphoses*, tr.	Elizabeth I reigning
1574	*A Mirror for Magistrates* (3rd ed.)	
1576	London's first playhouse built	
1578	John Lyly, *Euphues*	
1579	North, Plutarch's *Lives*, tr. Spenser, *Shepherd's Calender*	
1587	Marlowe, *I Tamburlaine*	Mary Queen of Scots executed
1588	Holinshed's *Chronicles* (2nd ed.)	Defeat of Spanish Armada
1589	Kyd, *Spanish Tragedy* Marlowe, *Jew of Malta*	Civil war in France
1590	Spenser, *Faerie Queene*, Bks I–III	
1591	Sidney, *Astrophel and Stella*	Proclamation against Jesuits
1592	Marlowe, *Dr Faustus* & *Edward II*	Scottish witchcraft trials Plague closes theatres from June
1593	Marlowe killed	
1594	Nashe, *Unfortunate Traveller*	Theatres reopen in summer
1594–6		Extreme food shortages
1595	Sidney, *An Apologie for Poetry*	Riots in London
1596		Calais captured by Spanish Cadiz expedition
1597	Bacon, *Essays*	

Year	*Age*	*Life*
1597–8		*The Merry Wives of Windsor* & *2 Henry IV*
1598	34	*Much Ado About Nothing*
1598–9		*Henry V*
1599	35	*Julius Caesar*. One of syndicate responsible for building the Globe in Southwark, where the Lord Chamberlain's Men now play
1599–1600		*As You Like It*
1600–1		*Hamlet*
1601	37	*Twelfth Night*. His father is buried in Stratford
1602	38	*Troilus and Cressida*. Invests £320 in land near Stratford[2]
1603	39	*Measure for Measure*. The Lord Chamberlain's Men become the King's Men. They play at court more than all the other companies combined
1603–4		*Othello*
c.1604	40	Shakespeare sues Philip Rogers of Stratford for debt
1604–5		*All's Well That Ends Well*
1605	41	*Timon of Athens*. Invests £440 in Stratford tithes
1605–6		*King Lear*
1606	42	*Macbeth* & *Antony and Cleopatra*
1607	43	*Pericles*. Susanna marries the physician John Hall in Stratford
1608	44	*Coriolanus*. The King's Men lease Blackfriars, an indoor theatre. His only grandchild is born. His mother dies
1609	45	*The Winter's Tale*. 'Sonnets' and 'A Lover's Complaint' published
1610	46	*Cymbeline*
1611	47	*The Tempest*
1613	49	*Henry VIII*. Buys house in London for £140
1613–14		*The Two Noble Kinsmen*
1616	52	Judith marries Thomas Quiney, a vintner, in Stratford. On 23 April he dies, and is buried two days later
1623		Publication of the First Folio. His widow dies in August

2 A schoolmaster would earn around £20 a year at this time.

Year	Literary Context	Historical Events
1598	Marlowe and Chapman, *Hero and Leander*	Rebellion in Ireland
	Jonson, *Every Man in his Humour*	
1599	Children's companies begin playing	Essex fails in Ireland
	Thomas Dekker's *Shoemaker's Holiday*	
1601	'War of the Theatres'	Essex rebels and is executed
	Jonson, *Poetaster*	
1602		Tyrone defeated in Ireland
1603	Florio, Montaigne's *Essays*, tr.	Elizabeth I dies, James I accedes
		Raleigh found guilty of treason
1604	Marston, *The Malcontent*	Peace with Spain
1605	Bacon, *Advancement of Learning*	Gunpowder plot
1606	Jonson, *Volpone*	
1607	Tourneur, *The Revenger's Tragedy*, published	Virginia colonized
		Enclosure riots
1609		Oath of allegiance
		Truce in Netherlands
1610	Jonson, *Alchemist*	
1611	Authorised Version of the Bible	
	Donne, *Anatomy of the World*	
1612	Webster, *White Devil*	Prince Henry dies
1613	Webster, *Duchess of Malfi*	Princess Elizabeth marries
1614	Jonson, *Bartholomew Fair*	
1616	Folio edition of Jonson's plays	

Biographical note, chronology and plot summary compiled by John Lee, University of Bristol, 1993.

FOREWORD by Hal Holbrook

So many great minds have written about *King Lear* that one is humbled by the sheer weight of scholarship laid upon this play. Rather than add any small ounce of tonnage to the scales, I would like to remove some. I am an actor and what follows are the discoveries of one actor who has played the role of King Lear.

There are those who have said that this play is not producible, but these are mostly literary folk like Charles Lamb and I believe they are wrong. I think it is very difficult to do the play well – to make the story, relationships, and intentions clear and to soar in performance to its imperious height – and I believe this is the reason it has seemed so daunting. But Shakespeare wrote this play for actors, so it is as an actor who has tried to scale this height that I speak to you. If I confine myself mainly to the character of Lear I hope you will forgive me. I see the play through him.

An actor approaching the role of King Lear must first look past the word 'King' and search for the human being. What I have missed in most performances of *King Lear* is this human being in Lear. The man I can identify with. The person I know. Too often he has seemed a sonorous figure in a long gown growling and howling his way through the scenery; or so physically fragile at the start that a full development of the character's arc is unattainable and his ability to carry Cordelia on at the end unconvincing.

Lear is an eighty-year-old patriarch who has fought his way to the top in a sometimes brutal and primitive world, and as this play begins he is finally confronting the fact that he is going to die. I say 'finally' because I doubt he's ever considered himself vulnerable enough to die. Death is for the weak and Lear scorns weakness. He is a man bursting with the primal energy of life, even at eighty years old; a warrior and a hunter, a tribal chieftain in ancient Britain. His sword, not divine right, has made him King.

But his mind is slipping. The paranoia of age is stalking him and he cannot fight it off. His memory has sudden blank spots in it, his flesh has fallen and his joints cry out in pain. These are real devils because they produce the humiliation that comes with age. They make Lear angry and impatient and even more arrogant as he – in his ironic phrase – 'crawl[s] toward Death'.

So in the opening scene of the play he gathers his three daughters to him in front of his entire court and makes a senile game of his confrontation with the spectre of death. He requires his daughters to state publicly 'which of you, shall we say, doth love us most'. It's a shock to them. The two older daughters play the game smoothly, telling him exactly what he wants to hear. They are interested in real estate, not truth. But Cordelia, his youngest daughter and the star of his heart, refuses to play the game. Lear is humiliated. He chokes on this bile, banishes her from his kingdom, and thus the wheel of fire begins to turn.

Goneril and Regan, having been awarded possession of the kingdom, suffer their father's presence but thinly. When Lear returns to Goneril's castle from the hunt, it becomes clear that he has no intention of giving over his powers to anyone. With his train of a hundred loud and sweaty men, 'breaking forth in rank and not-to-be-endur'd Riots', Lear is like a bull. It is important to take note of Lear's excesses because they are an integral part of the fabric of his character. He is a very, very difficult old man. Boisterous, demanding, arrogant. He expects absolute obedience.

> Idle Old Man,
> That still would manage those Authorities
> That he hath given away.

Infuriated by his behaviour, Goneril belittles her father and threatens to restrict his freedom, enraging Lear to such a pitch that he lays a curse on her and leaves.

It is in this scene that the theme of ingratitude is sounded loudly. This is a theme to which Lear will return over and over again throughout the play. The ingratitude of his daughters is the wound which festers in Lear's heart. It bewilders him and leads him towards the brink of the madness which he fears. 'I prythee, Daughter, do not make me Mad', he begs in the next scene when both daughters face him, attacking his manhood by reminding him that he is old, attacking his pride by scorning him. They gang up on him, jabbing verbal darts into his ancient flesh like matadors. When they cut his hundred men down to a single one, Lear's rage bursts all fetters. His fury past control, Lear hurls these words of defiance at them and roars out into the storm:

> You think I'll weep,
> No, I'll not weep. I have full Cause of Weeping,
> But this Heart shall break into a hundred thousand Flaws
> Or ere I'll weep.

By this point in the story we have been made aware of Edmund's treachery against his brother and father and of Gloucester's gullibility. Cornwall's treachery has been hinted at. We are beginning to get the picture of a kingdom that is up for grabs, one that is essentially leaderless now and where corruption and greed are going to thrive. The smell of corruption is heavy in the play. It is said that Shakespeare chose to set the story of Lear in a pagan environment where the earthy innocence of such a society could be corrupted by sophistication and cynicism, by such schemers as Edmund, Cornwall, Oswald, Goneril, and Regan.

Shakespeare makes it clear to me that Lear is not a man of conscious intellect. If he were, he would see the bitter humour of his foolishness and not go mad. But the Fool is an intellectual and the relationship between them is constantly that of the teacher (Fool) trying to make the adult student (Lear) understand what is happening, what is being done to him and what he is doing to himself.

> LEAR Dost thou call me Fool, Boy?
> FOOL All thy other Titles thou hast given away,
> that thou wast borne with.

Lear can brutalize the Fool one minute, knock him down, and then be humoured or touched by him in the next. Their relationship is very volatile. In some places it is tender, as in the scene between them after Lear has cursed Goneril. The Fool warns him:

> Thou should'st not have been Old till thou
> hadst been Wise.

The storm. Lear now presents himself to the gods, calling upon them to destroy everything – the earth itself – with thunder, lightning, wind, and rain. It is a duel between flesh and the universe and Lear is beaten – 'I will be the pattern of all patience. I will say nothing.'

But only for a moment. Now his focus shifts to the world at large, to mankind's enemies and his: the murderers, the perjurers, the simulators of virtue, the hypocrites, and those who conceal their guilt. He exhorts the gods to punish them and forgive him: 'I am a man more sinned against than sinning.' His pleas are drowned out by their indifference as the storm howls on.

Then, exhausted, Lear does something strange – for King Lear. For the first time he shows concern for his fellow man in the person of the Fool. 'Art cold? I am cold myself', he says, and takes him inside the shelter. This moment is the first conscious turning away of Lear's mind from his rage and, strangely, the turn is towards sympathy for another human being. Interesting. Could this mean that beneath the wintry bluster there is a soft heart? That love hides somewhere there?

In the very next scene a great moment of self-realization begins to dawn in Lear. He has clung steadfastly to the conviction that he is a loving father, despite all evidence to the contrary. He says:

> O Regan, Goneril,
> Your old kind father, whose frank heart gave all –

He pauses. Note Shakespeare's dash. It means something. Then:

> O, that way madness lies, let me shun that!
> No more of that.

Shun what? No more of what?? For the longest time the meaning of these lines escaped me. I grew to hate them. I complained to our director, Gerald Freedman, that I didn't understand what in the hell Lear was talking about here and how stupid could he be to think he was a 'kind father'. Performances of a tremulous, pathetic Lear full of self-pity retched in my mind and blinded me to what Shakespeare was saying. Jerry remained quiet and waited for me to see the obvious – the obvious, which is sometimes the most elusive truth of all. One night, as I cried 'your old kind father, whose frank heart gave all –', the darkness in my mind parted. I thought, 'My God, I *believe* this! I am *trying* to be kind. I think I am kind. I gave my kingdom to them, didn't I?' Then the shadow of doubt fell on me – 'Maybe I wasn't kind . . .' – and doubt begat the line:

> O, that way madness lies, let me shun that!
> No more of that.

The light, the light had struck my poor mind. Now stunned by uncertainty I turned to John Woodson (Kent) and said:

> Prythee, go in thyself; seek thine own Ease,
> This tempest will not give me leave to ponder
> *On things would hurt me more . . .*

There it was. The turning point in the play.

Lear prays. He does not acknowledge his lack of kindness, his failure as a father. Instead, he prays for the poor naked wretches who have no home. Like himself. In this moment of self-realization I believe Lear slips into madness. I think it happens here, not earlier, and is the direct result of Lear's refusal to face the awful truth that has exploded in his mind. His very next line in the scene is one of derangement. It comes upon Edgar's entrance. Lear sees this naked wretch and says:

> Didst thou give all to thy daughters? And
> art thou come to this?

He listens to this babbling outcast, another of the 'discarded fathers' of this world, and decides to learn from him: '. . . let me talk with this philosopher'.

The mock trial comes next. Lear arraigns his daughters in an imaginary court, crying 'is there any cause in nature that makes these hard hearts?' Then his tired brain stops spinning and he falls into a frantic, restless sleep.

We don't see Lear again for a long time. Meanwhile the coils of Evil spread and fester in the subplot of the play, its tentacles ensnaring all. Gloucester is blinded. The conspirators begin to turn upon one another in a frenzy of greed and self-gratification. When Edgar escorts his sightless father to Dover, Lear wanders into the play again, leaves and flowers in his hair, mind aflame with plans to mount an army and go on the march against his enemies. He stares at Gloucester: 'Ha! Goneril, with a White Beard!' And then: 'They flatter'd me like a Dog. . . ! To say "Ay" and "No" to everything that I said . . .' (Who's he talking about? Gloucester?) 'I pardon that Man's Life. What was thy Cause? Adultery?' (Gloucester committed adultery.) '. . . Die for Adultery! No; the Wren goes to 't . . .'

Gloucester has jested about his adultery in the opening scene of the play. Lear is focusing his scorn on him now. Gloucester, the good-hearted adulterer, the old friend at court who is a yes-man to Lear ('They are not men o' their words'), who has played the diplomatic game at court and been betrayed by his own bastard son; who has banished his true son, Edgar, crouching like Tom o' Bedlam nearby. Gloucester has been a blind fool. 'I remember thine eyes well enough . . . blind Cupid.'

Now, worn down by the intensity of his own scathing tirades against the hypocrisy and hatefulness of a world he at last sees clearly, Lear acknowledges Gloucester, this man who, like himself, has been blind to the corruption around him:

LEAR If thou wilt weep my Fortunes, take my Eyes.
I know thee well enough; thy name is Gloucester.
Thou must be Patient. We came crying hither:
Thou know'st the first time that we smell the Air
We wawl and cry. I will preach to thee. Mark.
GLOUCESTER Alack, alack the Day!
LEAR When we are borne, we cry that we are come
To this great stage of fools.

The wheel of fire upon which Lear has spun throughout his long torture rolls to a momentary stop here. It pauses while the great truth of life comes home to these two old brokenhearted fools. I believe this is the moment of greatest philosophic penetration in the play as well as one of deep emotional catharsis for us all. Lear not only sees the truth of his utter vulnerability, he shares it with another human being in pain.

The rest of this sad story moves like a great symphony towards the final bitter coda, the unsweet taste of truth. After being found by Cordelia, the daughter Lear loves and has banished, the two of them are captured, imprisoned, and she is killed in front of him. He bears her forth, howling the primal cry of all pain-struck creatures, and lays her down upon the ground. He grieves for her and lies down by her side and dies.

This play touches me to my heart and soul and I think that even in the final scene of death there is beauty. The beauty of truth. The truth about the pain that stalks us all if we do not learn to love in time; and which may strike us even then.

From his early days with the Lincoln Center Repertory in New York through fifty-odd feature and television films, HAL HOLBROOK has become known as an actor's actor. The recipient of four Emmys, the Tony and Peabody Awards, his one-man show *Mark Twain Tonight!* has become a classic of the American theatre.

The rest of [illegible] moves [illegible]
the final [illegible]
[illegible]
[illegible]
[illegible]
[illegible]
[illegible]

This play [illegible]
[illegible]
[illegible]
[illegible]

[illegible]
[illegible]
[illegible]
[illegible]
[illegible] theatre.

EDITOR'S INTRODUCTION TO *King Lear*

Can you make no use of Nothing, Nuncle?
(I.iv.139–40)

The clown who asks what sounds like a frivolous question is a self-professed Fool. He claims no wisdom, and he possesses no authority. As the King's jester, he doesn't even pretend to syntactic coherence. But in a world that exhibits less reason than do the rhymes of an imbecile, his 'Matter and Impertinency mix'd' will prove altogether to the point.

By emphasizing a noun that reverberates from the beginning of the drama to its end, the Fool calls attention to the paradox at the core of *King Lear*. His query echoes the pivotal exchange of the opening scene, where Lear asks his youngest daughter, Cordelia, what she can say to win her father's amplest bounty, and she responds with 'Nothing'. It recalls Lear's angry rejoinder, when he warns his favourite child that 'Nothing will come of Nothing' and entreats her to 'Mend [her] Speech a little'. It evokes the domestic scene that follows the conflagration at court: a private encounter in which the Earl of Gloucester's illegitimate son Edmund pretends to conceal a letter he says was written by his half-brother Edgar, and the gullible progenitor of both sons insists that 'the Quality of Nothing hath not such need to hide it self'.

Meanwhile the Fool's words reinforce the assessment he offers his master in I.iv, where he observes that an octogenarian who has disinherited his beloved Cordelia and divided his estate between her conniving older sisters has reduced himself to a cipher, an impotent 'O without a Figure'. Like a worthless steward, Lear's 'all-licens'd' satirist implies, a King who has always been assured that he was 'every thing' is now to be discarded as 'an unnecessary Letter'. Unless he can find some 'use' for the 'Nothing' he has become, he's doomed to finish his days in frustration and ignominy.

But of course *King Lear* is not the only Shakespearean play in which the characters – and audiences who involve themselves vicariously in those characters' destinies – are obliged to make something out of 'Nothing'. The same applies to *Much Ado About Nothing*, where the fourth word of the title plays on 'Noting' and alludes to the Elizabethan notion that a 'weaker vessel' (1 Peter 3:7), whether female in actuality or only in metaphorical terms, is deficient in part because it possesses 'no thing'.

A variation on what might be labelled 'the Nothing riddle' occurs in the Prison Scene (V.v) of *Richard II*, where a monarch who has deposed himself in IV.i with the clause 'I must nothing be' muses that

> Nor I nor any Man that but Man is
> With Nothing shall be pleas'd till he be eas'd
> With being Nothing.

A similar perspective on the conundrum informs the final act of *Timon of Athens*, where the disillusioned, misanthropic Timon expresses relief that

> My long Sickness
> Of Health and Living now begins to mend,
> And Nothing brings me All Things.

Yet another exploration of the enigma occupies *Coriolanus*, where an even more vengeful exile is depicted as 'a kind of Nothing, Titleless', until he has 'forg'd himself a Name a'th' Fire / Of burning Rome'. Here a warrior who has been described earlier as a 'Thing of Blood', as a 'Noble Thing', and as a 'thing / Made by some other Deity than Nature', is at least provisionally defined, not by what he is, but by what he is not. Something will emerge from the 'kind of Nothing' for which he stands; what it will be, however, and what the metamorphosis will signify, is left for the tragedy's interpreters to ponder.

The ambiguity associated with negation is one of the most salient features of *King Lear*. In the 'trial' that commences the action Goneril says that she honours her father with 'A Love that makes Breath poor, and Speech unable'. The meaning the King's eldest daughter expects the old man to derive is that her devotion to him is too boundless, too rich, to be conveyed verbally. But her subsequent treatment of Lear shows Goneril's 'Breath' to be 'poor' in a more elemental sense: like the counterfeit 'Love' it puts into circulation, and 'like the Breath of an unfeed Lawyer', its value is less than meets the ear of an unwary auditor.

Meanwhile Goneril's 'Love' renders Cordelia's 'Breath poor' too, first because corrupt 'Speech' leaves the youngest of Lear's offspring momentarily speechless, second because Cordelia knows that Goneril's 'glib and oily Art / To speak and purpose not' will make any plain and honest profession of love seem 'poor' by comparison, and third because the end product of Goneril's foul 'Breath' will be a Cordelia whose capacity for 'Speech' is terminally disabled as she lies limp in her grieving father's arms.

In the culminating moments of *King Lear* the enfeebled monarch asks his silent daughter 'Ha: / What is't thou sayst?' Hearing no reply, he rationalizes that 'Her Voice was ever Soft, / Gentle, and Low, an excellent thing in Woman.' A brief interval later, having resigned himself to the knowledge that she'll 'come no more', he cries, 'Why should a Dog, a Horse, a Rat have Life, / And thou no Breath at all?' For the King who had resolved to set his rest on Cordelia's 'kind Nursery', this interrogation of the cosmos is devastating, so much so that within seconds he too will be struggling for his final gasps of air. Five times he moans 'Never'. And as he cradles the heir his own miscalculations have reduced to nought, the old man's bowed composure reminds us of the stumbling that has brought him to this pass.

We remember the outrage with which Lear discounted his daughter's 'little seeming Substance'. We remember 'thy Truth then be thy Dow'r.' We remember Kent's prayer that 'the Gods to their dear Shelter' take the maiden a crazed King has exposed to 'Disasters of the World'. We remember France's portrait of this 'unpriz'd precious' bride as a treasure 'Most Choice Forsaken, and most Lov'd Despis'd'. And we remember the play's reiteration of such biblical passages as 2 Corinthians 6:10, where the Apostle Paul refers to the lot of the faithful in this life 'as sorrowful, yet alway rejoicing; as poor, yet making many rich; as having nothing, and yet possessing all things'.

As the drama draws to a close, Cordelia's lifeless form is an image of the horrifying nothing that has come of the 'Nothing' she has spoken. But a tableau that has been likened to Michelangelo's *Pietà* can also be construed positively, and in that light Cordelia's corpse can be viewed as the ultimate embodiment of Lear's eventual realization that

> The Art of our Necessities is strange,
> And can make vild things precious.

Though the King has cast her aside like a piece of refuse, 'Unfriended, new adopted to our Hate', Cordelia alone of Lear's progeny has remained true to her 'Bond'. She alone has returned those 'Duties back as are right Fit'. She alone has gone about her father's 'Business' with 'no blown Ambition' to advance any selfish designs. And even though she alone has had cause to condemn a parent who has treated her vilely, as Lear himself confesses, she has instead cherished and forgiven him with a devotion that 'redeems Nature from the general Curse' her two sisters have brought it to. Small wonder, then, that when a spent King awakens to Cordelia's beatific countenance after his traumatic night in the storm, his initial inference is that the daughter he rejected is now 'a Soul in Bliss'.

Like the Gloucester who serves as Lear's minister of state, the ruler to whom we're introduced at the outset of the tragedy is a 'Lust-dieted Man', a sovereign so accustomed to 'Pomp', so used to having all his needs met and all his whims pampered, that he has never even conceived of the hardships of ordinary mortals. To his astonishment Lear finds himself afflicted by the 'Injuries' his own vices have procured. At first he has only curses for the 'Pelican Daughters' who seem hell bent on devouring the 'Flesh' that 'begot' them. And he maintains, quite rightly, that he is 'a Man / More sinn'd against than sinning'. Before long, however, Lear's 'Manhood' becomes shaken in a way he would once have found shameful. He sheds the tears that accompany 'Noble Anger'; but what is more important, he goes on to weep tears of compassion. In the tempest that objectifies his inner turmoil, he takes pity on 'Poor Tom', the naked madman who becomes, for the King, a symbol of 'Unaccommodated Man'. Scrutinizing this 'Bare Forked Animal', this emaciated manifestation of essential humanity, Lear suddenly discovers that it is a disadvantage to be 'Sophisticated'. He recognizes, as Gloucester will phrase it later, that all too frequently 'Our Means secure us, and our mere Defects / Prove our Commodities'. Like the Earl whose downfall mirrors his own, Lear learns that what we think of as good fortunes are often bad for us, because they insulate us from reality and foster a complacency that can be our undoing; on the other hand our bad fortunes, our severest handicaps and our heaviest losses, can be our shrewdest counsellors and our most priceless assets.

Once he has registered this lesson, Lear begins stripping off the 'Lendings' that differentiate a proud potentate from his humblest subjects. He hurls scorn at the 'Robes and Furr'd Gowns' that shield the wealthy from the sword of Justice; he upbraids the 'Excess' that permits an idle aristocrat to indulge himself in luxury while a lowly peasant scrapes the floor for crumbs from the rich man's feast. Lear acts on a statement he'd earlier emitted in sarcasm, that 'Our basest Beggars / Are in the Poorest Thing Superfluous.' And by exposing himself 'to feel what Wretches feel', he finds a way to profit from 'Nothing' and 'shew the Heavens more Just'.

In the process, like the Gloucester who must be deprived of his sight before he can perceive things 'feelingly', the King is forced to the awareness that 'A Man may see how this World goes with no Eyes.' Once he reaches this juncture, Lear is 'cut to the Brains'. But he remains 'every Inch a King', and now in a sense that could never have been applied to the tyrant who strutted onto 'this great Stage of Fools' for the explosion that propelled him into contention with 'the fretful Elements'.

By the time his excruciating pilgrimage approaches its destination, Lear has discerned some of the 'Uses of Adversity' (*As You Like It*, II.i.12). Like Gloucester, like Edgar, and like Kent, he has come to 'within a Foot / Of th' extreme Verge'. He has been cured of 'the great Rage' that earlier made him lash out at anyone or anything that crossed him. He has surrendered any aspiration to command 'the Cause of Thunder'. So Job-like has his patience become, indeed, that he envisages Cordelia and himself as

'Sacrifices', submissive instruments of heaven, who will reverently take upon themselves 'the Mystery of Things'.

But what are we to make of the King we witness at the end of Act V? Is the old man who re-enters with exclamations of 'Howl, howl, howl' a reversion to the earlier, heaven-defying Lear? Is the invalid who pleads for help to 'undo this Button' removing his last 'Lendings' in contempt of a world that has proven too 'tough' to be tolerated any longer? To put the inquiry in the starkest theological terms, does Lear die persuaded that his agonies add up to no more than 'A Tale / Told by an idiot, full of Sound and Fury, / Signifying nothing' (*Macbeth*, V.iii.26–28)? Or do his dying words about Cordelia's lips hint that, in some sense not disclosed to anyone else, he is granted 'a Chance which does redeem all Sorrows'?

Most of us would like to believe that, like Gloucester's, the old King's 'flaw'd Heart' bursts 'smilingly', with at least a shred of faith and hope intact. We'd prefer to think he achieves what T. S. Eliot was later to call 'A condition of complete simplicity / (Costing not less than everything)'. In the final reckoning, however, the only thing we can affirm with certainty is that Lear's legacy is a 'gor'd State' whose shattered survivors are left to assume the burdens of 'this Sad Time' with few, if any, signs of support from above.

Date and Sources

Shakespeare seems to have completed *King Lear* in 1605 or 1606. He adapted, and gave a tragic ending to, an anonymous *True Chronicle History of King Leir*, which was probably written around 1590 and in which he himself may have acted when the play was being performed at the Rose playhouse in April 1594. Whether the poet reread the *True Chronicle* when he began working on his own *King Lear* in 1604 or 1605 is uncertain. The old *Leir* was printed in a 1605 quarto, but its appearance at that time may have been prompted by the popularity of Shakespeare's new version of the Lear story.

The tale that inspired the playwright's profoundest tragedy had roots in Celtic lore. It had been connected with the history of

Britain since the twelfth century, when Geoffrey of Monmouth depicted Lear as one of the kings who descended from the kingdom's titular founder, Brutus, whose lineage was said to go back to the Trojan hero Aeneas. We don't know whether Shakespeare was familiar with Geoffrey's *Historia Regum Britanniae*, but there is no reason to doubt that he knew, and drew upon, several other redactions of the Lear legend, among them the accounts to be found in Raphael Holinshed's *Chronicles of England, Scotland, and Ireland* (1577, 1588), in Edmund Spenser's *Faerie Queene* (1590), and in John Higgins's portion of the multi-author *Mirror for Magistrates* (1574, 1587).

In the old play, and in all the narratives that preceded it, the French invasion to restore Lear to the throne he has abdicated turns out successfully. The King enjoys a blessed reconciliation with the daughter he has scorned, and he rules peacefully for two more years before dying quietly of natural causes. Unfortunately, according to Holinshed, Higgins, and Spenser, Cordelia's fate is less happy. Five years after she succeeds her father, she is captured, imprisoned, and driven to suicide by the sons of Goneril and Regan, who rebel against their aunt and seize her throne. Unlike the author of the *True Chronicle History of King Leir*, Shakespeare decided to incorporate Cordelia's death into his drama. His Cordelia doesn't survive her father, of course, and she doesn't take her own life; but she does die by the hangman's rope (a detail Shakespeare took from Spenser's version of the story), as ordered by an Edmund who plans 'To lay the Blame upon her own Despair, / That she for-did her self'.

For the parallel plot that focuses on Gloucester and his sons Shakespeare went to Sir Philip Sidney's *Arcadia* (a prose narrative that had been written in the 1580s and published in 1590), which included an episode about the tribulations of a blind King of Paphlagonia. For details about witchcraft and demonic possession, and for the names of many of the devils Edgar enumerates in his persona as Tom o' Bedlam, the playwright ransacked Samuel Harsnett's *Declaration of Egregious Popish Impostors* (1603). For his depiction of the amoral 'Nature' invoked by the atheistic Bastard, Shakespeare appropriated philosophical reflections from John Florio's 1603 translation of Michel de Montaigne's *Essays*. Shakespeare appears to have been fascinated by the wry 'Apology for Raymond Sebonde', and particularly by Montaigne's withering scepticism about the intelligence and dignity that supposedly made human beings superior to the rest of Earth's creatures.

For his presentation of the unworldly 'foolishness' of Christian behaviour, as exemplified by such characters as Cordelia, Kent, the Fool, Edgar, and Albany, Shakespeare drew inspiration from the Gospels and from the Epistles of Paul, especially 1 Corinthians 1–2. No doubt he also derived some of his insights from Desiderius Erasmus's meditations on the topic in *The Praise of Folly*, which had been translated into English in 1549 by Sir Thomas Chaloner.

John F. Andrews, 1993

THE TEXT OF THE EVERYMAN SHAKESPEARE

Background

THE EARLY PRINTINGS OF SHAKESPEARE'S WORKS

Many of us enjoy our first encounter with Shakespeare when we're introduced to *Julius Caesar* or *Macbeth* at school. It may therefore surprise us that neither of these tragedies could ever have been read, let alone studied, by most of the playwright's contemporaries. They began as scripts for performance and, along with seventeen other titles that never saw print during Shakespeare's lifetime, they made their inaugural appearance as 'literary' works seven years after his death, in the 1623 collection we know today as the First Folio.

The Folio contained thirty-six titles in all. Of these, half had been issued previously in the small paperbacks we now refer to as quartos.* Like several of the plays first published in the Folio, the most trustworthy of the quarto printings appear to have been set either from Shakespeare's own manuscripts or from faithful copies of them. It's not impossible that the poet himself prepared some of these works for the press, and it's intriguing to imagine him reviewing proof-pages as the words he'd written for actors to speak and embody were being transposed into the type that readers would filter through their eyes, minds, and imaginations. But, alas, there's no indisputable evidence that Shakespeare had any direct involvement with the publication of these early editions of his plays.

What about the scripts that achieved print for the first time in the Folio? Had the dramatist taken any steps to give the permanency of book form to those texts? We don't know. All we

* Quartos derived their name from the four-leaf units of which these small books were comprised: large sheets of paper that had been folded twice after printing to yield four leaves, or eight pages. Folios, volumes with twice the page-size of quartos, were put together from two-leaf units: sheets that had been folded once after printing to yield four pages.

can say is that when he fell fatally ill in 1616, Shakespeare was denied any opportunities he might otherwise have taken to ensure that his 'insubstantial Pageants' survived the mortal who was now slipping into the 'dark Backward and Abysm of Time'.

Fortunately, two of the playwright's colleagues felt an obligation, as they put it, 'to procure his Orphans Guardians'. Sometime after his death John Heminge and Henry Condell made arrangements to preserve Shakespeare's theatrical compositions in a manner that would keep them vibrant for all time. They dedicated their endeavour to two noblemen who had helped see England's foremost acting company through some of its most trying vicissitudes. They solicited several poetic tributes for the volume, among them a now-famous eulogy by fellow writer Ben Jonson. They commissioned an engraved portrait of Shakespeare to adorn the frontispiece. And they did their utmost to display the author's dramatic works in a style that would both dignify them and make them accessible to 'the great Variety of Readers'.

As they prepared Shakespeare's plays for the compositors who would set them into stately Folio columns, Heminge and Condell (or editors designated to carry out their wishes) revised and augmented many of the entrances, exits, and other stage directions in the manuscripts. They divided most of the works into acts and scenes.* For a number of plays they appended 'Names of the Actors', or casts of characters. Meanwhile they made every effort to guarantee that the Folio printers had reliable copy-texts for each of the titles: authoritative manuscripts for the plays that had not been published previously, and good quarto printings (annotated in some instances to insert staging details, mark script changes, and add supplementary material) for the ones that had been issued prior to the Folio. For several titles they supplied texts that were substantively different from, if not always demonstrably superior to, the quarto versions that preceded them.

Like even the most accurate of the printings that preceded it, the Folio collection was flawed by minor blemishes. But it more than fulfilled the purpose of its generous-minded compilers: 'to keep

* The early quartos, reflecting the unbroken sequence that probably typified Elizabethan and Jacobean performances of the plays, had been printed without the structural demarcations usual in Renaissance editions of classical drama.

the memory of so worthy a Friend and Fellow alive as was our Shakespeare'. In the process it provided a publishing model that remains instructive today.

MODERN EDITIONS OF THE PLAYS AND POEMS

When we compare the First Folio and its predecessors with the usual modern edition of Shakespeare's works, we're more apt to be impressed by the differences than by the similarities. Today's texts of Renaissance drama are normally produced in conformity with twentieth-century standards of punctuation and usage; as a consequence they look more neat, clean, and, to our eyes, 'right' than do the original printings. Thanks to an editorial tradition that extends back to the early eighteenth century, most of the rough spots in the early printings of Shakespeare have long been smoothed away. Textual scholars have ferreted out redundancies and eradicated inconsistencies. They've mended what they've perceived to be errors and oversights in the playscripts, and they've systematically attended to what they've construed as misreadings by the copyists and compositors who transmitted these playscripts to posterity. They've added '[Within]' brackets and other theatrical notations. They've revised stage directions they've judged incomplete or inadequate in the initial printings. They've regularized disparities in the speech headings. They've gone back to the playwright's sources and reinstated the proper forms for many of the character and place names which a presumably hasty or inattentive author got 'wrong' as he conferred identities on his dramatis personae and stage locales. They've replaced obsolete words like *bankrout* with their modern heirs (in this case *bankrupt*). And in a multitude of other ways they've accommodated Shakespeare to the tastes, interests, and expectations of latter-day readers.

The results, on the whole, have been splendid. But interpreting the artistic designs of a complex writer is always problematical, and the task is especially challenging when that writer happens to have been a poet who felt unconstrained by many of the 'rules' that more conventional dramatists respected. The undertaking becomes further complicated when new rules, and new criteria of linguistic and social correctness, are imposed by subsequent generations of artists and critics.

To some degree in his own era, but even more in the neoclassical period (1660–1800) that came in its wake, Shakespeare's most ardent admirers thought it necessary to apologize for what Ben Jonson hinted at in his allusion to the 'small Latin, and less Greek' of an untutored prodigy. To be sure, the 'sweet Swan of Avon' sustained his popularity; in fact his reputation rose so steadily that by the end of the eighteenth century he'd eclipsed Jonson and his other peers and become the object of universal Bardolatry. But in the theatre most of his plays were being adapted in ways that were deemed advisable to tame their supposed wildness and bring them into conformity with the decorum of a society that took pride in its refinement. As one might expect, some of the attitudes that induced theatre proprietors to metamorphose an unpolished poet from the provinces into something closer to an urbane man of letters also influenced Shakespeare's editors. Persuaded that the dramatist's works were marred by crudities that needed expunging, they applied their ministrations to the canon with painstaking diligence.

Twentieth-century editors have moved away from many of the presuppositions that guided a succession of earlier improvers. But a glance at the textual apparatus accompanying virtually any modern publication of the plays and poems will show that emendations and editorial procedures deriving from such forebears as the sets published by Nicholas Rowe (1709), Alexander Pope (1723–5, 1728), Lewis Theobald (1733, 1740, 1757), Thomas Hanmer (1743–5, 1770–1), Samuel Johnson (1765), Edward Capell (1768), George Steevens (1773), and Edmond Malone (1790) retain a strong hold on today's renderings of the playwright's works. The consequence is a 'Shakespeare' who offers the tidiness we've come to expect in our libraries of treasured authors, but not necessarily the playwright a 1599 reader of the Second Quarto of *Romeo and Juliet* would still be able to recognize as a contemporary.

OLD LIGHT ON THE TOPIC

Over the last two decades we've learned from art curators that paintings by Old Masters such as Michelangelo and Rembrandt look a lot brighter when centuries of grime are removed from their surfaces – when hues that had become dulled with soot and other extraneous matter are allowed to radiate again with something approximating their pristine luminosity. We've learned from conductors like Christopher Hogwood that there are aesthetic rewards to be gained from a return to the scorings and instruments with which Renaissance and Baroque musical compositions were first presented. We've learned from twentieth-century experiments in the performance of Shakespeare's plays that an open, multi-level stage, analogous to that on which the scripts were originally enacted, does more justice to their dramaturgical techniques than does a proscenium auditorium devised for works that came later in the development of Western theatre. We've learned from archaeological excavations in London's Bankside area that the foundations of playhouses such as the Rose and the Globe look rather different from what many historians had previously expected. And we're now learning from a close scrutiny of Shakespeare's texts that they too look different, and function differently, when we accept them for what they are and resist the impulse to 'normalize' features that strike us initially as quirky, unkempt, or unsophisticated.

The Aims that Guide the Everyman *Text*

Like other modern editions of the dramatist's plays and poems, The Everyman Shakespeare owes an incalculable debt to the scholarship that has led to so many excellent renderings of the author's works. But in an attempt to draw fresh inspiration from the spirit that animated those remarkable achievements at the outset, the Everyman edition departs in a number of respects from the usual post-Folio approach to the presentation of Shakespeare's texts.

RESTORING SOME OF THE NUANCES OF RENAISSANCE PUNCTUATION

In its punctuation, Everyman attempts to give equal emphasis to sound and sense. In places where Renaissance practice calls for heavier punctuation than we'd normally employ – to mark the caesural pause in the middle of a line of verse, for instance –

Everyman sometimes retains commas that other modern editions omit. Meanwhile, in places where current practice usually calls for the inclusion of commas – after vocatives and interjections such as 'O' and 'alas', say, or before 'Madam' or 'Sir' in phrases such as 'Ay Madam' or 'Yes Sir' – Everyman follows the original printings and omits them.

Occasionally the absence of a comma has a significant bearing on what an expression means, or can mean. At one point in *Othello*, for example, Iago tells the Moor 'Marry patience' (IV.i.90). Inserting a comma after 'Marry', as most of today's editions do, limits Iago's utterance to one that says 'Come now, have patience.' Leaving the clause as it stands in the Folio, the way the Everyman text does, permits Iago's words to have the additional, agonizingly ironic sense 'Be wed to Patience.'

The early texts generally deploy exclamation points quite sparingly, and the Everyman text follows suit. Everyman also follows the early editions, more often than not, when they use question marks in places that seem unusual by current standards: at the ends of what we'd normally treat as exclamations, for example, or at the ends of interrogative clauses in sentences that we'd ordinarily denote as questions in their entirety.

The early texts make no orthographic distinction between simple plurals and either singular or plural possessives, and there are times when the context doesn't indicate whether a word spelled *Sisters*, say, should be rendered *Sisters*, *Sisters'*, or *Sister's* in today's usage. In such situations the Everyman edition prints the word in the form modern usage prescribes for plurals.

REVIVING SOME OF THE FLEXIBILITY OF RENAISSANCE SPELLING

Spelling had not become standardized by Shakespeare's time, and that meant that many words could take a variety of forms. Like James Joyce and some of the other innovative prose and verse stylists of our own century, Shakespeare revelled in the freedom a largely unanchored language provided, and with that in mind Everyman retains original spelling forms (or adaptations of those forms that preserve their key distinctions from modern spellings) whenever there is any reason to suspect that they might have a bearing on how a word was intended to be pronounced or on what it meant, or could have meant, in the playwright's day. When there is any likelihood that multiple forms of the same word could be significant, moreover, the Everyman text mirrors the diversity to be found in the original printings.

In many cases this practice affects the personalities of Shakespeare's characters. One of the heroine's most familiar questions in *Romeo and Juliet* is 'What's in a Name?' For two and a half centuries readers – and as a consequence actors, directors, theatre audiences, and commentators – have been led to believe that Juliet was addressing this query to a Romeo named 'Montague'. In fact 'Montague' *was* the name Shakespeare found in his principal source for the play. For reasons that will become apparent to anyone who examines the tragedy in detail, however, the playwright changed his protagonist's surname to 'Mountague', a word that plays on both 'mount' and 'ague' (fever). Setting aside an editorial practice that began with Lewis Theobald in the middle of the eighteenth century, Everyman resurrects the name the dramatist himself gave Juliet's lover.

Readers of *The Merchant of Venice* in the Everyman set will be amused to learn that the character modern editions usually identify as 'Lancelot' is in reality 'Launcelet', a name that calls attention to the clown's lusty 'little lance'. Like Costard in *Love's Labour's Lost*, another stage bumpkin who was probably played by the actor Will Kemp, Launcelet is an upright 'Member of the Commonwealth'; we eventually learn that he's left a pliant wench 'with Child'.

Readers of *Hamlet* will find that 'Fortinbras' (as the name of the Prince's Norwegian opposite is rendered in the First Folio and in most modern editions) appears in the earlier, authoritative 1604 Second Quarto of the play as 'Fortinbrasse'. In the opening scene of that text a surname that meant 'strong in arms' in French is introduced to the accompaniment of puns on *brazen*, in the phrase 'brazon Cannon', and on *metal*, in the phrase 'unimprooued mettle'. In the same play readers of the Everyman text will encounter 'Ostricke', the ostrich-like courtier who invites the Prince of Denmark to participate in the fateful fencing match that draws *Hamlet* to a close. Only in its final entrance direction for the obsequious fop does the Second Quarto call this character 'Osrick', the name he bears in all the Folio text's references to him and in most modern editions of Shakespeare's most popular tragedy.

Readers of the Everyman *Macbeth* will discover that the fabled 'Weird Sisters' appear only as the 'weyward' or 'weyard' Sisters. Shakespeare and his contemporaries knew that in his *Chronicles of England, Scotland, and Ireland* Raphael Holinshed had used the term 'weird sisters' to describe the witches who accost Macbeth and Banquo on the heath; but because he wished to play on *wayward*, the playwright changed their name to *weyward*. Like Samuel Johnson, who thought punning vulgar and lamented Shakespeare's proclivity to seduction by this 'fatal Cleopatra', Lewis Theobald saw no reason to retain the playwright's weyward spelling of the witches' name. He thus restored the 'correct' form from Holinshed, and editors ever since have generally done likewise.

In many instances Renaissance English had a single spelling for what we now define as two separate words. For example, *humane* combined the senses of 'human' and 'humane' in modern English. In the First Folio printing of *Macbeth* the protagonist's wife expresses a concern that her husband is 'too full o'th' Milke of humane kindnesse'. As she phrases it, *humane kindnesse* can mean several things, among them 'humankind-ness', 'human kindness', and 'humane kindness'. It is thus a reminder that to be true to his or her own 'kind' a human being must be 'kind' in the sense we now attach to 'humane'. To disregard this logic, as the protagonist and his wife will soon prove, is to disregard a principle as basic to the cosmos as the laws of gravity.

In a way that parallels *humane*, *bad* could mean either 'bad' or 'bade', *borne* either 'born' or 'borne', *ere* either 'ere' (before) or 'e'er' (ever), *least* either 'least' or 'lest', *lye* either 'lie' or 'lye', *nere* either 'ne'er' or 'near' (though the usual spellings for the latter were *neare* or *neere*), *powre* either 'pour' or 'power', *then* either 'than' or 'then', and *tide* either 'tide' or 'tied'.

There were a number of word-forms that functioned in Renaissance English as interchangeable doublets. *Travail* could mean 'travel', for example, and *travel* could mean 'travail'. By the same token, *deer* could mean *dear* and vice versa, *dew* could mean *due*, *hart* could mean *heart*, and (as we've already noted) *mettle* could mean *metal*.

A particularly interesting instance of the equivocal or double meanings some word-forms had in Shakespeare's time is *loose*, which can often become either 'loose' or 'lose' when we render it in modern English. In *The Comedy of Errors* when Antipholus of Syracuse compares himself to 'a Drop / Of Water that in the Ocean seeks another Drop' and then says he will 'loose' himself in quest of his long-lost twin, he means both (a) that he will release himself into a vast unknown, and (b) that he will lose his own identity, if necessary, to be reunited with the brother for whom he searches. On the other hand, in *Hamlet* when Polonius says he'll 'loose' his daughter to the Prince, he little suspects that by so doing he will also lose his daughter.

In some cases the playwright employs word-forms that can be translated into words we wouldn't think of as related today: *sowre*, for instance, which can mean 'sour', 'sower', or 'sore', depending on the context. In other cases he uses forms that do have modern counterparts, but not counterparts with the same potential for multiple connotation. For example, *onely* usually means 'only' in the modern sense; but occasionally Shakespeare gives it a figurative, adverbial twist that would require a nonce word such as 'one-ly' to replicate in current English.

In a few cases Shakespeare employs word-forms that have only seeming equivalents in modern usage. For example, *abhominable*, which meant 'inhuman' (derived, however incorrectly, from *ab*, 'away from', and *homine*, 'man') to the poet and his contemporaries, is not the same word as our *abominable* (ill-omened, abhorrent). In his advice to the visiting players Hamlet complains about incompetent actors who imitate 'Humanity so abhominably' as to make the characters they depict seem unrecognizable as men. Modern readers who don't realize the distinction between Shakespeare's word and our own, and who see *abominable* on the page before them, don't register the full import of the Prince's satire.

Modern English treats as single words a number of word-forms that were normally spelled as two words in Shakespeare's time. What we render as *myself*, for example, and use primarily as a reflexive or intensifying pronoun, is almost invariably spelled *my self* in Shakespeare's works; so also with *her self*, *thy self*, *your self*, and *it self* (where *it* functions as *its* does today). Often there is no discernible difference between Shakespeare's usage and our own. At other times there is, however, as we are reminded when we come across a phrase such as 'our innocent self' in *Macbeth* and think how strained it would sound in modern parlance, or as we observe when we note how naturally the self is objectified in the balanced clauses of the Balcony Scene in *Romeo and Juliet*:

> Romeo, doffe thy name,
> And for thy name, which is no part of thee,
> Take all my selfe.

Yet another difference between Renaissance orthography and our own can be exemplified with words such as *today*, *tonight*, and *tomorrow*, which (unlike *yesterday*) were treated as two words in Shakespeare's time. In *Macbeth* when the Folio prints 'Duncan comes here to Night', the unattached *to* can function either as a preposition (with *Night* as its object, or in this case its destination) or as the first part of an infinitive (with *Night* operating figuratively as a verb). Consider the ambiguity a Renaissance reader would have detected in the original publication of one of the most celebrated soliloquies in all of Shakespeare:

> To morrow, and to morrow, and to morrow,
> Creeps in this petty pace from day to day,
> To the last Syllable of Recorded time:
> And all our yesterdayes, have lighted Fooles
> The way to dusty death.

Here, by implication, the route 'to morrow' is identical with 'the way to dusty death', a relationship we miss if we don't know that for Macbeth, and for the audiences who first heard these lines spoken, *to morrow* was not a single word but a potentially equivocal two-word phrase.

RECAPTURING THE ABILITY TO HEAR WITH OUR EYES

When we fail to recall that Shakespeare's scripts were designed initially to provide words for people to hear in the theatre, we sometimes overlook a fact that is fundamental to the artistic structure of a work like *Macbeth*: that the messages a sequence of sounds convey through the ear are, if anything, even more significant than the messages a sequence of letters, punctuation marks, and white spaces on a printed page transmit through the eye. A telling illustration of this point, and of the potential for ambiguous or multiple implication in any Shakespearean script, may be found in the dethronement scene of *Richard II*. When Henry Bullingbrook asks the King if he is ready to resign his crown, Richard replies 'I, no no I; for I must nothing be.' Here the punctuation in the 1608 Fourth Quarto (the earliest text to print this richly complex passage) permits each *I* to signify either 'ay' or 'I' (*I* being the usual spelling for 'ay' in Shakespeare's time). Understanding *I* to mean 'I' permits additional play on *no*, which can be heard (at least in its first occurrence) as 'know'. Meanwhile the second and third soundings of *I*, if not the first, can also be heard as 'eye'. In the context in which this line occurs, that sense echoes a thematically pertinent passage from Matthew 18:9: 'if thine eye offend thee, pluck it out'.

But these are not all the implications *I* can have here. It can also represent the Roman numeral for '1', which will soon be reduced, as Richard notes, to 'nothing' (0), along with the speaker's title, his worldly possessions, his manhood, and eventually his life. In Shakespeare's time, to become 'nothing' was, *inter alia*, to be emasculated, to be made a 'weaker vessel' (1 Peter 3:7) with 'no thing'. As the Fool in *King Lear* reminds another monarch who has abdicated his throne, a man in want of an 'I' is impotent, 'an O without a Figure' (I.iv.207). In addition to its other dimensions, then, Richard's reply is a statement that can be formulated mathematically, and in symbols that anticipate the binary system behind today's computer technology: '1, 0, 0, 1, for 1 must 0 be.'

Modern editions usually render Richard's line 'Ay, no; no, ay; for I must nothing be.' Presenting the line in that fashion makes good sense of what Richard is saying. But as we've seen, it doesn't make total sense of it, and it doesn't call attention to Richard's paradoxes in the same way that hearing or seeing three undifferentiated *I*'s is likely to have done for Shakespeare's contemporaries. Their culture was more attuned than ours is to the oral and aural dimensions of language, and if we want to appreciate the special qualities of their dramatic art we need to train ourselves to 'hear' the word-forms we see on the page. We must learn to recognize that for many of what we tend to think of as fixed linkages between sound and meaning (the vowel 'I', say, and the word 'eye'), there were alternative linkages (such as the vowel 'I' and the words 'I' and 'Ay') that could be just as pertinent to what the playwright was communicating through the ears of his theatre patrons at a given moment. As the word *audience* itself may help us to remember, people in Shakespeare's time normally spoke of 'hearing' rather than 'seeing' a play.

In its text of *Richard II*, the Everyman edition reproduces the title character's line as it appears in the early printings of the tragedy. Ideally the orthographic oddity of the repeated *I*'s will encourage today's readers to ponder Richard's utterance, and the play it epitomizes, as a characteristically Shakespearean enigma.

OTHER ASPECTS OF THE EVERYMAN TEXT

Now for a few words about other features of the Everyman text.

One of the first things readers will notice about this edition is its bountiful use of capitalized words. In this practice as in others, the Everyman exemplar is the First Folio, and especially the works in the Folio sections billed as 'Histories' and 'Tragedies'.* Everyman makes no attempt to adhere to the Folio printings with literal exactitude. In some instances the Folio capitalizes words that the Everyman text of the same passage lowercases; in other instances Everyman capitalizes words not uppercased in the Folio. The objective is merely to suggest something of the flavour, and what appears to have been the rationale, of Renaissance capitalization, in the hope that today's audiences will be made continually aware that the works they're contemplating derive from an earlier epoch.

* The quarto printings employ far fewer capital letters than does the Folio. Capitalization seems to have been regarded as a means of recognizing the status ascribed to certain words (*Noble*, for example, is almost always capitalized), titles (not only King, Queen, Duke, and Duchess, but Sir and Madam), genres (tragedies were regarded as more 'serious' than comedies in more than one sense), and forms of publication (quartos, being associated with ephemera such as 'plays', were not thought to be as 'grave' as the folios that bestowed immortality on 'works', writings that, in the words of Ben Jonson's eulogy to Shakespeare, were 'not of an age, but for all time').

Readers will also notice that instead of cluttering the text with stage directions such as '[Aside]' or '[To Rosse]', the Everyman text employs unobtrusive dashes to indicate shifts in mode of address. In an effort to keep the page relatively clear of words not supplied by the original printings, Everyman also exercises restraint in its addition of editor-generated stage directions. Where the dialogue makes it obvious that a significant action occurs, the Everyman text inserts a square-bracketed phrase such as '[Fleance escapes]'. Where what the dialogue implies is subject to differing interpretations, however, the Everyman text provides a facing-page note to discuss the most plausible inferences.

Like other modern editions, the Everyman text combines into 'shared' verse lines (lines divided among two or more speakers) many of the part-lines to be found in the early publications of the plays. One exception to the usual modern procedure is that Everyman indents some lines that are not components of shared verses. At times, for example, the opening line of a scene stops short of the metrical norm, a pentameter (five-foot) or hexameter (six-foot) line comprised predominantly of iambic units (unstressed syllables followed by stressed ones). In such cases Everyman uses indentation as a reminder that scenes can begin as well as end in mid-line (an extension of the ancient convention that an epic commences *in media res*, 'in the midst of the action'). Everyman also uses indentation to reflect what appear to be pauses in the dialogue, either to allow other activity to transpire (as happens in *Macbeth*, II.iii.87, when a brief line 'What's the Business?' follows a Folio stage direction that reads 'Bell rings. Enter Lady') or to permit a character to hesitate for a moment of reflection (as happens a few seconds later in the same scene when Macduff responds to a demand to 'Speak, speak' with the reply 'O gentle Lady, / 'Tis not for you to hear what I can speak').

Everyman preserves many of the anomalies in the early texts. Among other things, this practice pertains to the way characters are depicted. In *A Midsummer Night's Dream*, for example, the ruler of Athens is usually identified in speech headings and stage directions as 'Theseus', but sometimes he is referred to by his title as 'Duke'. In the same play Oberon's merry sprite goes by two different names: 'Puck' and 'Robin Goodfellow'.

Readers of the Everyman edition will sometimes discover that characters they've known, or known about, for years don't appear in the original printings. When they open the pages of the Everyman *Macbeth*, for example, they'll learn that Shakespeare's audiences were unaware of any woman with the title 'Lady Macbeth'. In the only authoritative text we have of the Scottish tragedy, the protagonist's spouse goes by such names as 'Macbeth's Lady', 'Macbeth's Wife', or simply 'Lady', but at no time is she listed or mentioned as 'Lady Macbeth'. The same is true of the character usually designated 'Lady Capulet' in modern editions of *Romeo and Juliet*. 'Capulet's Wife' makes appearances as 'Mother', 'Old Lady', 'Lady', or simply 'Wife'; but she's never termed 'Lady Capulet', and her husband never treats her with the dignity such a title would connote.

Rather than 'correct' the grammar in Shakespeare's works to eliminate what modern usage would categorize as solecisms (as when Mercutio says 'my Wits faints' in *Romeo and Juliet*), the Everyman text leaves it intact. Among other things, this principle applies to instances in which archaic forms preserve idioms that differ slightly from related modern expressions (as in the clause 'you are too blame', where 'too' frequently functions as an adverb and 'blame' is used, not as a verb, but as an adjective roughly equivalent to 'blameworthy').

Finally, and most importantly, the Everyman edition leaves unchanged any reading in the original text that is not manifestly erroneous. Unlike other modern renderings of Shakespeare's works, Everyman substitutes emendations only when obvious problems can be dealt with by obvious solutions.

The Everyman *Text of* King Lear

King Lear survives in two seventeenth-century versions, a First Quarto (Q1) text that was published in 1608, and a First Folio (F1) text that emerged a decade and a half later in 1623.

A number of passages in the First Quarto printing appear mangled in ways that suggest mishearing rather than misreading.* For this reason editors of *King Lear* once believed that the manuscript behind Q1 was compiled entirely or almost entirely through aural means, either by a 'reporter' who had taken detailed notes during performances of the play, or by a group of actors who had relied upon memory to recall lines they'd delivered or heard delivered as members of the cast. Theories of aural transmission have in no sense disappeared from discussions of the First Quarto *King Lear*, but in the last quarter of a century they've yielded ground to the more encouraging hypothesis that Q1 was set primarily, if not totally, from Shakespeare's 'foul papers' (his unpolished draft of a script that would have been refined in various respects as the play was rehearsed and produced in the theatre). In either case the handwriting the Quarto compositors worked from must have been difficult for them to decipher: the extant copies of Q1 exhibit no fewer than 167 instances of proof correction.

The First Folio version of the play inspires more confidence than does the Quarto text that preceded it. For all its virtues, however, the F1 *King Lear* can be almost as disconcerting as its forebear. One problem is that in a number of places the Folio seems to have been contaminated by the Quarto text it was devised to supersede, either directly (by way of a partially uncorrected exemplar of Q1 that the Folio compositors may have drawn upon as they set type from the promptbook that supplied most of the readings particular to the 1623 text) or indirectly (by way of a 1619 Second Quarto reprint of Q1 that scholars now believe to have had an even stronger influence on the Folio publication of the play than did the First Quarto itself). A more serious problem is that many of the traits that make the Folio *King Lear* distinct from the Quarto text may have been the result of factors over which Shakespeare had no control.

The Folio introduces scores of variations in phrasing and punctuation, many of them significant both in themselves and in their bearing on larger thematic patterns. Meanwhile it inserts more than a hundred lines or part-lines that hadn't been present in the First Quarto text. In all probability the majority of these modifications and additions represent authorial revisions; but some of the minor ones could just as easily be 'improvements'

* For example, 'a dogge, so bade in office' at IV.vi.158, as opposed to the Folio's 'a Dog's obey'd in Office'.

volunteered by others (including the Folio's notoriously high-handed 'Compositor B') to regularize verse lines, 'sophisticate' language that seemed insufficiently formal or elevated, and correct what were judged to be authorial lapses in style or content.

At the same time that it alters the text preserved in the Quarto and augments it with supplementary material, the Folio *King Lear* omits nearly three hundred of the lines Q1 had included in its rendering of the play. Among the Quarto passages absent from the Folio are one brief scene (IV.iii), large segments of a second scene (III.vi), and multi-line sequences from several other scenes (I.ii, I.iii, I.iv, II.ii, III.i, III.vii, IV.i, IV.ii, IV.vii, V.i, and V.iii). Some of the Folio deletions look as if they were motivated by a desire to streamline the dramatic action, either by abbreviating reflective pauses or by eliminating what might have been construed as redundancies in the dialogue or excrescences in the development of the plot. Other cuts look as if they might have been dictated by a requirement to downplay or avoid subjects that were socially, politically, or religiously sensitive. But how many of these excisions – and, if not all of them, precisely which ones – were authorial in origin is difficult, if not impossible, to determine.

Taken together, the Folio's modifications of the Q1 script result in a text with subtle differences from the Quarto in its portrayal of several characters (especially Albany, Edgar, and Kent), a text that impresses many observers as more dramaturgically coherent than the Quarto, and a text that seems less bleak than the Quarto in its depiction of Lear's final moments.

For a century the Folio *King Lear* was the only version of Shakespeare's tragedy that the average reader was in a position to know. It was reprinted with little change in the 1632, 1663–4, and 1685 Folios (F2, F3, and F4), and it was the sole basis for Nicholas Rowe's edition of the play in 1709. During this period the 1608 Quarto text was reprinted twice, first in 1619 (Q2) and then again in 1655 (Q3), but it probably had little impact on the way people thought about *King Lear* until 1723, when Alexander Pope's edition took the crucial step of piecing out the Folio *King Lear* with several of the Q1 passages omitted from the 1623 printing. Following Pope's lead, Lewis Theobald and Edward

Capell carried the process further, and by 1790 Edmond Malone was offering the buyers of his collection a fully conflated text of the play. From that point on it became standard practice not only to augment the Folio *King Lear* with passages F1 had omitted, but also to replace Folio readings with Quarto readings in many instances where the two editions proffered parallel passages.

For two centuries the Pope–Theobald–Malone approach to the presentation of *King Lear* went largely unchallenged. During the last three decades, however, a number of critics have subjected that tradition to intense scrutiny. They've cast doubt on the justification sometimes offered for composite texts of the play: the notion that an authoritative, 'complete' *King Lear* stood behind the supposedly incomplete versions that have come down to us through the Quarto and Folio publications. They've argued that the Folio text (with its cuts as well as its additions and other alterations) is a comprehensive Shakespearean recasting of the material the playwright first scripted in the Q1 version of *King Lear*. And they've maintained that the only thing a responsible editor can do today is to respect the author's wishes and treat the Quarto and Folio renderings of the play as discrete entities: an early dramatization of the subject matter that probably dates from 1605–6, and a more mature and somewhat more focused representation of the same material that may date from as late as 1609 or 1610.

We've learned a great deal from the current reexamination of the early printings of *King Lear*, and it's heartening to note that one modern-spelling edition and one facsimile edition now give readers an opportunity to contemplate the two versions of Shakespeare's tragedy in separate, non-conflated texts.* But

* *The Oxford Shakespeare*, ed. Stanley Wells and Gary Taylor (Oxford: Clarendon Press, 1986), and *The Complete 'King Lear', 1608–1623*, ed. Michael Warren (Berkeley: University of California Press, 1989). Michael Warren gave the two-text movement its impetus with an International Shakespeare Association paper on the Quarto *King Lear* in 1976. Seven years later he and Gary Taylor published a collection, *The Division of the Kingdoms: Shakespeare's Two Versions of 'King Lear'* (Oxford: Clarendon Press, 1983), that established what is now the prevailing view on the subject. For a useful overview, see Stanley Wells's 'The Once and Future *King Lear*' in *The Division of the Kingdoms*, and consult Richard Knowles's critical review of the anthology in the Spring 1985 issue (Volume 36) of *Shakespeare Quarterly*. Meanwhile, for a more recent compendium of information about the textual problems of *King Lear*, see Jay L. Halio's new edition of the play for *The New Cambridge Shakespeare* (Cambridge: Cambridge University Press, 1992). Halio anchors his *King Lear* on the Folio printing, with an appendix of Quarto passages omitted from the Folio and a thorough examination of all the Quarto–Folio variants.

whether the distinctions between the 1608 and 1623 versions of the play are as absolute as some would insist is a question that remains unsettled.

Given the present state of our knowledge, it seems wisest to assume that, notwithstanding the corruptions it almost certainly contains, the Folio *King Lear* transmits a 'riper', and in most ways better, drama than does the Quarto. A modern editor will therefore be well advised to designate the Folio as control copy and to proceed on the premise that F1's additions to and alterations of the Quarto text are more than likely to reflect Shakespeare's intent. Given that *modus operandi*, an editor should resist the temptation to substitute Quarto readings for Folio readings – even when the Quarto version of a passage seems in some way 'superior' to what the Folio contains – unless there is good reason to infer that the F1 readings in question, considered purely on their own merits, have failed to convey an authoritative 1623 script accurately.

But should a modern editor feel obliged to accord the same deferential treatment to the Folio's omissions from the Quarto? Not necessarily. Virtually no one today doubts that the Quarto passages deleted from the Folio version of *King Lear* are authentically Shakespearean. No one has demonstrated to everyone's satisfaction that *King Lear* is a better play without all these passages, and no one has yet proven that the playwright himself was responsible for, or even a willing party to, their excision. All or most of the Folio cuts may in fact be authorial in origin. But since we can't be certain that they were authorial, it would seem wisest to retain the Quarto-only passages, but to do so in a way that makes it easy for the reader to experience the play without them.

In accordance with this rationale, the Everyman Shakespeare incorporates most if not all of the Quarto-only passages, but does so in a manner that will also allow – indeed encourage – readers to ponder *King Lear* in its Folio-only version. In the pages that follow, then, and again in the facing-page notes that accompany the text, the Everyman edition offers an accessible guide to the passages that derive from the Quarto rather than from the Folio. The reader who wishes to mark those passages for deletion –

either literally or mentally – will be able to construct a Folio-only text from this edition of *King Lear*. Meanwhile that reader will also be in a position to assemble any conceivable combination of Folio–Quarto compilations.

As an additional service, the facing-page notes to the Everyman edition indicate all of the passages in *King Lear* that derive solely from the Folio text. This, too, should be helpful to readers who wish to see how the Folio version of the play differs from the Quarto.

To a degree that makes it unusual among twentieth-century editions, *The Everyman Shakespeare* adheres to the First Folio in those portions of the text for which the 1623 version of the play is the control copy.* Unless it is manifest that the Folio text is erroneous in particular instances, *The Everyman Shakespeare* abides by F1's representation of the script. By the same token, in those passages of *King Lear* for which the Quarto is a modern editor's only authority, the Everyman edition retains every Q1 reading that can reasonably be defended.

In compliance with the Folio, Everyman treats as a single scene (II.ii) what most editions reconfigure as three scenes (II.ii, II.iii, and II.iv). Everyman's one departure from the segmentation to be found in the Folio occurs in Act IV, where the insertion of what is rendered here and in most of today's editions as IV.iii adds one scene to the six included in Act IV of the Folio.

In keeping with its usual practice, the Everyman text retains most of the names and titles the early texts deploy to designate the play's characters. Thus, for example, Oswald frequently appears in the Everyman speech headings and stage directions as 'Steward'. In similar fashion, Edmund (whose name is spelled *Edmund* in the Quarto, but both *Edmond* and *Edmund* in the Folio) is usually designated here as 'Bastard'.

The Everyman text also retains a number of spellings that most editions modernize, among them *abhominable* (abominable), *adew* (adieu), *Benizon* (benison), *comptrol* (control), *Curriors* (curriers), *Despight* (despite), *guilded* (gilded), *hether* (hither),

* Including both *The New Cambridge Shakespeare* and *The Oxford Shakespeare*, whose Folio-based texts of *King Lear* incorporate numerous emendations not only from the Quarto but also from a number of later editions.

Maister (master), *ought* (aught), *Preheminence* (preeminence), *pue* (pew), *shew* (show), *sixt* (sixth), *strook* (struck), *vild* (vile), and *whether* (whither).

In the passages listed below the Everyman edition supplements the Folio text with material from the First Quarto.

I.i.	34	*one bearing a Coronet; then*
	69	Speak.
	105	To . . . all.
	158	a
	217	best
I.ii.	107–9	BASTARD . . . Earth!
	149	Fut
	151	Edgar –
	163–72	as . . . come,
I.iii.	17–21	Not . . . abus'd.
	25–26	I . . . speak.
	27	very
I.iv.	159–65	that . . . snatching.
	245–48	LEAR . . . Father.
	271	– O . . . come?
	318	Is't . . . this?
II.i.	72	I [the second one in this line]
	79	I . . . him.
II.ii.	40	*(with his Rapier drawn)*
	138–41	His . . . with.
	147	For . . . Legs.
	169	*Sleeps.*
	183	bare
	202–4	LEAR . . . have.
III.i.	7–15	tears . . . all.
	30–42	But . . . you.
III.iii.	0	*with Lights*
III.vi.	18–56	Edgar . . . scape?
	99–102	KENT . . . Cure.
	104–17	EDGAR . . . lurk.
III.vii.	76	*Draw and fight.*
	78	*She . . . behind.*
	97–105	1 SERVANT . . . *Exeunt.*

IV.i.	57–62	Five . . . Master.
IV.ii.	28	*Exit.*
	31–48	I . . . Deep.
	52–58	that . . . so?'
	61–66	ALBANY . . . mew –
IV.iii.	1–57	*Enter . . . Exeunt.*
IV.v.	39	him
IV.vi.	34	*He kneels.*
	41	*He falls.*
	80	*mad*
	194	ay . . . Dust
	197	my
	242	*They fight.*
	248	*He dies.*
IV.vii.	23–24	CORDELIA . . . there.
	32–35	To . . . Helm?
	57	No Sir,
	77–78	And . . . lost.
	83	*Manent . . . Gentlemen.*
	84–94	GENTLEMEN . . . *Exit.*
V.i.	11–13	BASTARD . . . hers.
	17–18	GONERIL . . . me.
	22–27	Where . . . Nobly.
	32	BASTARD . . . Tent.
	34	you
V.iii.	37–39	CAPTAIN . . . do't.
	47	and appointed Guard
	54–59	At . . . Place.
	108	CAPTAIN . . . Trumpet!
	115	*at the Third Sound*
		a Trumpet before him
	204–21	EDGAR . . . Slave.
	221	*Enter . . . Knife.*

In the passages that follow, the Everyman text adopts Quarto readings in preference to Folio readings. For each listing the first entry, in boldface type, is the Everyman reading (adopted from Q1), and the second is the reading to be found in F1.

I.i.	163	LEAR KEAR
		KENT LENT

	227	**Majesty,** Majesty.
I.ii.	10	**Bastardy** Barstadie
I.iv.	55	**Daughter** Daughters
	212	**nor Crumb** not crumb
II.i	2	**you** your
	41	**stand's** stand
	124	**thought** though
II.ii.	149	**Duke's** Duke
	168	**shameful** shamefnll
	186	**Sheep-coats** Sheeps-Coates
	195	**thy** ahy
	199	**Man's** man
	244	**With** Wirh
	247	**the** the the
	260	**have** hause
	312	**you** your
	314	**Mother's** Mother
	487	**to** too
III.i	45	**Out-wall,** out-wall;
III.iv.	10	**thy** they
	51	**through Fire** though Fire
	93	**deeply** dearly
III.vii.	8	**Advise** Advice
	33	**I am** I'm
IV.vi.	63	**Tyrant's** Tyranrs
	269	**indistinguish'd** indinguish'd
	271	**the** rhe
IV.vii.	17	**long** long?
	46	**scald** scal'd
V.iii.	13	**hear poor Rogues** heere (poore Rogues)
	84	**Sister** Sisters
	97	**he is** hes
	106	**Trumpet** Trumper
	132	**Despight** Despise
	255	**you** your
	286	**You're** You are

In the following passages the Everyman text emends either the Folio text or the Quarto text (depending upon which edition has been adopted as control copy in a particular instance) with readings from other texts. In each listing the first entry, in boldface type, is the Everyman reading, and the second is the reading to be found in the F1 or Q1 copy-text. When the adopted reading derives from a seventeenth-century edition, the first entry so indicates in the parenthesis that follows it.

I.i.	65	**rich'd,** rich'd
	70	**self** selfe-
I.ii.	167	**needless** needles
I.iv.	357	**You** (F2) Your
I.v.	8	**were't** wert
II.i.	20	**Fortune,** Fortune
II.ii.	196	**Garters.** (F2) Garters
	285	**tends** tends,
	420	**What,** What
	465	**Earth!** Earth?
III.iv.	7	**Skin so** (F2) skinso (F1); skin, so (Q1, Q2)
III.vi.	26	**Trial** (Q2) tral
IV.iii.	23	**dropp'd. In** (Q2) dropt in (Q1)
	51	**so,** so (Q1)
	53	**him. Some** him some (Q1)
IV.vi.	57	**Bourn.** bourne (F1); borne, (Q1, Q2)
	67	**Cliff,** (Q2) Cliff.
IV.vii.	34	**Lightning?** Lightning
	35	**Helm?** (Q2) helm
	81	**Will't** Wilt
V.iii.	90	**Trumpet** (F2) Trmpet
	108	***Trumpet*** (F2) *Tumpet*
	207	**Extremity.** (Q2) extremity

In the following passages, the Everyman text adheres to First Folio or First Quarto readings that many, if not most, of today's editions emend. For each listing the first entry, in boldface type, is the Everyman reading, and the second is the reading to be found in other modern editions. When the usual emendation derives from a seventeenth-century text, that edition is listed in the parenthesis that follows the second entry.

I.i.

5 **Qualities** equalities (Q1)
21 **Account,** account:
22 **for:** for,
36 **Lord Liege** (Q1)
52 **most,** most?
56 **Word** words (Q1)
60 **ere** e'er (so also in I.iv.183, V.i.36)
67 **Issues** issue (Q1)
75 **professes** possesses (Q1)
86 **Interest** interess'd
87 **opilent** opulent (Q1)
Sisters sisters'
96 **Least** lest (so also in II.ii.256, IV.iv.18, IV.vi.23, 229)
106 **I** Ay (so also in I.ii.175, I.iv.349, I.v.10, II.i.72, II.ii.2, 206, 283, IV.i.71, IV.vi.100, 101, 109, 155)
111 **Miseries** mysteries (F2; mistresse Q1, Q2)
153 **Rashness,** rashness:
Judgement: judgement,
159 **nere** nor (Q1) *or* ne'er (compare I.iv.177)
fear fear'd
loose lose (compare I.i.251, 266, I.iv.317, III.iii.26, IV.vi.281, V.i.17, V.iii.15)
166 **thy Physician** the physician (Q1)
171 **Vows** vow (Q1)
173 **Sentences** sentence (Q1)
181 **death, away.** death. Away!
183 **King,** King;
sith since
191 **CORNWALL** GLOUCESTER
198 **less?** less. (F4)
201 **little seeming** little-seeming
208 **her.** her?
215 **Then** Than (compare I.iv.74, 136, V.i.17, V.iii.68)
229 **will** well (Q1; compare I.iv.1)
235 **still soliciting** still-soliciting
243 **stands** stand
253 **Respect and Fortunes** respects of fortune (Q1)
290 **to night** tonight (compare I.ii.24, II.i.16, 60, IV.v.16, V.iii.40, 53)
294 **hath been** hath not been (Q1)
304 **Way-wardness** waywardness
308 **complement** compliment (so also in V.iii.233)
310 **sit** hit (Q1)

I.ii.

4 **me?** me,

10 **Baseness,** baseness?
15 **a Sleep** asleep
21 to top
61 **wake** wak'd (Q1)
74 **his.** his? (Q1)
106 **Monster** monster –
109 **him,** him.
132 **True-harted** true-hearted
140 **Predominance.** predominance,
145 **on** to (Q1)
150 **Maidenlest** maidenliest (F3)
152 **Pat:** and pat
192 **Brother?** brother!
196 **faintly.** faintly, (Q1)

I.iv. 1 **will** well (Q1; compare I.i.229)
23 **he's** he is
35 **Counsail** counsel (compare I.iv.149)
45 **Dinner,** dinner.
60 **not?** not!
99 **to, have you Wisdom, so.** to. Have you wisdom? So!
105 **my Boy** Fool
134 **in a Door** in-a-door
135 **more,** more
163 **Lodes** ladies
170 **Crowns** crown (Q1)
177 **nere** ne'er
190 **Fool** fools (Q1)
203 **Daughter?** daughter!
218 **Riots, Sir.** riots. Sir,
230 **it's** it (Q1)
242 **so?** so!
271 **Will, / Speak, Sir?** will? Speak, sir.
310 **Death,** death! (Q1)
327 **ho?** ho!
335 **Knights?** knights!
337 **Knights:** knights?
347 **Oswald?** Oswald!
357 **at task** attax'd
361 **the 'vent** th' event

I.v. 0 *Gentleman* (deleted in most editions)
35 **Nature,** nature.
Father? father!

II.i. 8 **abroad,** abroad?
9 **Ear-kissing** ear-bussing (Q1)

16 **to night?** tonight!
16 **better** better,
46 **revenging** revengive (Q1)
53 **latch'd** lanch'd (Q1)
58 **uncaught** uncaught;
59 **found;** found –
71 **should I** I should (Q1)
78 **Villain,** villain!
80 **where** why (Q1)
88 **Strangeness** strange news (Q1)
119 **you?** you –
122 **Advise** advice (Q2)

II.ii.
11 **Woosted** worsted (Q1)
18 **Clamours** clamorous (Q1)
23 **thee?** thee!
25 **me?** me!
29 **you, you** you. You
42 **if** and (Q1)
48 **King?** king.
51 **Valour,** valour.
63 **you will** you'll (Q1)
74 **t'intrince** too intrince
76 **the** their (Q1)
77 **Revenge** renege (reneag Q1)
78 **Gall** gale (Q1)
81 **Smoile** Smile (F4)
82 **if** and (Q1)
97 **take it** take't (Q1)
105 **flicking** flick'ring
121 **dead** dread (Q1)
123 **there** their (Q1)
124 **reverent** reverend
128 **Respects** respect (Q1)
132 **Noon?** noon!
140 **'temnest** contemnest
142 **The King his Master needs must** The King must
148 **my Lord** my good Lord
152 **travail'd** travell'd (so also in II.ii.272)
155 **too blame** to blame (Q1)
165 **From** For
172 **unus'al** unusual (Q1)
184 **Wodden** wooden (so also in II.ii.199, where, unlike here, Q1 prints *wooden*)
188 **Tom,** Tom!
191 **Messengers** messenger (Q1)

194 **Ha?** Ha!

196 **Cruel** crewel (Q1)

215 **painting** panting (Q1)

218 **those** whose (Q1)

230 **wil'd** wild (F2)

241 **Oh** O (compare II.ii.303, 320, III.vii.79, 80, IV.i.21, IV.ii.26, 29, 60, 67, IV.vi.243, 269, V.i.35)

242 **Historica** Hysterica (F4)
climing climbing

271 **me?** me!

272 **Fetches,** fetches, ay (Q1)

331 **his** her (Q1)

351 **blister** blister her

368 **easy borrowed** easy-borrow'd

369 **fickly** fickle (Q1) *or* sickly (F3)

383 **You?** you!

394 **Pinch.** pinch!
her? her!

395 **bloodied** blooded (F1 uncorrected)

398 **her?** her!

406 **Bile** boil

422 **many? Sith** many, sith

471 **Blame** blame;

476 **Whether** Whither

481 **high** bleak (Q1)

III.i. 10 **outscorn** outstorm

27 **hath** have (F2)

III.ii. 3 **drown** drown'd (Q1)

14 **Belly full** bellyful

23 **Battailes** battles (compare IV.vi.206, V.i.17, 37, 61, 65)

74 **little-tyne** little tine *or* little tiny

91–92 **Then . . . Confusion** (Some editions place this passage after line 83.)

III.iii. 19 **for it** for't (Q1)

III.iv. 7 **Skin so;** skin: so (As noted above, the *Everyman* text follows F2 in correcting F1's *skinso* to *skin so*.)

12 **the** this (Q1 corr.)

31 **lop'd** loop'd (Q1)

52 **Sword** ford (Q1)

58 **Bliss** Bless (Q1; so also in III.iv.59)

64 **Has** What, has (Q1)

85 **Sweet-heart** sweet heart (Q1)

87 **Servingman?** servingman, (Q1)
103 **nonny** hey no nonny
104 **Sesey** sessa
110 **Ha?** Ha!
121 **at** till the (Q1)
122 **squints** squinnies
125 **old** wold
128 **Troth-plight** troth plight (Q1)
135 **Tod-pole** tadpole
140–41 **stock'd, punish'd** stock-punish'd (Q1)
141 **hath** hath had (Q1)
144 **Dear** deer
175 **this?** this!

III.v. 11 **Just?** just!
Letter which letter (Q1)
27 **dear** dearer (Q1)

III.vi. 23 **Justice** justicer
24 **No** Now (Q2)
25 **glars,** glares
Wanst Want'st (Q2)
27 **Broom** bourn
36 **Cushings** cushions (Q2)
38 **robbed** robed
46 **Pur the** Purr, the
47 **Goneril, I** Goneril. I
48 **Assembly,** assembly, she (Q2)
54 **an** on
67 **Mongril, Grim** Mongrel grim
68 **Hym** lym
69 **tight** tike (Q1)
Troudle trundle (Q1)
72 **leapt** leap (Q1)
73 **sese** Sessa *or* Cessez
78 **make** makes (Q1)
Hard-hearts hard hearts

III.vii. 9 **festivate** festinate (F2; festuant Q1, Q2)
14 **now?** now!
32 **Lady,** lady (Q1)
42 **simple answer'd** simple-answer'd
56 **stick** rash (Q1)
61 **stern** dearn (Q1)
73 **Dog?** dog!

75 **What . . . mean?** (Many editions reassign this question to Regan; but both the Quartos and the First Folio give it to the Servant.)
76 **Villain?** Villain!
78 **thus?** thus!
83 **Comfortless?** comfortless:

IV.i.
2 **flatter'd, to be worst:** flatter'd. To be worst,
10 **poorly led** parti-ey'd (Q1)
41 **Get** Then, prithee get (Q1)
54 **Gate** gait (so also in IV.vi.233, V.iii.175)
55 **scarr'd** scar'd (Q1)
57–58 **of Lust, as Obdicut** as Obdicut, of lust
60 **Stiberdigebit, of Mobing; and Mohing,** Flibbertigibbet, of mopping and mowing;
63 **Heavens'** Heavens,

IV.ii.
27 **my** A (Q1)
28 **Body** bed (Q1)
29 **Whistle** whistling (Q1)
46 **the** these
56 **Helm;** helm
thereat to threat
59 **seems** shews (Q1)
64 **dislecate** dislocate
66 **mew** – mew!
69 **Eyes.** eyes? (Q1)
72 **Threat-enrag'd** thereat enrag'd (Q1)
76 **Justices** justicers (Q1)

IV.iii.
9 **Monsier** Monsieur
12 **I say** Ay sir
17 **'streme** strove
18 **goodliest, you have seen,** goodliest. You have seen
20 **like a** like, a
21 **seem** seem'd
28 **prest** press'd
31 **beleeft** believ'd (Q2)
33 **And Clamour moisten'd her; then** And, clamour-moisten'd, then
37 **since.** since? (Q2)
50 **not.** not? (Q2)

IV.iv.
3 **Fenitar** fumiter *or* femiter
4 **Hardokes** burdocks
6 **Centery** century (Q1)
9 **Sense,** sense? (Q2)

18 **Desires** distress (Q1)
28 **Rite** right (Q1)

IV.v. 25 **Eliads** oeilliads
27 **Madam?** madam!

IV.vi. 9 **Y'are** You're
10 **y'are** You're
17 **walk'd** walk (Q1)
30 **off,** off;
49 **Gozemore** goss'mer
57 **Somnet** summit
71 **wealk'd** whelk'd
enraged enridg'd (Q1)
83 **Crying** coining (Q1)
125 **Fiends** fiend's *or* fiends'
156 **Cur.** cur?
160 **thy** thine (Q1)
163 **great** small (Q1)
164 **Place Sins** Plate sin
169 **Glass-Eyes** glass eyes (Q1)
183 **shoo** shoe
187 **him, Sir** him. Sir,
195 **What?** What!
202 **a Daughter** one daughter (Q1)
206 **Battell** battle (compare III.ii.3)
213 **ever gentle** ever-gentle
222 **happy** happy!
228 **Dar'st** Durst (Q1)
256 **Manners:** manners,
not not:
257 **Minds;** minds,
Hearts, hearts;
262 **done. If** done if
263 **Conqueror,** conqueror;
279 **Sorrows?** sorrows!

IV.vii. 6 **clipt** clipp'd
12 **GENTLEMAN** DOCTOR (Q1)
23 **doubt of** doubt not of (Q1)
25 **Restauration** restoration
31 **jarring** warring (Q1)
32 **dread bolted** dread-bolted
47 **Spirit** spirit,
47 **where** when (Q2)
50 **Day Light** daylight

68 **am:** am,

V.i. 11 **Forefended** forfended
16 **Fear not** Fear me not (Q1)
17 **Battaile, then** battle than (cf. III.ii.23, V.i.37)
25 **bold's** bolds
29 **particurlar** particular
44 **loves** love (Q1)

V.ii. 11 **all come on.** all. Come on.

V.iii. 17 **Gods** gods' *or* God's
24 **Good Years** good-years *or* goodyears
50 **imprest** impress'd
67 **himself,** himself
70 **ALBANY** GONERIL
76 **is** are
83 **Arrest** attaint (Q1)
85 **bare** bar
87 **Banes** banns
88 **Loves** love (Q1)
100 **not,** not?
121 **lost** lost:
122 **Tooth:** tooth
130 **Honours** honour
135 **illustirous** illustrious (Q1)
148 **scarely** scarcely (Q1)
155 **stop** stopple (Q1)
160 **BASTARD** GONERIL (Q1)
191 **Despair.** despair, (Q1)
196 **our** my (Q1)
213 **threw me** threw him
217 **crack twice;** crack; twice
248 **Sword,** Sword the Captain (Q1)
249 **EDGAR** ALBANY (Q1)
262 **Horror.** horror? (Q2)
267 **you Murderers** you, murderers
275 **him** them (Q1)
307 **her?** her.
Look Look,
311 **Wrack** rack (F4)
320 **Waight** weight

KING LEAR

NAMES OF THE ACTORS

LEAR, King of Britain

GONERIL, REGAN, CORDELIA — Daughters to Lear

KING OF FRANCE
DUKE OF BURGUNDY
DUKE OF ALBANY, Husband to Goneril
DUKE OF CORNWALL, Husband to Regan
EARL OF KENT
EARL OF GLOUCESTER
EDGAR, Legitimate Son to Gloucester
EDMUND [BASTARD], Illegitimate Son to Gloucester

FOOL to Lear

CURAN, a Courtier
OSWALD, Steward to Goneril
OLD MAN, Tenant to Gloucester
DOCTOR
CAPTAIN, employed by Edmund
GENTLEMAN, attendant on Cordelia
HERALD
Two SERVANTS to Cornwall
KNIGHTS of Lear's Train
GENTLEMEN
OFFICERS
MESSENGERS
SOLDIERS
ATTENDANTS

I.i The play opens at the palace of King Lear in pre-Christian Britain.

1 **had more affected** was more favourably disposed to.

3 **us** either (a) me, or (b) the rest of us.

5–7 **for . . . Moi'ty** for their favour with the King appears so equal that the most careful scrutiny can establish neither as his preference. Most editors adopt the Quarto's 'equalities' rather than the Folio's 'qualities' (substances, merits). *Moi'ty* (moiety) normally means 'half' (a sense that fits Gloucester's image of a balance scale, and one that will take on additional import by the end of the scene), but it can also mean 'share'.

8 **this** Edmund. Whether he is a party to the conversation before he is addressed in lines 25–26 is unclear.

9 **Breeding** both (a) conception, and (b) rearing.
at my Charge both (a) my responsibility (one I've been forced to 'acknowledge', line 10), and (b) under my tutelage. *Charge* can also refer to 'weight' and to material to be discharged (as in the firing of a gun); compare 2 *Henry IV*, II.iv.121–22.

11 **braz'd** brazened (plated with brass), hardened. Gloucester's tone is itself brazen (impudent, smug). He refers to an illicit 'Sport' (line 23) for which he appears to have no remorse and for which, indeed, he seems to feel more than a little male pride. And, given the name he applies to his offspring (line 24), Gloucester seems to have had scant respect for Edmund's mother. Whether or not Edmund's mother was a 'whore' in the usual modern sense, she was clearly a 'good Sport' to a man who was already the father of a legitimate son (lines 19–20).

12 **conceive** understand (literally, 'take in' or 'take together'). In the next line Gloucester gives Kent's verb a copulative sense.

16 **smell a Fault** detect an irregularity. *Fault* alludes both to Gloucester's breach of propriety and to the breach in the 'weaker vessel' (1 Peter 3:7) his senses led him to. Compare IV.vi.123–31.

17–18 **I . . . proper** I cannot wish the sin uncommitted, since it yielded such a handsome result. *Undone* plays on the copulative sense of *do*.

19 **by . . . Law** under the normal laws of matrimony.

20–21 **Dearer . . . Account** more valued a possession. *Account* (accounting, estimation) hints at an English derivative of *cunnus* (the Latin word for the female 'Fault').

ACT I

Scene 1

Enter Kent, Gloucester, and Edmund.

KENT I thought the King had more affected the Duke of Albany than Cornwall.

GLOUCESTER It did always seem so to us; but now in the Division of the Kingdom it appears not which of the Dukes he values most, for Qualities are so weigh'd that Curiosity in neither can make Choice of either's Moi'ty.

KENT Is not this your Son, my Lord?

GLOUCESTER His Breeding, Sir, hath been at my Charge. I have so often blush'd to acknowledge him that now I am braz'd to't.

KENT I cannot conceive you.

GLOUCESTER Sir, this young Fellow's Mother could, whereupon she grew Round-womb'd, and had indeed, Sir, a Son for her Cradle ere she had a Husband for her Bed. Do you smell a Fault?

KENT I cannot wish the Fault undone, the Issue of it being so proper.

GLOUCESTER But I have a Son, Sir, by order of Law, some Year elder than this, who yet is no Dearer in my Account, though this Knave came something

21 **something** somewhat.

22 **saucily** forwardly, boldly.

31 **I . . . better** [Because of your noble breeding,] I hold you in high regard, and desire to become better acquainted.

32 **study Deserving** endeavour to make myself worthy of your esteem.

33 **out** away from the court; abroad. Lines 33–34 can refer either to Edmund or to Kent; in either case they prove prophetic.

S.D. **one . . . then** These words derive from the 1608 First Quarto text. They do not appear in the 1623 First Folio printing.

35 **Attend** tend to the needs of; be prepared to escort. Whether Edmund exits with his father (line 36) is not specified in the early texts.

37 **darker** as yet undisclosed; obscure. Subsequent events will activate the more sinister potential in Lear's word choice.

39 **fast** fixed, firm. But *fast* can also mean 'hasty', and that sense will quickly emerge as pertinent.

40 **shake all Cares** shake down (like fruit being harvested, or trees being 'unburthen'd') all duties ('Business') and concerns. *Cares* (responsibilities) can also refer to human ties and familial bonds. Lear little imagines how literally his 'darker Purpose' will be realized. Lines 41–46 (from 'while' to 'now') appear only in the Folio text; so also with the parenthetical lines 50–51.

44 **constant** unswerving, consistent; 'fast' (line 39).
publish make public; announce.

45 **several Dowers** individual inheritances.

50–51 **divest . . . State** disrobe ourselves (that is, myself) of monarchy, property, kingly vestments, and royal responsibilities.

53 **extend** offer; hand out.

saucily to the World before he was sent for: yet was his Mother fair, there was good Sport at his Making, and the Whoreson must be acknowledged. – Do you know this Noble Gentleman, Edmund?

EDMUND No, my Lord.

GLOUCESTER My Lord of Kent: remember him hereafter as my Honourable Friend.

EDMUND My Services to your Lordship.

KENT I must love you, and sue to know you better.

EDMUND Sir, I shall study Deserving.

GLOUCESTER He hath been out nine Years, and away he shall again. The King is coming.

Sennet. Enter one bearing a Coronet; then King Lear, Cornwall, Albany, Goneril, Regan, Cordelia, and Attendants.

LEAR Attend the Lords of France and Burgundy, Gloucester.

GLOUCESTER I shall, my Lord. *Exit.*

LEAR Mean time we shall express our darker Purpose.
Give me the Map there. Know that we have divided
In three our Kingdom; and 'tis our fast Intent
To shake all Cares and Business from our Age,
Conferring them on Younger Strengths, while we
Unburthen'd crawl toward Death. – Our Son of Cornwall,
And you, our no less loving Son of Albany,
We have this Hour a constant Wish to publish
Our Daughters' several Dowers, that future Strife
May be prevented now. The Princes, France and Burgundy,
Great Rivals in our youngest Daughter's Love,
Long in our Court have made their amorous Sojourn,
And here are to be answer'd. – Tell me, my Daughters
(Since now we will divest us both of Rule,
Interest of Territory, Cares of State),
Which of you shall we say doth love us most,
That we our largest Bounty may extend

54 **Nature . . . challenge** a loving disposition competes with other forms of deserving to prove the recipient's worthiness.

55 **eldest borne** both (a) first-carried, and (b) earliest born. The verse lineation suggests a pause before Goneril says 'Sir'.

56 **wield the Matter** shape the substance. *Wield* (manipulate) hints at *weal.*

57 **Space** freedom to move about at will.
Liberty freedom from behavioural restraints.

58 **valued** (a) calculated, and (b) treasured.

60 **found** both (a) proved, discovered, and (b) found himself loved. *Ere* means both (a) ere (before), and (b) e'er (ever).

61 **makes Breath poor** is so great as to render beggarly even the richest words brought forward to express it. But this phrase can also mean (a) makes words worthless, and (b) impoverishes breath (a sense that will be fulfilled in V.iii.260–61, 269–72).
unable incapable of functioning adequately. Goneril's words will soon be borne out by Cordelia (lines 63, 77–79).

63 **Love . . . Silent** [let her] love and say nothing.

64 **Bounds** bounded territories. This word anticipates *Bond*, line 94.

65 **Champains** open plains, not 'shadowy' (shaded with trees). Lines 65–66 (from 'and' to 'Rivers') appear only in the Folio text.

66 **wide-skirted Meads** broad meadows.

70 **self Mettle** same metal (substance). *Self* hints at 'selfish'. *Speak* (line 69) is inserted from the Quarto text; compare lines 55, 87.

71 **prize . . . Worth** value myself as equivalent to her in merit.

72 **Deed** both (a) pledge, contractual bond, and (b) manifestation.

73 **Onely** only, except [that]. Here the original spelling (a reminder that the word derives from *one*) hints at the upright I with which a man becomes 'all one' with a woman's 'most precious Square of Sense' (line 75). Compare *The Two Gentlemen of Verona*, II.i.147; II.v.30–31, 33–35.

74 **Joys** Regan's phrasing hints at the sense that relates to a physical 'Deed of Love' (compare line 17, and see *Pericles*, III.v.7–10), here implying a forbidden affinity. Compare line 83.

Where Nature doth with Merit challenge. – Goneril,
Our eldest borne, speak first.

GONERIL Sir,
I love you more than Word can wield the Matter,
Dearer than Eyesight, Space, and Liberty,
Beyond what can be valued, rich or rare,
No less than Life, with Grace, Health, Beauty, Honour;
As much as Child ere lov'd, or Father found.
A Love that makes Breath poor, and Speech unable,
Beyond all manner of so much I love you.

CORDELIA – What shall Cordelia speak? Love, and be
Silent.

LEAR Of all these Bounds, even from this Line to this,
With shadowy Forests, and with Champains rich'd,
With plenteous Rivers and wide-skirted Meads,
We make thee Lady. To thine and Albany's Issues
Be this perpetual. – What says our Second Daughter?
Our dearest Regan, Wife of Cornwall? Speak.

REGAN I am made of that self Mettle as my Sister,
And prize me at her Worth. In my true Heart
I find she names my very Deed of Love:
Onely she comes too short, that I profess
My self an Enemy to all other Joys
Which the most precious Square of Sense professes,

76 **felicitate** fulfilled, made happy. *Alone* plays on 'all one'.

79 **ponderous** weighty, substantial.

82 **Space, Validity** geographical extent, value. Compare line 57.

86 **Strive . . . Interest** vie to become linked (inter-essed) through matrimony. Compare line 51. Lines 84–86 (from 'to' to 'Interest') appear only in the Folio.

87 **opilent** opulent, rich. Lines 89–90 are unique to the Folio text; so is the word 'Speak' in line 87.

92 **Unhappy . . . am** both (a) unfortunate though I am in this regard, and (b) unhappy though it makes me.

heave cast. Cordelia's verb hints at nausea, a heaving of the gorge (see *Othello*, II.i.238–39). Cordelia's words recall 1 John 3:18, 'My little children, let us not love in words, neither in tongue: but in deed and in truth.'

94 **According . . . Bond** in accordance with my filial obligations.

95 **Mend** both (a) repair, and (b) amend, augment (to make less 'poor', line 61).

96 **Least** lest. Here the original spelling provides a reminder that Cordelia will receive the least if she says the least. Compare lines 84, 154.

97 **begot** begotten, conceived.

98 **right Fit** most proper (as distinguished from the kind of 'wrong fit' insinuated by her sisters; compare lines 70–77 and 104–5). Lines 97–99 echo Exodus 20:12, 'Honour thy father and thy mother: that thy days may be long upon the land which the Lord thy God hath given thee.'

101 **Happily** both (a) happily, and (b) appropriately.

102 **take my Plight** receive my trothplight (pledge of fidelity). By the end of the scene (see lines 255–58), Cordelia's 'Lord' will take her 'Plight' in another sense (taking her predicament on himself, and taking her into the bargain).

106 **I** both (a) I (my self), and (b) ay (yes). *Heart* plays on the name of Lear's favourite daughter: *cor* means 'heart' in Latin. Line 105 appears only in the Quarto version of the play.

And find I am alone felicitate
In your dear Highness' Love.
CORDELIA – Then poor Cordelia,
And yet not so, since I am sure my Love's
More ponderous than my Tongue.
LEAR To thee and thine hereditary ever
Remain this ample Third of our fair Kingdom,
No less in Space, Validity, and Pleasure
Than that conferr'd on Goneril. – Now our Joy,
Although our Last and Least; to whose young Love
The Vines of France and Milk of Burgundy
Strive to be Interest. What can you say, to draw
A Third more opilent than your Sisters? Speak.
CORDELIA Nothing, my Lord.
LEAR Nothing?
CORDELIA Nothing.
LEAR Nothing will come of Nothing, speak again.
CORDELIA Unhappy that I am, I cannot heave
My Heart into my Mouth: I love your Majesty
According to my Bond, no more nor less.
LEAR How, how, Cordelia? Mend your Speech a little,
Least you may mar your Fortunes.
CORDELIA Good my Lord,
You have begot me, bred me, lov'd me: I
Return those Duties back as are right Fit,
Obey you, Love you, and most Honour you.
Why have my Sisters Husbands, if they say
They love you all? Happily when I shall wed,
That Lord whose Hand must take my Plight shall carry
Half my Love with him, half my Care and Duty;
Sure I shall never marry like my Sisters,
To love my Father all.
LEAR But goes thy Heart with this?
CORDELIA I, my good Lord.
LEAR So Young, and so Untender?
CORDELIA So Young, my Lord, and True.
LEAR Let it be so, thy Truth then be thy Dow'r:
For by the sacred Radiance of the Sun,

111 **Miseries . . . Night** afflictions visited on earthlings by the goddess of the Moon and of Witchcraft (as in *Macbeth*, II.v, and IV.i). Most editors emend *Miseries* to *mysteries*; the Quarto prints *mistresse*. Compare II.ii.162–63.

115 **Propinquity . . . Blood** closeness and relatedness through blood and its claims. *Care* echoes line 40.

117 **this** both (a) this time, and (b) this breast (line 116).
Scythian a warrior from an Asian tribe proverbial for its savagery.

118 **makes . . . Messes** turns his own offspring into meals. Compare line 129, where *digest* means 'divide between you'.

120 **reliev'd** assisted in time of need.

121 **sometime** one-time, erstwhile; former.

124–25 **thought . . . Nursery** planned to spend all the rest of my days at rest with her to take care of me. In the card game Primero *set my Rest* meant 'stake all my holdings on the cards in my hand'. Lear's imagery suggests another variation on unnatural father–daughter relationships, this time an inversion that would turn an old man into a child requiring 'Paternal Care' (line 114). *Rest* anticipates line 138.

127 **from her** away from her; in such a way as to exclude her.
who stirs? Why is no one instantly ready to obey my command?

130 **Plainness** honest directness. This word anticipates line 150.

131 **invest . . . Power** bestow my power on the two of you. Compare line 50.

132 **Preheminence** preeminence; sole authority.

137 **Addition to** titular respect and prerogatives accorded to.

138–39 **Sway . . . Sons** authority, income, and executive power that remains, dear sons-in-law. See lines 124–25. Lear will soon 'sway' in a way that makes it clear that the 'Name' is not necessarily synonymous with 'all th' Addition to a King'.

140 **Coronet** small crown worn by a member of the upper nobility. See *Henry VIII*, IV.i.54–55, where *Coronet* plays on *cornuto* (Italian for 'cuckold').

144 **make . . . Shaft** stand back from the arrow about to be released. In line 145 *Fork* refers to an arrowhead with two points, a 'forkhead' (like *Fork*, another term for a cuckold). See the notes to I.iv.165–208, I.v.27–34.

The Miseries of Hecat and the Night,
By all the Operation of the Orbs,
From whom we do exist, and cease to be,
Here I disclaim all my Paternal Care,
Propinquity and Property of Blood,
And as a Stranger to my Heart and me
Hold thee from this for ever. The barbarous Scythian,
Or he that makes his Generation Messes
To gorge his Appetite, shall to my Bosom
Be as well neighbour'd, pitied, and reliev'd
As thou my sometime Daughter.

KENT Good my Liege –

LEAR Peace, Kent,
Come not between the Dragon and his Wrath;
I lov'd her most, and thought to set my Rest
On her kind Nursery. Hence and avoid my Sight:
So be my Grave my Peace, as here I give
Her Father's Heart from her. – Call France, who stirs?
Call Burgundy. – Cornwall, and Albany,
With my two Daughters' Dow'rs digest the third.
Let Pride, which she calls Plainness, marry her:
I do invest you jointly with my Power,
Preheminence, and all the large Effects
That troop with Majesty. Our self by Monthly Course,
With Reservation of an hundred Knights,
By you to be sustain'd, shall our Abode
Make with you by due Turn; onely we shall retain
The Name and all th' Addition to a King;
The Sway, Revenue, Execution of the rest,
Beloved Sons, be yours, which to confirm
This Coronet part between you.

KENT Royal Lear,
Whom I have ever honour'd as my King,
Lov'd as my Father, as my Master follow'd,
As my great Patron thought on in my Prayers –

LEAR The Bow is bent and drawn, make from the Shaft.

KENT Let it fall rather, though the Fork invade

146 **unmannerly** lacking in proper deference and courtesy.

149 **to Flattery bows** curtsies to pleasing lies. Compare line 144.

151 **Reserve thy State** preserve (retain possession of) your throne and kingdom.

152 **Consideration** sound judgement (the opposite of 'Rashness').
check both (a) impede, block (as in chess, a sense continued in line 158), and (b) correct, control.

153 **answer . . . Judgement** even if it costs me my life to have given you my candid opinion.

155 **Low** quiet, inaudible. This line anticipates V.iii.270–71.

156 **Reverb no Hollowness** do not reverberate like hollow drums.

158 **Pawn** (a) pledge (as in the gauntlet cast down to engage a man in chivalric combat), (b) lowly servant, and (c) humble chess piece.

159 **nere** 'ne'er', but here with a sense that approximates *nor*, the word the Quarto supplies (followed by some modern editions).
loose (a) discharge, (b) cast off, and (c) lose.

162 **Blank** centre, pupil (by analogy with the white centre of a target). Compare lines 144, 159. *Still* (line 161) means both (a) yet, and (b) ever.

163 **Apollo** the Olympian god associated with wisdom, prophecy, health, harvest, and civic order. Apollo is the god who visits plagues on those who disturb the balance of nature or disrupt societies (as Lear is now doing). He plays a prominent role in such Greek tragedies as Sophocles' *Oedipus* cycle. Fittingly, given the context in which his name is invoked here, Apollo is associated with the Sun (and thus with clarity of vision) and with archery.

165 **Vassal! Miscreant** slave, infidel (misbeliever).
forbear restrain your anger.

167 **Revoke thy Gift** withdraw the bequest you have just announced. Lines 166–67 echo Matthew 9:12 and Luke 4:23–24; compare *Macbeth*, V.i.83, V.iii.37–47.

170 **Recreant** traitor (enemy of the Faith, violator of 'Allegiance').

171 **That** because

172 **strain'd** overextended, arrogant. Compare line 144.

The Region of my Heart; be Kent unmannerly
When Lear is mad. What wouldest thou do, Old Man?
Thinkst thou that Duty shall have dread to speak
When Power to Flattery bows?
To Plainness Honour's bound
When Majesty falls to Folly. Reserve thy State,
And in thy best Consideration check
This hideous Rashness, answer my Life my Judgement:
Thy Youngest Daughter does not love thee Least,
Nor are those Empty-hearted whose Low Sounds
Reverb no Hollowness.

LEAR Kent, on thy Life no more.

KENT My Life I never held but as a Pawn
To wage against thine Enemies, nere fear to loose it,
Thy Safety being Motive.

LEAR Out of my Sight.

KENT See better, Lear, and let me still remain
The true Blank of thine Eye.

LEAR Now by Apollo –

KENT Now by Apollo, King,
Thou swear'st thy Gods in vain.

LEAR O Vassal! Miscreant.

ALBANY, CORNWALL Dear Sir, forbear.

KENT Kill thy Physician, and thy Fee bestow
Upon the foul Disease. Revoke thy Gift,
Or whilst I can vent Clamour from my Throat
I'll tell thee thou dost Evil.

LEAR Hear me, Recreant, on thine Allegiance hear me;
That thou hast sought to make us break our Vows,
Which we durst never yet, and with strain'd Pride

173 **Sentences** both (a) sententiae (wise pronouncements), and (b) judgements on wrongdoers.

174 **nor . . . bear** neither my character as a man nor my position as a monarch can tolerate.

175 **Our . . . good** [to assure you that] my power remains in force.

176–77 **for . . . World** to gather such provisions as will protect you from the world's dangers. Lear's sentence recalls lines 33–34.

180 **Trunk** body.

181 **Jupiter** Zeus (Jove) the lightning-thrower; ruler of the Olympian gods.

183 **sith . . . appear** since this is the face you choose to wear.

187 **And . . . approve** and may your [Cordelia's sisters'] 'Good Effects' prove your fulsome words to be more than empty promises.

189 **adew** adeiu (farewell; literally, 'to God' and his care, as in line 185, a concept Shakespeare frequently associates with *dew*, manna, in accordance with Exodus 16:11–19). Here as elsewhere the spelling in the original printing provides an eye-rhyme.

191 CORNWALL Most editors follow the Quarto and assign this speech to Gloucester; a few interpret the Folio's *Cor.* to refer to Cordelia.

192 **My . . . Burgundy** This half-line is here indented to indicate the time between Burgundy's entrance and Lear's 'address toward' him. Burgundy (Bourgogne) is a region in southeastern France; but the Duke of Burgundy also controlled the Netherlands during the Renaissance.

196 **Most** This word appears only in the Folio text.

198 **Nor . . . less?** and surely you aren't thinking of offering less? Most editions disregard the question mark in the Quarto and Folio texts.

199 **Dear to us** (a) lovingly disposed to me, and (b) treasured by me. Compare lines 20–21, 57, 77, 185, 219.

201 **ought . . . Substance** anything within what now appears to be so insubstantial. Lear means 'little-seeming' (of no 'Price' or value); but in fact Cordelia's plight is a result of her 'little seeming' (her refusal to 'seem' to be other than she is). Hyphenating the phrase, as modern editions normally do, obscures the ambiguity.

To come betwixt our Sentences and our Power,
Which nor our Nature nor our Place can bear,
Our Potency made good, take thy Reward.
Five Days we do allot thee for Provision,
To shield thee from Disasters of the World,
And on the Sixt to turn thy hated Back
Upon our Kingdom; if on the Tenth Day following
Thy banish'd Trunk be found in our Dominions
The Moment is thy Death, away. By Jupiter,
This shall not be revok'd.

KENT Fare thee well, King, sith thus thou wilt appear,
Freedom lives hence, and Banishment is here.
– The Gods to their dear Shelter take thee, Maid,
That justly thinkst and hast most rightly said.
– And your large Speeches may your Deeds approve,
That Good Effects may spring from Words of Love.
– Thus Kent, O Princes, bids you all adew;
He'll shape his Old Course in a Country New. *Exit.*

Flourish. Enter Gloucester with France and Burgundy, Attendants.

CORNWALL Here's France and Burgundy, my noble Lord.

LEAR My Lord of Burgundy,
We first address toward you, who with this King
Have rivall'd for our Daughter; what in the least
Will you require in present Dower with her
Or cease your Quest of Love?

BURGUNDY Most royal Majesty,
I crave no more than hath your Highness offer'd,
Nor will you tender less?

LEAR Right noble Burgundy,
When she was Dear to us, we did hold her so,
But now her Price is fallen. Sir, there she stands:
If ought within that little seeming Substance,

202 **piec'd** pieced out; augmented. Compare lines 66, 95.

205 **Infirmities she owes** defects she possesses (and owes to her 'Plainness', her unmended plain-speaking, lines 130, 150).

206 **adopted** Lear's phrasing is a reminder that a beloved child has been accorded the opposite of adoption ('stranger'd', treated like a stranger). Compare Gloucester's treatment of a real bastard (lines 24–25, echoed in lines 215–16).

209 **Election . . . Conditions** choice does not function (make up or 'mend' the 'Infirmities') under such circumstances. Here *Election* has New Testament implications; see the notes to *The Merchant of Venice*, II.ix.3, 43, 82. A daughter who lacks her father's grace ('Election', blessing) is not acceptable for a Burgundy.

210 **Powre** power. See the note to I.ii.24.

211 **tell you** both (a) calculate for you, and (b) announce to you.

212 **make . . . Stray** commit such a transgression (departure from the right way of dealing with a fellow monarch).

214 **avert . . . Way** turn your affections in a more advantageous direction.

215 **Then** Lear means 'than' (which is normally spelled *then* in Shakespeare's plays); but the usual modern sense of *then* (which can be synonymous with *therefore* in Shakespeare) is also applicable here. Compare *Macbeth*, III.ii.7, III.iv.12, and *The Merchant of Venice*, III.ii.161, III.v.45.

217 **best Object** most prized possession. *Best* derives from the Quarto.

218 **Argument** chief instance; highest exemplar; main theme.
Balm . . . Age soothing ointment for your old age (compare lines 124–25).

219 **Trice** moment (the time required for one tug or pull on a rope).

220 **dismantle** remove, strip off; 'divest' (line 50).

223 **monsters it** makes it appallingly abhorrent.
fore-vouch'd (a) previously sworn, (b) formerly bound to.

228 **for . . . Art** because I lack that smooth and unctuous artifice.

229 **will intend** will resolve. Most editors adopt the Quarto's *well*. Compare line 39.

231 **vicious Blot** taint deriving from vice.

235 **still soliciting** constantly soliciting (urging, seducing).

Or all of it, with our Displeasure piec'd,
And nothing more, may fitly like your Grace,
She's there, and she is yours.
BURGUNDY I know no Answer.
LEAR Will you with those Infirmities she owes,
Unfriended, new adopted to our Hate,
Dow'r'd with our Curse, and stranger'd with our Oath,
Take her or leave her.
BURGUNDY Pardon me, Royal Sir,
Election makes not up in such Conditions.
LEAR Then leave her, Sir, for by the Powre that made
me,
I tell you all her Wealth. – For you, great King,
I would not from your Love make such a Stray
To match you where I hate, therefore beseech you
T' avert your Liking a more worthier Way,
Then on a Wretch whom Nature is asham'd
Almost t' acknowledge hers.
FRANCE This is most Strange,
That she whom even but now was your best Object,
The Argument of your Praise, Balm of your Age,
The Best, the Dearest, should in this Trice of Time
Commit a thing so monstrous, to dismantle
So many Folds of Favour. Sure her Offence
Must be of such Unnatural Degree
That monsters it, or your fore-vouch'd Affection
Fall into Taint, which to believe of her
Must be a Faith that Reason without Miracle
Should never plant in me.
CORDELIA I yet beseech your Majesty,
If for I want that glib and oily Art
To speak and purpose not, since what I will intend
I'll do't before I speak, that you make known
It is no vicious Blot, Murther, or Foulness,
No Unchaste Action or Dishonoured Step,
That hath depriv'd me of your Grace and Favour,
But even for want of that for which I am richer,
A still soliciting Eye, and such a Tongue

237 **lost . . . Liking** 'stranger'd' me; lost me my position as one who is like you (an heir of your blood).

238 **borne** (a) carried by your mother, (b) born, and (c) reared.

239 **Tardiness** slowness; reticence, shyness, modesty.

240 **History** story; narrative. Compare II.ii.242.

243–44 **mingled . . . Point** mixed (adulterated) with considerations that have nothing to do with what is of central importance. France's phrasing is a reminder that Cordelia's stand against hypocrisy (line 200) has prompted Burgundy to stand 'aloof' from a daughter who has elected not to be a party to 'such Conditions' as Lear has imposed upon 'Election' to his bounty (line 209). France insists that true love 'stands' (holds true to its position or established destination) only when directed to the 'Point' ('Object') of true 'Love', whether or not it stands (resides) within an angry father's 'Grace' (line 278). His words echo the archery and target imagery of lines 75, 123, 144, 161–62, 173, 177, 181, 251.

249 **Nothing** This word echoes lines 88–91, 203.
firm unbending. Compare lines 39, 44, 144, 205.

251 **loose** (a) lose, (b) unleash, and (c) release. See line 159.

253 **Respect** (a) respectability, social standing, reputation, and (b) 'Regards', in the sense defined in lines 243–44.

255–56 **most . . . Despis'd** France's words echo such biblical passages as Isaiah 53:3 (associating Cordelia with the suffering servant described in Isaiah 52:13–53:12), Matthew 5:3, 1 Corinthians 1:28, 2 Corinthians 6:10, 8:9, and Philippians 2:5–8.

258 **Be . . . away** if I may be permitted to salvage this discarded object. *Cast away* echoes *heave*, line 92.

260 **enflam'd Respect** a blazing fire of 'Respect' (here a recognition of Cordelia's transcendent virtues), the highest form of love; 'best Consideration' (line 152).

263 **wat'rish Burgundy** France's adjective connotes thinness (as in wine or milk diluted with water), inconstancy (for which water was proverbial), and weakness. See lines 85, 192; and compare Revelation 3:14–17.

264 **unpriz'd** unvalued. Compare lines 70–71, 199–204, 210–11.

265 **though unkind** (a) though they are unkind (unnatural), and (b) though you have been declared unkind (unrelated to their kind, lines 207, 237).

That I am glad I have not, though not to have it
Hath lost me in your Liking.

LEAR Better thou
Hadst not been borne than not t' have pleas'd me
better.

FRANCE Is it but this? A Tardiness in Nature,
Which often leaves the History unspoke
That it intends to do? – My Lord of Burgundy,
What say you to the Lady? Love's not Love
When it is mingled with Regards that stands
Aloof from th' entire Point. Will you have her?
She is herself a Dowry.

BURGUNDY – Royal King,
Give but that Portion which your self propos'd,
And here I take Cordelia by the Hand,
Duchess of Burgundy.

LEAR Nothing, I have sworn, I am firm.

BURGUNDY I am sorry then you have so lost a Father
That you must loose a Husband.

CORDELIA Peace be with Burgundy:
Since that Respect and Fortunes are his Love,
I shall not be his Wife.

FRANCE Fairest Cordelia, that art most Rich being Poor,
Most Choice Forsaken, and most Lov'd Despis'd,
Thee and thy Virtues here I seize upon,
Be it lawful I take up what's cast away.
– Gods, Gods! – 'Tis Strange that from their cold'st
Neglect
My Love should kindle to enflam'd Respect.
– Thy Dow'rless Daughter, King, thrown to my
Chance,
Is Queen of us, of ours, and our fair France:
Not all the Dukes of wat'rish Burgundy
Can buy this unpriz'd precious Maid of me.
– Bid them farewell, Cordelia, though unkind,

266 **loosest** losest. Compare lines 159, 250–51 for additional implications. *Find* echoes line 60.

270 **Benizon** benison, benediction; blessing.

273 **wash'd** tearful, here meaning (a) cleansed, (b) pure.

275 **loath** reluctant, unwilling.

279 **prefer** (a) commend, 'commit', (b) advance, and (c) wish. *Stood* (line 278) echoes lines 242–44.

281 **Prescribe . . . Duty** Don't presume to dictate our responsibilities.

283 **At Fortune's Alms** as a scrap bestowed on a beggar by Fortune.
scanted withheld like a miser; neglected.

284 **Want . . . wanted** deprivation that your own stinginess (want of loving expression) earned you. *Want* echoes line 228.

285 **Time . . . hides** Time will disclose (open up or strip bare) what pleated (folded) deceit covers over. *Unfold* echoes lines 220–21 and continues the clothing and sheltering imagery of lines 40–41, 50–51, 66, 109, 130–33, 185, 190, 202, 250–51; *plighted* recalls lines 102–3.

286 **Who . . . derides** Whoever conceals blemishes will in time be mocked by the shame of exposure, blots and all (line 231). Lines 285–86 echo Proverbs 28:13, 'He that covereth his sins shall not prosper: but whoso confesseth and forsaketh them shall have mercy.'

289 **nearly appertains** intimately pertains.

290 **to night** tonight. But see the note to I.ii.24.

294–95 **The . . . little** we have made little comment on a flaw that we have both noted individually. Most editions follow the Quarto and insert *not* before *been*.

297 **appears too grossly** is too obvious and unsightly to overlook. *Infirmity* (line 298) echoes lines 205, 304.

Thou loosest here a better where to find.
LEAR Thou hast her, France, let her be thine, for we
Have no such Daughter, nor shall ever see
That Face of hers again; therefore be gone,
Without our Grace, our Love, our Benizon.
– Come, noble Burgundy. *Flourish. Exeunt*
[*all but France, Cordelia, Goneril, and Regan*].
FRANCE Bid farewell to your Sisters.
CORDELIA The Jewels of our Father, with wash'd Eyes
Cordelia leaves you. I know you what you are,
And like a Sister am most loath to call
Your Faults as they are named. Love well our Father:
To your professed Bosoms I commit him,
But yet alas, stood I within his Grace,
I would prefer him to a better Place.
So farewell to you both.
REGAN Prescribe not us our Duty.
GONERIL Let your Study
Be to content your Lord, who hath receiv'd you
At Fortune's Alms. You have Obedience scanted,
And well are worth the Want that you have wanted.
CORDELIA Time shall unfold what plighted Cunning
hides,
Who covers Faults, at last with Shame derides:
Well may you prosper.
FRANCE Come, my fair Cordelia.
Exit with Cordelia.
GONERIL Sister, it is not little I have to say
Of what most nearly appertains to us both.
I think our Father will hence to night.
REGAN That's most certain, and with you; next
Month with us.
GONERIL You see how full of Changes his Age is.
The Observation we have made of it hath been
little; he always lov'd our Sister most, and
with what poor Judgement he hath now cast her
off appears too grossly.
REGAN 'Tis the Infirmity of his Age, yet he hath

300 **Time** 'Age', both (a) age group and (b) era (now old-fashioned).

303 **ingraffed Condition** deeply implanted disposition.

304 **Choleric** prone to choler (a humour associated with anger). *Way-wardness* (waywardness) anticipates I.ii.79–83. The Folio spelling may have been influenced by the end-of-line word-division in the Quarto text; but it may also preserve an authorial pun on *ward* (dependent minor).

306 **Unconstant Starts** quirky outbursts. Compare lines 44, 249. Here *like* means 'likely'.

308 **complement** completing; complying with formal courtesy.

310 **sit together** put our heads together [and plot our strategies]. Most editors adopt the Quarto's *hit* (reinforcing line 314).

311–12 **last Surrender** most recent submission to irrationality. Goneril's phrasing is a reminder of everything else Lear has surrendered.

314 **i'th' Heat** immediately (striking while the iron is hot).

I.ii This scene takes place in the castle of the Earl of Gloucester.

2–4 **Wherefore . . . me?** Why should I allow myself to be discriminated against by the arbitrary traditions that have kept good men down in one nation after another? Edmund (who is normally designated 'Bastard' from this point forward in the Folio text) refers to primogeniture, a 'Custom' that deprives younger sons, and especially illegitimate ones, of any claims on their fathers' estates. *Curiosity* echoes I.i.5–6.

5 **Moonshines** months (here figuratively likened to insubstantial glimmers of dim, reflected light).

6 **Lag of** lagging behind; younger than.
Base low, of no esteem. Edmund plays on the first syllable of *Bastard*.

7 **Dimensions . . . Compact** proportions are as well composed.

8 **Generous** noble (from the Latin *generosus*, 'well born').

11–12 **in . . . Quality** from the untamed ferocity and fecundity that resulted in our conception derive more strength and fiery vigour.

14 **Fops** limp ('dull, stale') fools. Compare *Foppery*, line 134.

ever but slenderly known himself.

GONERIL The Best and Soundest of his Time hath been but Rash; then must we look from his Age to receive not alone the Imperfections of long ingraffed Condition, but therewithal the unruly Way-wardness that Infirm and Choleric Years bring with them.

REGAN Such Unconstant Starts are we like to have from him as this of Kent's Banishment.

GONERIL There is further complement of Leave-taking between France and him: pray you let us sit together. If our Father carry Authority with such Disposition as he bears, this last Surrender of his will but offend us.

REGAN We shall further think of it.

GONERIL We must do something, and i'th' Heat. *Exeunt.*

Scene 2

Enter Bastard.

BASTARD Thou, Nature, art my Goddess: to thy Law
My Services are bound. Wherefore should I
Stand in the Plague of Custom, and permit
The Curiosity of Nations to deprive me?
For that I am some twelve or fourteen Moonshines
Lag of a Brother? Why Bastard? Wherefore Base?
When my Dimensions are as well Compact,
My Mind as Generous, and my Shape as True
As Honest Madam's Issue? Why brand they us
With Base? With Baseness, Bastardy? Base, Base?
Who in the lusty Stealth of Nature take
More Composition and fierce Quality
Than doth within a dull, stale, tired Bed
Go to th' Creating a whole Tribe of Fops
Got 'tween a Sleep and Wake? – Well then,

19 **speed** succeed in its purpose; 'thrive'.

21 **to th' Legitimate** rise to the level of the legitimate brother (and supplant him). Most editors prefer the Quarto's *top* to *to*. In the Folio version of this passage Edmund plays on *to* in lines 14, 17–18.

grow become larger. Edmund's verb hints at genital potency and fertility (compare 'stand up', line 22, and I.i.14); it also recalls such organic imagery as I.i.85–86, 175, 224–26, 301–5. *Intention* recalls I.i.39, 229–30.

22 **Now . . . Bastards** Compare I.i.185, 206.

23 **Choler** anger. This word echoes I.i.304. France's 'Choler' is expressed in I.i.221–26, 261–66. Evidently France has then tried to make amends: see I.i.308–9.

24 **to night** Gloucester means *tonight*; but the Renaissance spelling of what we now treat as a single word allows the Earl's question to resonate with implications unintended by the speaker. The King's 'darker Purpose' will convey him (and others, including Gloucester) 'to night' in several senses.

Powre power. In *Macbeth*, I.iii.98, I.v.28, and IV.i.18, *powre* is the spelling for *pour*. Soon Lear's decision to prescribe (limit) his power will prove to have been a decision to prescribe pouring rain as a medicine for the King's own ills.

24–25 **Prescrib'd . . . Exhibition?** Put prescribed limits on his power, circumscribing himself to merely ceremonial appearances and a small allowance of funds and attendants? Compare I.i.131–40, 281.

26 **Upon the Gad** goaded by impulse (likened here to a sharp prod).

32 **Nothing** Like Lear's offspring in the previous scene, Edmund replies in a manner that will drive a gullible father to make much ado about something that really *is* nothing. Compare I.i.249.

33–34 **terrible Dispatch** terrified, urgent thrusting away.

34 **Quality** essence, nature. Compare I.i.5–7, 201.

39–40 **that . . . o'er-read** which I have not finished perusing.

41 **fit** suitable. This word echoes I.i.98, 203, and anticipates lines 80, 189, 205.

43 **detain** hold back.

45 **blame** blameworthy. So also in II.ii.155.

Legitimate Edgar, I must have your Land.
Our Father's Love is to the Bastard Edmund
As to th' Legitimate. – Fine Word: 'Legitimate'.
– Well, my Legitimate, if this Letter speed,
And my Intention thrive, Edmund the Base
Shall to th' Legitimate: I grow, I prosper.
– Now Gods, stand up for Bastards.

Enter Gloucester.

GLOUCESTER Kent banish'd thus? And France in Choler parted?
And the King gone to night? Prescrib'd his Powre,
Confin'd to Exhibition? All this done
Upon the Gad? Edmund, how now? What News?

BASTARD So please your Lordship, none.

GLOUCESTER Why so earnestly seek you to put up that Letter?

BASTARD I know no News, my Lord.

GLOUCESTER What Paper were you reading?

BASTARD Nothing, my Lord.

GLOUCESTER No? What needed then that terrible
Dispatch of it into your Pocket? The Quality
of Nothing hath not such need to hide it self.
Let's see: come, if it be Nothing, I shall not
need Spectacles.

BASTARD I beseech you, Sir, pardon me; it is a
Letter from my Brother, that I have not all
o'er-read; and for so much as I have perus'd,
I find it not fit for your o'er-looking.

GLOUCESTER Give me the Letter, Sir.

BASTARD I shall offend either to detain or give
it: the Contents, as in part I understand them,
are too blame.

GLOUCESTER Let's see, let's see.

BASTARD I hope, for my Brother's Justification,

48 **Taste** test (as in the custom whereby a monarch had one of his attendants sample his food to be sure that the ruler would not be poisoned by a meal prepared for him by others).

50 **Policy . . . Age** cunning craftiness by which the older generation keeps the younger reverent (respectful and subservient). *Best* echoes I.i.217, 300–1.

53 **relish** enjoy (playing on 'Taste', line 48).

54 **idle and fond** irresponsible and foolish (doting, senile).

55 **sways** rules. Edmund will try to make 'Age' sway in another sense (totter, become unstable). Compare I.i.138–39.

56 **suffer'd** permitted, tolerated.

57–58 **till . . . him** for ever [since the writer of the letter plans to put the old man to sleep for good].

64 **breed it** beget it. Compare I.i.9, 97.

68 **Casement . . . Closet** hinged window of my private chamber. Compare *Julius Caesar*, I.ii.319–24, II.i.35–57.

69 **Character** handwriting (supposedly expressing 'character' in the usual modern sense).

71 **Matter** subject matter.
durst would dare.

73 **fain** gladly prefer to. So also in I.iv.31 and in IV.vii.37.

74 **It is his** Most editions follow the Quarto and conclude line 74 with a question mark. The Folio punctuation suggests that Gloucester is already persuaded by Edmund's insinuations.

77 **sounded** tested; sounded you out, plumbed you for the depth of your affection to your father.

80 **at perfect Age** once they become adults in their prime. *Fit* echoes I.i.98.

81 **declin'd** losing their powers; literally, fallen off.

81–82 **as . . . Son** under the son's guardianship. Compare I.i.124–25. *Ward* echoes *Way-wardness*, I.i.304.

he wrote this but as an Essay, or Taste of my Virtue.

GLOUCESTER *reads* 'This Policy and Reverence of Age makes the World bitter to the Best of our Times, keeps our Fortunes from us till our Oldness cannot relish them. I begin to find an idle and fond Bondage in the Oppression of Aged Tyranny, who sways not as it hath Power but as it is suffer'd. Come to me, that of this I may speak more. If our Father would sleep till I wak'd him, you should enjoy half his Revenue for ever, and live the Beloved of your Brother. Edgar.'

Hum? Conspiracy? 'Sleep till I wake him, you should enjoy half his Revenue.' My Son Edgar, had he a Hand to write this? A Heart and Brain to breed it in? When came you to this? Who brought it?

BASTARD It was not brought me, my Lord; there's the Cunning of it. I found it thrown in at the Casement of my Closet.

GLOUCESTER You know the Character to be your Brother's?

BASTARD If the Matter were good, my Lord, I durst swear it were his; but in respect of that, I would fain think it were not.

GLOUCESTER It is his.

BASTARD It is his Hand, my Lord; but I hope his Heart is not in the Contents.

GLOUCESTER Has he never before sounded you in this Business?

BASTARD Never, my Lord. But I have heard him oft maintain it to be fit, that Sons at perfect Age, and Fathers declin'd, the Father should be as Ward to the Son, and the Son manage his Revenue.

GLOUCESTER O Villain, Villain: his very Opinion in the Letter. Abhorred Villain; unnatural,

87 **Sirrah** This term is normally reserved for a social inferior; here it serves as a reminder of the way Gloucester has always thought of 'the Whoreson' (I.i.24).

88 **Abhominable** inhuman. This word was thought to derive from *ab + homine*, Latin for 'away from humanity'. Here that sense is synonymous with 'unnatural' and 'brutish'.

90 **suspend your Indignation** hold your righteous anger in suspension. Compare *forbear* in I.i.165.

92–93 **run . . . Course** proceed along a well-marked, safe path (with no fear of being misled or going astray). Compare I.i.301–5.

93 **where** whereas.
violently hastily and forcibly.

95 **Gap** breach, hole.
shake both (a) frighten, and (b) shatter. Compare I.i.40.

97 **pawn down** pledge as surety. Compare I.i.158.

98 **feel** make trial of. Compare lines 48, 77–78.

99 **Pretence of Danger** dangerous intent.

103 **Auricular Assurance** the certainty that comes from hearing with your own ears. Compare *Othello*, III.ii.350.

104 **Satisfaction** full confirmation. Lines 107–9 ('BASTARD . . . Earth!') occur only in the Quarto; so also with 'Fut' and 'Edgar' (lines 149, 151).

110 **wind . . . him** worm your way into his confidence for me.

111–12 **I . . . Resolution** I would forgo my entire estate to have all my doubts duly resolved. Compare I.i.37–42, 50–51, 151.

115 **withal** therewith; with all [I've arranged].

117 **portend** bode, forecast. Eclipses were in fact seen in England in September and October of 1605. Since *Sun* is a symbol of royalty (see *Hamlet* I.ii.67), Gloucester's words can also refer to the 'late Eclipses' of Lear's majesty.

117–18 **the . . . and thus** those who trust in the scientific study of Nature believe that they can explain it this way or that.

119 **scourg'd . . . Effects** injured (whipped) by the events that follow.

122 **Bond** familial tie. Compare I.i.93–94.

detested, brutish Villain; worse than brutish. Go Sirrah, seek him: I'll apprehend him. Abhominable Villain, where is he?

BASTARD I do not well know, my Lord. If it shall please you to suspend your Indignation against my Brother till you can derive from him better Testimony of his Intent, you should run a Certain Course; where, if you violently proceed against him, mistaking his Purpose, it would make a great Gap in your own Honour and shake in Pieces the Heart of his Obedience. I dare pawn down my Life for him, that he hath writ this to feel my Affection to your Honour, and to no other Pretence of Danger.

GLOUCESTER Think you so?

BASTARD If your Honour judge it meet, I will place you where you shall hear us confer of this, and by an Auricular Assurance have your Satisfaction, and that without any further Delay than this very Evening.

GLOUCESTER He cannot be such a Monster.

BASTARD Nor is not, sure.

GLOUCESTER To his Father, that so tenderly and entirely loves him, Heaven and Earth! Edmund, seek him out; wind me into him, I pray you; frame the Business after your own Wisdom. I would unstate my self, to be in a due Resolution.

BASTARD I will seek him, Sir, presently: convey the Business as I shall find Means, and acquaint you withal.

GLOUCESTER These late Eclipses in the Sun and Moon portend no good to us: though the Wisdom of Nature can reason it thus, and thus, yet Nature finds it self scourg'd by the sequent Effects. Love cools, Friendship falls off, Brothers divide. In Cities, Mutinies; in Countries, Discord; in Palaces, Treason; and the Bond crack'd 'twixt Son and Father. This Villain

124 **comes . . . Prediction** is one of the things the eclipses portend. Lines 123–29 (from 'This' to 'Graves') appear only in the Folio text.

125–26 **Bias of Nature** the disposition Nature has placed in him. Gloucester's image derives from the game of bowls, played with a ball whose bias (off-centre weight) causes it to swerve (roll with a bias).

127 **Machinations** treacherous manipulation; deceitful 'Hollowness' (compare I.i.155–56). *Best* echoes line 51 and anticipates line 193.

132 **harted** both (a) harted (like a noble stag), and (b) hearted.

136 **Surfeits** nausea or other illnesses resulting from overindulgence. *Disasters* (line 137) recalls I.i.177.

140 **Treachers** traitors; treacherous persons.

143 **Thrusting-on** prompting. Edmund's phrasing suggests both the spurring of erotic desire and the in-forced 'Compulsion' of rape. His imagery alludes profanely to the immaculate conception of Christ (Luke 1:30–38).

144–46 **to . . . Star** to lay the blame for his lechery on a star (to credit 'Spherical Predominance', or 'Planetary Influence', lines 140, 142).

146 **compounded** combined; literally, 'pounded together'.

147 **the Dragon's Tail** *Dragon* refers to the constellation Draco, located near 'Ursa Major' (Big Bear), line 148. *Tail* is one meaning of the Latin word *penis*, and Edmund's mother was 'under' more than one 'Dragon's Tail'.

Nativity birth (another blasphemous allusion to the Virgin Birth).

149 **Fut** a contemptuous expletive (short for 'God's foot'), here echoing another word that accords with 'Rough and Lecherous'.

150 **Maidenlest** most maiden-like (virginal). But the Folio spelling suggests that this 'Star' (planet) was maidenless and thus prone to induce maiden-lust, lust for (and in) maidens.

152 **Catastrophe** denouement, resolution.

154 **Tom o' Bedlam** a lunatic from Bedlam (the Bethlehem hospital, London's insane asylum). Edmund's 'Cue' (both signal and role) will soon be Edgar's.

of mine comes under the Prediction: there's Son against Father, the King falls from Bias of Nature, there's Father against Child. We have seen the Best of our Time. Machinations, Hollowness, Treachery, and all ruinous Disorders follow us disquietly to our Graves. Find out this Villain, Edmund, it shall lose thee nothing, do it carefully. And the Noble and True-harted Kent banish'd, his Offence Honesty. 'Tis Strange. *Exit.*

BASTARD This is the excellent Foppery of the World, that when we are Sick in Fortune, often the Surfeits of our own Behaviour, we make Guilty of our Disasters the Sun, the Moon, and Stars, as if we were Villains on Necessity, Fools by Heavenly Compulsion, Knaves, Thieves, and Treachers by Spherical Predominance. Drunkards, Liars, and Adulterers by an inforc'd Obedience of Planetary Influence; and all that we are Evil in by a Divine Thrusting-on. An admirable Evasion of Whore-master Man, to lay his Goatish Disposition on the Charge of a Star. My Father compounded with my Mother under the Dragon's Tail, and my Nativity was under Ursa Major, so that it follows I am Rough and Lecherous. Fut, I should have been that I am had the Maidenlest Star in the Firmament twinkled on my Bastardizing. Edgar –

Enter Edgar.

Pat: he comes like the Catastrophe of the Old Comedy. My Cue is villainous Melancholy, with a Sigh like Tom o' Bedlam. – O these Eclipses

155 **Fa . . . Me** Edmund sings four notes (a musical cue, here to signify 'Melancholy'), using their names from the gamut (musical scale).

165 **Dearth** deprivation (lines 2–4), as with Cordelia and Kent. **ancient Amities** time-honoured leagues (ties, allegiances). Lines 162–64 recall Matthew 10:21, 'And the brother shall deliver up the brother to death, and the father the child: and the children shall rise up against their parents, and cause them to be put to death.'

166 **Maledictions** evil-speakings; curses and threats.

167 **needless Diffidences** unwarranted suspicions (compare *King John*, I.i.65). Lines 163–72 ('as . . . come') are from the Quarto. The Quarto prints *needles*.

168 **Dissipation of Cohorts** dispersing of companies (such as the entourage of troops Lear has reserved for himself, I.i.134–35).

169 **Nuptial Breaches** ruptures of matrimonial bonds. As in line 168, Edmund describes some 'Effects' yet to 'succeed'.

170–71 **Sectary Astronomical** member of the astrological sect (those who put their faith in readings of the Heavens).

175 **I** both (a) ay (yes), and (b) I. Compare I.i.106.

179 **Bethink your self** think hard, try to recall.

180 **forbear** avoid; deprive yourself of. Compare I.i.165.

181 **qualified** diluted, lessened. Compare I.i.242–44, 263. Edmund will be doing his best to qualify Gloucester's 'Displeasure' in a different sense: 'Heat' it in such a way as to distil it to a concentrate of its essential quality (line 34), its nature.

183–84 **with . . . allay** even his harming you (doing 'Mischief' to your 'Person') would scarcely end it.

186–87 **have . . . Forbearance** restrain (contain) any impulse you have to see him. See line 180. Lines 186–91 (from 'I' to 'abroad') appear only in the Folio.

do portend these Divisions. Fa, Sol, La, Me.

EDGAR How now, brother Edmund, what serious Contemplation are you in?

BASTARD I am thinking, Brother, of a Prediction I read this other Day, what should follow these Eclipses.

EDGAR Do you busy your self with that?

BASTARD I promise you, the Effects he writes of succeed unhappily, as of Unnaturalness between the Child and the Parent, Death, Dearth, Dissolutions of ancient Amities, Divisions in State, Menaces and Maledictions against King and Nobles, needless Diffidences, Banishment of Friends, Dissipation of Cohorts, Nuptial Breaches, and I know not what.

EDGAR How long have you been a Sectary Astronomical?

BASTARD Come, come, when saw you my Father last?

EDGAR The Night gone by.

BASTARD Spake you with him?

EDGAR I, two Hours together.

BASTARD Parted you in Good Terms? Found you no Displeasure in him, by Word nor Countenance?

EDGAR None at all.

BASTARD Bethink your self wherein you may have offended him; and at my Entreaty forbear his Presence until some little Time hath qualified the Heat of his Displeasure, which at this Instant so rageth in him that with the Mischief of your Person it would scarcely allay.

EDGAR Some Villain hath done me wrong.

BASTARD That's my Fear, I pray you have a continent Forbearance till the Speed of his Rage goes slower; and as I say, retire with me to my Lodging, from whence I will fitly bring you to hear my Lord speak. Pray ye go, there's my Key. If you do stir abroad, go arm'd.

EDGAR Arm'd, Brother?

194 **Good Meaning** benign 'Intent' (I.iv.2). Edmund speaks the truth: it is the Bastard's 'Meaning' (purpose) that Edgar needs to be concerned about.

196 **faintly** in a 'qualified' fashion (line 181). Compare Edmund's earlier references to weak 'Composition' (mixture) in lines 11–15, 48–49.

Image true (undiminished) likeness.

199 **serve you** both (a) labour in your behalf (the meaning Edgar hears), and (b) work to undo you (Edmund's private meaning).

200 **Credulous** disposed to believe what he is told. Claudius speaks similarly about his nephew in *Hamlet*, IV.vii.131–36; and Iago relies on the same kind of trusting nobility in his intended victim, as he notes in *Othello*, I.iii.406–9.

204 **Wit** intelligence, cunning. See the note to I.iv.201.

205 **fit** aptly. This word recalls lines 41, 189.

I.iii This scene takes place at the residence of the Duke of Albany. We learn later that the 'Steward' (chief servant) of Albany's duchess is named Oswald (see I.iv.327).

2 **Chiding . . . Fool** rebuking his court jester.

4 **By . . . Night** an oath, here one that is synonymous with 'Every Hour'.

5 **flashes** ignites, erupts. Compare the references to Lear's 'unruly Way-wardness' and 'Unconstant Starts' in I.i.303–6.

7 **Riotous** unruly, disorderly.

10 **slack . . . Services** less obedient to his commands than in the past.

11 **the . . . answer** I'll bear the responsibility for your lapses.

13 **Put . . . please** adopt what unhelpful manner you wish, pretending that you are too tired. Goneril's clothing metaphor recalls I.i.285.

14 **come to Question** become an issue; come to a head (like a boil).

15 **distaste** dislike. Compare I.ii.48.

17 **Idle** (a) unemployed, (b) foolish, and (c) irritating. Lines 17–21 occur only in the First Quarto printing; so also with lines 25–26 ('I would . . . speak') and 'very' (identical) in line 27.

BASTARD Brother, I advise you to the best; I am no
Honest Man if there be any Good Meaning toward
you. I have told you what I have seen and heard:
but faintly. Nothing like the Image and Horror
of it. Pray you away.
EDGAR Shall I hear from you anon?
BASTARD I do serve you in this Business. *Exit Edgar.*
– A Credulous Father, and a Brother Noble,
Whose Nature is so far from doing Harms
That he suspects none: on whose foolish Honesty
My Practices ride easy. I see the Business.
Let me, if not by Birth, have Lands by Wit;
All with me's meet that I can fashion fit. *Exit.*

Scene 3

Enter Goneril and Steward.

GONERIL Did my Father strike my Gentleman for
Chiding of his Fool?
STEWARD Ay, Madam.
GONERIL By Day and Night, he wrongs me. Every Hour
He flashes into one gross Crime or other
That sets us all at Odds; I'll not endure it.
His Knights grow Riotous, and himself upbraids us
On every Trifle. When he returns from Hunting,
I will not speak with him; say I am Sick.
If you come slack of former Services,
You shall do well; the Fault of it I'll answer.
STEWARD He's coming, Madam, I hear him.
GONERIL Put on what weary Negligence you please,
You and your Fellows. I'd have it come to Question;
If he distaste it, let him to my Sister,
Whose Mind and mine I know in that are one,
Not to be overrul'd. Idle Old Man,
That still would manage those Authorities

20 **Babes again** like untrained children. Lear is about to find out what kind of 'kind Nursery' he has set his rest on (I.i.124–25). Compare I.i.293–314.

20–21 **us'd . . . abus'd** treated with firm discipline for their own good when they are observed to be deceiving themselves. In II.ii.483–85 Regan will use similar imagery to sterner effect.

23 **Colder** less friendly; distant. Compare II.ii.221.

25 **breed . . . Occasions** create from these practices opportunities [to speak my mind to my father]. *Breed* echoes I.ii.9–16, 63–64.

26 **straight** straightway (straight away); immediately. *Course* (line 27) recalls I.ii.89–93.

I.iv This scene takes place at the Duke of Albany's palace.

1 **as will** as I choose. Most editions opt for the Quarto's *well* here. If that is Kent's meaning, *will* is probably an instance of the 'other Accents' he now must 'borrow'.

2 **defuse** disorder [and thereby disguise]. *Intent* recalls I.ii.19–21.

3 **Issue** both (a) emission, and (b) birth (outcome); compare I.i.17–18. In this speech *carry*, *stand*, and *come* can function as sexual metaphors, and *full of Labours* suggests both intercourse and incipient childbirth. Like France's (I.i.243–44), Kent's 'stand' is a 'Good Intent'.

4 **raz'd my Likeness** erased my normal appearance. Kent has now become 'unmannerly', donning a mask of peasant 'Plainness' in order to continue operating as the 'true Blank' of Lear's eye; his new likeness will allow him to 'shape his Old Course' in the 'Country New' that Lear's folly has begotten (I.i.146, 150, 162, 190).

9 **stay a iot** wait a jot (an instant as minuscule as an iota).

12 **What . . . profess?** What is your profession? As when he asks 'what art thou?' in line 10, Lear is seeking an occupational identity for this newcomer, so that he can relate to his social function. Kent's replies (lines 11, 14–19) give Lear's questions a philosophical twist. A *Man* can be a 'servant' (a serving-man); but the word's more fundamental meaning is 'human being'. Similarly, *profess* can refer to a vocation; but Kent relates it to a man's honesty, integrity, and faith (both fidelity and religious profession). Before this scene concludes, Lear's question will have modulated into 'Who is it that can tell me who I am?' (line 243).

That he hath given away. Now by my Life,
Old Fools are Babes again, and must be us'd
With Checks as Flatteries when they are seen abus'd.
Remember what I have said –

STEWARD Well, Madam.

GONERIL And let
His Knights have Colder Looks among you; what grows
Of it no matter. Advise your Fellows so.
I would breed from hence Occasions, and I shall,
That I may speak. I'll write straight to my Sister
To hold my very Course. Prepare for Dinner.

Exeunt.

Scene 4

Enter Kent.

KENT If but as will I other Accents borrow,
That can my Speech defuse, my Good Intent
May carry through it self to that full Issue
For which I raz'd my Likeness. – Now banished Kent,
If thou canst serve where thou dost stand condemn'd,
So may it come, thy Master whom thou lov'st
Shall find thee full of Labours.

Horns within. Enter Lear and Attendants.

LEAR Let me not stay a iot for Dinner, go get it ready. [*Exit at least one Attendant.*]
– How now, what art thou?

KENT A Man, Sir.

LEAR What dost thou profess? What wouldst thou with us?

14 **seem** both (a) appear to be, and (b) profess myself to be.

17 **fear Judgement** fear God [and live in a way that prepares me for the Last Judgement]. Kent has already shown in I.i. that he doesn't 'fear Judgement' (sentencing) in the sense that pertains to a monarch's lack of judgement (wisdom).

18 **choose** choose to do otherwise and retain my honour.

18–19 **eat no Fish** Kent probably means 'allow no one to make me do anything that undermines my integrity or demeans my manhood' (compare 2 *Henry IV*, IV.iii.98–102). He may also be saying that he will lead a clean life, abstaining from illicit liaisons; see *Romeo and Juliet*, I.i.31–34, *Hamlet*, II.ii.178, *1 Henry IV*, III.iii.140–46, and *Antony and Cleopatra*, II.v.15–18, for bawdy references to fish and fishing. In Shakespeare's time 'eat no fish' was sometimes associated with a refusal to return to Catholicism (which required one to eat fish, rather than red meat, on Fridays). See the note to lines 44–45.

21 **Honest-hearted** echoes I.ii.132.

35 **Counsail** counsel; confidentiality. Compare line 149.

36 **curious** artful, complicated. Compare *Curiosity* in I.i.6 (scrutiny) and I.ii.4 (arbitrary fastidiousness).

37 **bluntly** directly, with no ornamentation; plainly (compare I.i.150).

38 **fit** suited. Compare I.ii.205.
best best part or trait. This word echoes I.ii.127.

42 **dote on** blindly and foolishly idolize.

44–45 **if . . . Dinner** The original texts do not indicate whether this clause modifies what precedes it or what follows it. Most editors insert a semicolon either before or after the clause. *Follow me* echoes the calls to service in Matthew 4:19 (where Jesus promises to make his disciples 'fishers of men') 8:22, 9:9, 16:24 ('If any man will come after me, let him deny himself and take up his cross, and follow me'), and 19:21 ('If thou wilt be perfect, go and sell that thou hast, and give to the poor, and thou shalt have treasure in heaven; and come and follow me').

47 **Knave** Lear probably means his Fool, the boy who serves him as court jester. 'Knave' (villain) and 'Fool' were proverbially paired.

KENT I do profess to be no less than I seem: to serve him truly that will put me in Trust, to love him that is Honest, to converse with him that is Wise and says little, to fear Judgement, to fight when I cannot choose, and to eat no Fish.

LEAR What art thou?

KENT A very Honest-hearted Fellow, and as Poor as the King.

LEAR If thou be'st as Poor for a Subject as he's for a King, thou art Poor enough. What wouldst thou?

KENT Service.

LEAR Who wouldst thou serve?

KENT You.

LEAR Dost thou know me, Fellow?

KENT No Sir, but you have that in your Countenance which I would fain call Master.

LEAR What's that?

KENT Authority.

LEAR What Services canst thou do?

KENT I can keep Honest Counsail, ride, run, mar a curious Tale in telling it, and deliver a Plain Message bluntly; that which Ordinary Men are fit for, I am qualified in, and the best of me is Diligence.

LEAR How old art thou?

KENT Not so Young, Sir, to love a Woman for Singing, nor so Old to dote on her for any thing. I have Years on my Back forty-eight.

LEAR Follow me, thou shalt serve me, if I like thee no worse after Dinner, I will not part from thee yet. – Dinner, ho, Dinner. – Where's my Knave? My Fool? Go you and call my Fool hither. [*Exit another Attendant.*]

Enter Steward.

49 **Sirrah** a term for a subordinate; also spelled 'sirha' and 'sirrha'.

51–52 **Clot-pole** clodhead (with *pole* meaning *poll*, head). Most editors insert an '*Exit a Knight*' stage direction after this line and an '*Enter Knight*' after Lear's next sentence. But whether Lear's Knight would have time to leave the stage completely is doubtful. It may be that he catches the Steward before he completes his departure.

54 **Mungrel** mongrel; mixed-breed dog. Lear refers to the Steward (Oswald), who is obeying his mistress and being 'slack of' the 'Services' (I.iii.10) Lear is used to.

58 **Roundest** most direct and open (with no restraint).

59 **he would not** it was his will not to.

63–64 **as . . . wont** that you were accustomed to in the past.

64 **Abatement of Kindness** lessening of respect. *Kindness* can refer both to kindliness (courteous, loving manners) and to kind-ness (the behaviour fitting a particular kind of person). Compare I.i.265, and see the note to I.ii.88. The phrase 'of Kindness' appears only in the Folio text.

65 **general Dependants** servants who wait on the entire household.

71–72 **Thou . . . Conception** You only prompt my memory of what I have been thinking myself. Lear's phrasing is a reminder that it was he who conceived this unkind daughter, and it was later he who gave birth to the situation that he now finds so disagreeable; compare I.iii.25 and I.iv.2–4, and see the notes to I.i.12, I.ii.143, 147.

72 **faint** slight (and perhaps 'weary', as in I.iii.13). Compare I.ii.196.

74 **jealous Curiosity** suspicion aroused by his failure to exhibit the usual attentiveness.

then As in I.i.215, Lear means *than*; but again *then* can yield a pertinent sense.

75 **Pretence** intent. Compare I.ii.96–99.

80 **of that** mention of Cordelia's departure and the impact it has had on the Fool. Lear's resistance to any reference to what he has done to Cordelia suggests that he is beginning to feel some regrets over what he has done. By line 270 he is willing to speak about the matter himself. The word 'well' appears only in the Folio; so also with 'arise, away' in line 96.

– You, you, Sirrah, where's my Daughter?

STEWARD So please you – *Exit.*

LEAR – What says the Fellow there? Call the Clot-pole back. – Where's my Fool? Ho, I think the World's asleep. – How now? Where's that Mungrel?

KNIGHT He says, my Lord, your Daughter is not well.

LEAR Why came not the Slave back to me when I call'd him?

KNIGHT Sir, he answered me in the Roundest Manner, he would not.

LEAR He would not?

KNIGHT My Lord, I know not what the matter is, but to my Judgement your Highness is not entertain'd with that Ceremonious Affection as you were wont; there's a great Abatement of Kindness appears as well in the general Dependants as in the Duke himself also, and your Daughter.

LEAR Ha? Sayst thou so?

KNIGHT I beseech you pardon me, my Lord, if I be mistaken, for my Duty cannot be silent when I think your Highness wrong'd.

LEAR Thou but rememb'rest me of mine own Conception. I have perceived a most faint Neglect of late, which I have rather blamed as mine own jealous Curiosity, then as a very Pretence and Purpose of Unkindness; I will look further into't. But where's my Fool? I have not seen him this Two Days.

KNIGHT Since my young Lady's going into France, Sir, the Fool hath much pined away.

LEAR No more of that, I have noted it well; go you and tell my Daughter, I would speak with her. – Go you call hither my Fool.

[*Exeunt one or more Attendants.*]

Enter Steward.

86 **My Lord's Knave** Lear's epithet for the Steward.

87 **Slave** basest of peasants.

90 **bandy Looks** bat expressions to and fro. By lines 203–4 Lear will be accusing Oswald's mistress of equally disrespectful 'Looks'. Compare I.iii.23.

92 **Football** a rowdy forerunner of modern soccer.

96 **arise** The dialogue makes it clear that the Steward has yet to get up after being struck by Lear and tripped by the disguised Kent.

97 **Differences** (a) quarrelsomeness, (b) different forms of behaviour [as distinguished from the insolence you have just displayed to your superior], and (c) the difference between a monarch and a surly servant. Kent's reference to teaching is a reminder of what Goneril has said in I.iii.19–21.

97–98 **if . . . Length** if you will be laid full length on the ground. *Lubber* is a contemptuous term for a large, oafish, impotent person; Kent takes Oswald's 'measure' (puts him in his place). Compare *Romeo and Juliet*, III.iii.69–70.

99 **go to** out of here.

101 **Earnest** an initial payment. Lear gives his new man a gratuity.

102 **Coxcomb** fool's cap, with a red flannel crest like a cock's comb.

104 **were best** would do well to. The Fool addresses Kent. In line 105 many editions follow the Quarto, which has Kent reply 'Why, Fool?' *Best* echoes line 38.

106 **taking one's part** siding with; becoming a member of the party. The Fool may also be punning on bodily 'part', in this case the coxcomb Lear himself is now figuratively wearing.

107–8 **and . . . sits** if you can't tolerate or befriend the wind (by smiling in its direction to flatter it into lessening its blows).

109–10 **banish'd . . . Daughters** driven away two of his daughters [by bequeathing them new roles as wicked stepmothers].

110–11 **did . . . Blessing** The Fool probably means that the daughter who has been banished will turn out to be the one who has really received Lear's blessing. See Matthew 5:3–16, and compare I.i.185, 255, 266, and I.ii.22.

113 **Nuncle** a contraction of 'mine uncle'.

– O you, Sir, you, come you hither, Sir. Who am I, Sir?

STEWARD My Lady's Father.

LEAR 'My Lady's Father'? My Lord's Knave, you whoreson Dog, you Slave, you Cur.

STEWARD I am none of these, my Lord, I beseech your Pardon.

LEAR Do you bandy Looks with me, you Rascal?

STEWARD I'll not be strucken, my Lord.

KENT Nor tripp'd neither, you base Football Player.

LEAR I thank thee, Fellow. Thou serv'st me, and I'll love thee.

KENT Come Sir, arise, away, I'll teach you Differences. Away, away: if you will measure your Lubber's Length again, tarry. But away, go to, have you Wisdom, so. [*Exit Steward.*]

LEAR Now, my friendly Knave, I thank thee; there's Earnest of thy Service.

Enter Fool.

FOOL Let me hire him too, here's my Coxcomb.

LEAR How now, my pretty Knave, how dost thou?

FOOL – Sirrah, you were best take my Coxcomb.

LEAR Why, my Boy?

FOOL Why? For taking one's part that's out of Favour. – Nay, and thou canst not smile as the Wind sits, thou'lt catch Cold shortly: there, take my Coxcomb. Why this Fellow has banish'd two on's Daughters, and did the third a Blessing against his Will: if thou follow him, thou must needs wear my Coxcomb. – How now, Nuncle? Would I had two Coxcombs and two Daughters.

LEAR Why, my Boy?

FOOL If I gave them all my Living, I'd keep my Coxcombs my self. There's mine, beg another of thy Daughters.

120 **to Kennel** be driven into hiding.

121 **Brach** bitch.

129 **owest** (a) ownest (as in I.i.205), and (b) owest in debt. In lines 127–32, as in line 136 below, the early texts print *then*, not *than*; in some of those instances the ambiguity may relate to the Fool's riddles. Compare line 74.

130 **goest** walkest; with wordplay on *go* as a term for copulation.

131 **Learn . . . trowest** hear (acquire more information) more than you believe; be sceptical.

132 **Set . . . throwest** wager ('set') less than you have available for a throw of the dice; be careful. Compare I.i.124–25.

134 **in a Door** indoors (in of door).

136 **Score** sum of twenty. Since there are twenty shillings to a pound, the Fool's riddle probably involves wordplay on the sexual senses of *pound* (compare I.ii.146, and see *Henry VIII*, II.iii.64, 85) and *Score* (see 2 *Henry IV*, II.i.23–24), implying that a man who bids farewell to his 'Whore' will end up with 'more' on his ledger than the one who spends 'two Tens' on a 'Score'. See the note on *then* at line 129.

137 **Nothing** nonsense; of no value. Since *Nothing* ('no thing') was a common term for the 'Score' (notch) of a 'Whore', Kent's reply is to the point. See the note to I.i.16, and compare I.ii.32.

138 **unfeed** both (a) unpaid (given no fee), and (b) unfed (like the ravenous young cuckoos referred to in lines 229–30).

146 **Difference** Now the Fool will teach Lear 'Differences'.

149 **counsail'd** counselled; advised. Lines 149–50 allude to Luke 18:18–23, where Jesus tells a rich young ruler, 'sell all that thou hast, and distribute unto the poor, and thou shalt have treasure in heaven.' Compare *Othello* I.iii.386–89, and see the note to lines 44–45. The Fool's words also allude to the references to Christian folly in 1 Corinthians 1:18–31, 2:1–16.

155 **Motley** the particoloured costume of the traditional court jester.

156 **found out there** both (a) located over there, and (b) found out (discovered, detected) there. Compare lines 174–76.

LEAR Take heed, Sirrah, the Whip.

FOOL Truth's a Dog must to Kennel; he must be whipp'd out, when the Lady Brach may stand by th' Fire and stink.

LEAR A pestilent Gall to me.

FOOL Sirha, I'll teach thee a Speech.

LEAR Do.

FOOL Mark it, Nuncle.
Have more than thou showest,
Speak less than thou knowest,
Lend less than thou owest,
Ride more than thou goest,
Learn more than thou trowest,
Set less than thou throwest;
Leave thy Drink and thy Whore,
And keep in a Door,
And thou shalt have more,
Then two Tens to a Score.

KENT This is Nothing, Fool.

FOOL Then 'tis like the Breath of an unfeed Lawyer: you gave me Nothing for't. Can you make no use of Nothing, Nuncle?

LEAR Why no, Boy, nothing can be made out of Nothing.

FOOL – Prythee tell him, so much the Rent of his Land comes to; he will not believe a Fool.

LEAR A bitter Fool.

FOOL Dost thou know the Difference, my Boy, between a Bitter Fool and a Sweet one?

LEAR No, Lad, teach me.

FOOL That Lord that counsail'd thee
To give away thy Land,
Come place him here by me,
Do thou for him stand:
The Sweet and Bitter Fool
Will presently appear,
The one in Motley here,
The other found out there.

159 **borne** carried and born. Lines 149–65 ('That . . . snatching.') occur only in the Quarto.

160 **This . . . Fool** both (a) this is not mere foolishness, and (b) this Fool is not the imbecile his motley would suggest he is. Compare *Twelfth Night*, I.v.61–62, III.i.66–74.

163 **an't** on it; of it.
Lodes loads, perhaps with play on 'Ladies', the word most editors substitute here.

164 **all the Fool** a monopoly on folly (here alluding to sexual licence, with play on 'Fool' as a term for the male 'part').

165 **snatching** grasping for a piece of the action.

169 **Meat** substance. *Meat* referred to any food, not just flesh.

170 **clovest** cleaved; divided. Compare IV.vi.191.
Crowns (a) Lear's monarchial, 'Golden' crown, (b) the 'Bald Crown' of Lear's head (lines 173–74), and perhaps (c) the coronet originally intended for Cordelia's husband (see the note to I.i.140). Most editions adopt the Quarto's *crown*.

171 **boar'st** borest (bore). The Folio spelling suggests wordplay on *boar*, implying that Lear now roots in the 'Dirt'.

175–76 **finds it so** proves it to be the case (as in a law court). Compare I.i.60, 266.

177 **nere** ne'er, but possibly with play on 'nere'. Compare I.i.159.
Grace favour; special dispensations, privileges (see line 215).

178 **Foppish** foolish. Compare I.ii.14, 134–35.

180 **Apish** both (a) imitative, and (b) foolish.

181 **When . . . Songs** when in the past have you been so musical? In line 183 *us'd* means 'practised'; and *ere* can mean both 'ere' (before) and 'e'er' (ever), as in I.i.60.

186 **Breeches** pants (with a reminder of Lear's *breaches*, 'faults', as in I.i.16–18). Compare *Othello*, II.i.90.

189 **play Bo-peep** become a child again (playing hide-and-seek). See the note to I.i.124–25, and compare I.i.298–305, I.ii.79–83.

194 **whipp'd** flogged. But in line 198 the Fool plays on a sense of 'whipping' that relates to 'holding one's piece'. Compare *Love's Labour's Lost*, IV.iii.133 and V.i.150. In this line *And* means 'if'. The word 'Sirrah' appears only in the Folio text.

LEAR Dost thou call me Fool, Boy?

FOOL All thy other Titles thou hast given away, that thou wast borne with.

KENT This is not altogether Fool, my Lord.

FOOL No faith, Lords and Great Men will not let me. If I had a Monopoly out, they would have part an't, and Lodes too; they will not let me have all the Fool to my self; they'll be snatching. Nuncle, give me an Egg, and I'll give thee two Crowns.

LEAR What two Crowns shall they be?

FOOL Why, after I have cut the Egg i'th' Middle and eat up the Meat, the two Crowns of the Egg. When thou clovest thy Crowns i'th' Middle, and gav'st away both Parts, thou boar'st thine Ass on thy Back o'er the Dirt; thou hadst little Wit in thy Bald Crown when thou gav'st thy Golden one away. If I speak like my self in this, let him be whipp'd that first finds it so.

Fools had nere less Grace in a Year,
For Wise Men are grown Foppish,
And know not how their Wits to wear,
Their Manners are so Apish.

LEAR When were you wont to be so full of Songs, Sirrah?

FOOL I have us'd it, Nuncle, ere since thou mad'st thy Daughters thy Mothers, for when thou gav'st them the Rod and put'st down thine own Breeches,

Then they for sudden Joy did weep,
And I for Sorrow sung,
That such a King should play Bo-peep,
And go the Fool among.

Prythee Nuncle, keep a Schoolmaster that can teach thy Fool to lie; I would fain learn to lie.

LEAR And you lie, Sirrah, we'll have you whipp'd.

198 **Holding my Peace** here, refusing to speak. The Fool puns on *piece*, a word that could be applied to either (a) a woman (see *Pericles*, IV.iii.47–48), or (b) a man's own 'piece of Flesh' (*Romeo and Juliet*, I.i.31–32), the codfish (line 214) within his codpiece. See the note to V.iii.255.

200 **pared** (a) paired, (b) peeled, scored, (c) 'sheal'd' (line 214).

201 **Nothing** This word echoes lines 137–42. Since *Wit* often carries the same genital implications as *Will* (see *As You Like It*, IV.i.175–81, and *Othello*, II.iii.380–82), the Fool is implying that Lear has made himself not only stupid but impotent: 'an O without a Figure' (line 207), a eunuch who no longer counts for anything. See the notes to I.i.140, 144.

203–4 **What . . . on?** What makes you wear that frown? A *frontlet* or 'frowning cloth', was a band worn across the forehead at night to forestall or eliminate wrinkles.

207 **an . . . Figure** both (a) a zero without a preceding digit to turn it into a functioning number, and (b) an 'ungenitur'd Agent' (*Measure for Measure*, III.i.469), a man without a thing (lines 137, 208). The Fool is admonishing Lear that he's now paying the price for his earlier failure to 'smell a Fault' (I.i.16).

212 **keeps** preserves for himself, rather than discarding all that remains after he grows 'Weary' of it (line 213, echoing I.iii.13).

214 **sheal'd Pescod** shelled peascod (empty peapod). The Fool puns on 'she'ld pees-cod', a cod (scrotum) a she has turned into a 'she'. See the note to lines 18–19.

218 **rank . . . Riots** undisciplined and intolerable outbursts.

220 **a safe Redress** an inoffensive means of addressing the problem.

222 **put it on** encourage this 'Thrusting' against authority (I.ii.143); 'protect' this misbehaviour.

224–28 **Redresses . . . Proceeding** corrective measures fail to be applied, which in the service of a healthy commonwealth might do you the kind of injury which would otherwise be shameful but under the circumstances would be judged both necessary and prudent. *Fault* (line 223) echoes I.i.16.

FOOL I marvel what Kin thou and thy Daughters are: they'll have me whipp'd for Speaking True, thou'lt have me whipp'd for Lying, and sometimes I am whipp'd for Holding my Peace. I had rather be any kind o' thing than a Fool, and yet I would not be thee, Nuncle: thou hast pared thy Wit o' both Sides, and left Nothing i'th' Middle. Here comes one o' the Parings.

Enter Goneril.

LEAR How now, Daughter? What makes that Frontlet on? You are too much of late i'th' Frown.

FOOL Thou wast a Pretty Fellow when thou hadst no need to care for her Frowning; now thou art an O without a Figure. I am better than thou art now: I am a Fool, thou art Nothing. – Yes, forsooth I will hold my Tongue: so your Face bids me, though you say Nothing.

Mum, mum,
He that keeps nor Crust, nor Crumb,
Weary of all, shall want Some.

That's a sheal'd Pescod.

GONERIL – Not only, Sir, this your all-licens'd Fool,
But other of your insolent Retinue
Do hourly carp and quarrel, breaking forth
In rank and not-to-be-endur'd Riots, Sir.
I had thought, by making this well known unto you,
To have found a safe Redress, but now grow fearful,
By what your self too late have spoke and done,
That you protect this Course, and put it on
By your Allowance; which if you should, the Fault
Would not scape Censure, nor the Redresses sleep
Which, in the Tender of a wholesome Weal,
Might in the Working do you that Offence,
Which else were Shame, that then Necessity
Will call discreet Proceeding.

FOOL For you know, Nuncle,

229 **Cuckoo** baby cuckoo (the 'Young', line 230). Cuckoos were proverbial for laying their eggs in the nests of other birds. The Fool implies that Lear has been emasculated (figuratively cuckolded) by the 'Unkind Daughters' (III.iv.73) who now 'make Servants of / Their Betters' (lines 269–70).

230 **by it Young** (a) by the young cuckoo, and (b) by it while young. *It* was the usual form for modern *its*.

231 **Darkling** [to fend for ourselves] in the dark. Compare I.i.37.

234 **fraught** freighted, supplied (an image continued in *transport*).

235–36 **Dispositions . . . are** behaviours which are now carrying you away from your true self. Compare I.i.146–47, 298–99.

238 **Jug** a nickname for 'Joan' (often used of a whore), here a 'Cart' with a determination to 'transport' Lear into madness. See *The Taming of the Shrew*, I.i.55. Lines 237–38 allude to a common way of defining the word *preposterous*, whose literal meaning in Latin is that what should be in the rear (*posterus*) is in the prior (*prae*) position.

241–42 **Notion . . . lethargied** mind is failing, his senses are dulled.

245 **learn that** pursue that idea further. Lines 245–48 are to be found in the Quarto only.

247 **be false persuaded** be convinced only against all reason [that].

248 **Which . . . Father** Whom they will transform into a well-trained father. The Fool reminds Lear that Goneril is perverting the commandment that children obey their parents (Exodus 20:12, Ephesians 6:1–2). See the notes to I.i.124–25; I.iv.71–72, 109–11.

250 **Admiration** [pretence of] wonderment.
Savour flavour. Compare I.ii.48–49, I.iii.15.

255 **Debosh'd** debauched; given over to 'riotous living' (Luke 15:13), like a troop of prodigal sons.
Bold insolent, unruly.

257 **Shews . . . Inn** resembles a noisy 'Tavern' or whorehouse.
Epicurism indulgence of the fleshy appetites.

259 **grac'd** civilized, Christian. This word echoes line 177.

259–60 **speak . . . Remedy** cry out for immediate mending (I.i.95).

260 **desir'd** requested

262 **disquantity your Train** reduce the number of your followers.

The Hedge-Sparrow fed the Cuckoo so long
That it's had it Head bit off by it Young:
So out went the Candle, and we were left Darkling.

LEAR Are you our Daughter?

GONERIL I would you would make use of your good
Wisdom
(Whereof I know you are fraught) and put away
These Dispositions, which of late transport you
From what you rightly are.

FOOL May not an Ass know when the Cart draws the Horse? Whoop, Jug, I love thee.

LEAR Does any here know me? This is not Lear.
Does Lear walk thus? Speak thus? Where are his Eyes?
Either his Notion weakens, his Discernings
Are lethargied – Ha! Waking? 'Tis not so?
Who is it that can tell me who I am?

FOOL Lear's Shadow.

LEAR I would learn that, for by the Marks of Sovereignty, Knowledge, and Reason, I should be false persuaded I had Daughters.

FOOL Which they will make an obedient Father.

LEAR Your Name, fair Gentlewoman?

GONERIL This Admiration, Sir, is much o'th' Savour
Of other your new Pranks. I do beseech you
To understand my Purposes aright:
As you are Old and Reverend, should be Wise.
Here do you keep a hundred Knights and Squires,
Men so Disorder'd, so Debosh'd, and Bold,
That this our Court, infected with their Manners,
Shews like a Riotous Inn: Epicurism and Lust
Makes it more like a Tavern, or a Brothel,
Than a grac'd Palace. The Shame it self doth speak
For instant Remedy. Be then desir'd
By her that else will take the thing she begs,
A little to disquantity your Train,

263 **And . . . depend** and those dependants (servants, 'People', line 268) who remain.

264 **besort** befit, sort with.

265 **Which . . . you** who have self-control and understand the kind of man you are in your old age. Compare lines 235–36.

273 **Marble-hearted** cold, hard. Compare *Twelfth Night*, V.i.126. The first clause of line 270 ('O . . . come?') appears only in the Quarto printing.

275 **Sea-monster** Lear may be thinking of the biblical Leviathan (Psalm 104:26), the whale that swallowed the prophet Jonah, or the monsters slain by Hercules and Perseus. Compare I.i.221–23.

276 **Kite** a scavenging buzzard. Compare *Hamlet*, II.ii.616–17. Albany's interjection in line 276 appears only in the Folio; so also with the first half of line 288 (Of . . . you').

277 **Parts** attributes, qualities. See the note to line 106.

279–80 **exact . . . Name** fastidious manner (a) uphold the dignity implied by their titles as knights ('Worships'), and (b) support the 'Worships' (noblemen) in whose 'Name' they serve. Compare I.i.136–37.

280 **Fault** flaw, breach. Compare I.i.16–17, 274–76, 286; I.iii.11; I.iv.223–24.

282 **Engine** a mechanical device such as a torturing wheel, a rack, or a battering ram.

283 **the Fix'd Place** its normal position (here one that had 'set' its 'Rest' on retirement with the daughter on whom all its affection was fixed, I.i.124–25). Lear's phrasing hints at Ixion, a king who sought to seduce the goddess Hera (Juno) and was tricked into a dark encounter whereby he conceived the Centaurs, an unruly race of horse-men. Zeus (Jupiter) punished Ixion's presumption by fixing him to a fiery wheel in Hades.

284 **Gall** (a) bitterness, (b) yellow bile, and (c) chafing sore.

285 **Gate** Lear's head. As he speaks, Lear probably strikes his forehead; compare lines 170, 200–2, 214, 229–30. *Gate* can also mean 'gait' (compare IV.ii.54, IV.vi.233, V.iii.175), and here it serves to remind us of the 'gait' (self-indulgent 'walk') that let Lear's 'Folly' in.

And the Remainders that shall still depend,
To be such Men as may besort your Age,
Which know themselves, and you.

LEAR Darkness and Divels.
– Saddle my Horses; call my Train together.
– Degenerate Bastard, I'll not trouble thee;
Yet have I left a Daughter.

GONERIL You strike my People,
And your disorder'd Rabble make Servants of
Their Betters.

Enter Albany.

LEAR Woe, that too late repents –
– O Sir, are you come? Is it your Will,
Speak, Sir? – Prepare my Horses.
– Ingratitude! thou Marble-hearted Fiend,
More hideous when thou shew'st thee in a Child
Than the Sea-monster.

ALBANY Pray, Sir, be Patient.

LEAR – Detested Kite, thou liest:
My Train are Men of Choice and Rarest Parts,
That all particulars of Duty know
And in the most exact regard support
The Worships of their Name. – O most small Fault,
How ugly didst thou in Cordelia shew?
Which like an Engine wrench'd my Frame of Nature
From the Fix'd Place: drew from my Heart all Love,
And added to the Gall. O Lear, Lear, Lear!
Beat at this Gate that let thy Folly in,

286 **Go . . . People** It may be that Lear's knights exit after this line. But it seems equally likely that they remain and exit with him after line 303.

292 **Stirrility** sterility (with wordplay on *stir*, 'disturb').

294 **derogate** cursed, denatured.

295 **teem** reproduce, have functional 'Organs of Increase' (line 293).

296 **Spleen** spite. The spleen was regarded as one of the seats of distemper.

297 **thwart** perverted and perverse; thwarting.

299 **cadent** falling.
fret erode (by making her fret with vexation).

300 **Pains and Benefits** labours, nourishing care, and blessings.

301 **Laughter** scorn, mockery.

302 **Serpent's Tooth** the poisonous fang of a snake. Lear's phrasing echoes Psalm 140:3, 'They have sharpened their tongues like a serpent.'

304 **whereof comes this?** what is the reason for this outbreak of curses?

306 **Scope** range, latitude; freedom of movement.

307 **As . . . it** that the follies of age prompt it to.

311 **shake my Manhood** unsettle my masculinity (self-control). Lear's phrasing echoes lines 282–83, 292; and *shake* recalls I.i.40 and I.ii.95–96.

312 **perforce** unwillingly, despite my efforts to hold myself together.

314 **untented** untreated with a tent, a thin roll of lint to cleanse wounds.

315 **fond** doting; foolishly affectionate.

316 **Beweep . . . again** if you weep any more because of this. Lines 316–19 echo Matthew 18:9, where Jesus says 'if thine eye offend thee, pluck it out and cast it from thee'. Compare lines 322–24, where *cast off* continues the allusion to this passage.

317 **loose** both (a) release, and (b) lose.

And thy dear Judgement out. – Go, go, my People.
ALBANY My Lord, I am Guiltless, as I am Ignorant
Of what hath moved you.
LEAR It may be so, my Lord.
– Hear, Nature, hear, dear Goddess, hear:
Suspend thy Purpose if thou didst intend
To make this Creature fruitful.
Into her Womb convey Stirrility;
Dry up in her the Organs of Increase,
And from her derogate Body never spring
A Babe to honour her. If she must teem,
Create her Child of Spleen, that it may live
And be a thwart disnatur'd Torment to her.
Let it stamp Wrinkles in her Brow of Youth,
With cadent Tears fret Channels in her Cheeks,
Turn all her Mother's Pains and Benefits
To Laughter and Contempt: that she may feel
How sharper than a Serpent's Tooth it is
To have a Thankless Child. – Away, away. *Exit.*
ALBANY Now, Gods that we adore, whereof comes this?
GONERIL Never afflict your self to know more of it:
But let his Disposition have that Scope
As Dotage gives it.

Enter Lear.

LEAR What, Fifty of my Followers at a Clap?
Within a Fortnight?
ALBANY What's the matter, Sir?
LEAR I'll tell thee. – Life and Death, I am asham'd
That thou hast Power to shake my Manhood thus,
That these hot Tears, which break from me perforce,
Should make thee worth them. Blasts and Fogs upon
thee:
Th' untented Woundings of a Father's Curse
Pierce every Sense about thee. – Old fond Eyes,
Beweep this Cause again, I'll pluck ye out
And cast you with the Waters that you loose

318 **temper Clay** soften my firm flesh. 'Is't . . . this' appears in the Quarto only.

320 **Comfortable** able to bring me comfort; reassuring. *Kind* echoes line 64; see the note to line 229.

322 **flea** flay, strip bare. See lines 4, 214, and compare I.i.285.

323 **resume the Shape** once again put on the form. *Shape* recalls I.i.190; but Lear's phrasing also relates to the 'Figure' imagery of lines 135–42, 206–10, and to the imagery of form or deformity in lines 4, 37–38, 43, 155–56, 168–74, 179–80, 200–7, 230, 255, 273–75, 282–83, 295–99, 322.

324 **mark that** register what he says. Goneril refers to Lear's threat to take back the power he has 'cast off'.

327 **Knave** villain. Compare lines 46, 47, 86–87.

329 **take . . . thee** The Fool puns on a proverbial expression, with the implication that Lear will be taking two fools with him when he leaves, one of them the 'Fool' the King has shown himself to be. Compare lines 146–60.

330 **Fox** a creature proverbial for its cunning, particularly in the 'Politic' discourse associated with Machiavelli (line 336).

332–33 **Should . . . Halter** would certainly be executed if I could buy a hangman's noose with my coxcomb (compare line 102).

337 **At point** both (a) armed, and (b) under his command. Lines 335–37 are sarcastic. *Counsel* echoes line 149.

339 **enguard his Dotage** both (a) ornament (guard) his whims (here likened to a garment), and (b) 'protect this Course' (line 222).

340 **hold . . . Mercy** threaten us. See the note to line 324.

342 **trust too far** feel too secure [for your own good].

343 **still . . . Harms** ever remove the dangers.

344 **taken** captured; harmed by threats that could have been prevented.

345 **What . . . utter'd** Goneril is probably thinking primarily of what Lear has said in lines 322–24.

347 **shew'd th' Unfitness** warned her of the risks of doing so. *Unfitness* (inappropriateness) echoes lines 37–38, 339.

To temper Clay. Ha? Is't come to this?
Let it be so: I have another Daughter,
Who I am sure is Kind and Comfortable.
When she shall hear this of thee, with her Nails
She'll flea thy Wolvish Visage. Thou shalt find
That I'll resume the Shape which thou dost think
I have cast off for ever. *Exit.*
GONERIL Do you mark that?
ALBANY I cannot be so partial, Goneril,
To the great Love I bear you –
GONERIL Pray you content.
– What, Oswald, ho? – You Sir, more Knave than Fool,
After your Master.
FOOL Nuncle Lear, Nuncle Lear,
Tarry, take the Fool with thee.
A Fox, when one has caught her,
And such a Daughter,
Should sure to the Slaughter,
If my Cap would buy a Halter.
So the Fool follows after. *Exit.*
GONERIL This Man hath had good Counsel: a hundred
Knights?
'Tis Politic and Safe to let him keep
At point a hundred Knights: yes, that on every Dream,
Each Buzz, each Fancy, each Complaint, Dislike,
He may enguard his Dotage with their Powres
And hold our Lives in Mercy. – Oswald, I say.
ALBANY Well, you may fear too far.
GONERIL Safer than trust too far.
Let me still take away the Harms I fear,
Not fear still to be taken. I know his Heart,
What he hath utter'd I have writ my Sister;
If she sustain him and his hundred Knights
When I have shew'd th' Unfitness –

Enter Steward.

349 **I** both (a) I [have], and (b) ay (yes). Compare I.ii.175.

350 **Company** attendants; fellow servants.

351 **particular Fear** special sense of our insecurity. *Particular* also means 'personal'. See *Troilus and Cressida*, II.ii.9, where it puns on 'part-tickler'. And compare lines 106–7, 160–74, 278.

353 **compact it more** pack in material to build it up further.

355 **milky** effeminate, cow-like. Compare I.i.263, and *Macbeth*, I.v.19.

356 **under pardon** if you'll forgive my saying so.

357 **at . . . Wisdom** to be criticized (taken to task) for a risky (potentially 'harmful') lack of prudence (caution). Compare the reference to *Harms* in lines 343–44.

361 **the 'vent** let's see whom events prove to be correct. The Folio elision (*'vent* for *event*) accords with the imagery of eye-piercing in line 359; that figure will prove prophetic.

I.v This scene takes place en route to the Duke of Albany's palace.

3–4 **her . . . Letter** any question that may be prompted by the letter. Whether the 'Gloucester' of line 1 is the Earl or the town of that name is not clear. In Lear's mind the two destinations may be synonymous.

8–9 **were . . . Kybes** would he not run the risk of a brain with kibes (chilblains, a swelling or inflammation of the foot).

10 **I** Lear means 'ay'; but 'I' is here pertinent too. Compare I.iv.349.

12 **Slip-shod** slipper-shoe'd. In lines 11–12 the Fool may mean either (a) that Lear's mind will not be wearing slippers because Lear has no brains left to become sore, or (b) that Lear's brains cannot be in the heels that are making their way to his 'other Daughter' (line 14), since that is a foolish journey for the old man to take. The Fool anticipates the later sense of *slipshod*, 'down at the heels' or 'out at Heels' (II.ii.154). See the note to I.iv.285.

– How now, Oswald?
What, have you write that Letter to my Sister?

STEWARD I, Madam.

GONERIL Take you some Company, and away to Horse;
Inform her full of my particular Fear,
And thereto add such Reasons of your own
As may compact it more. Get you gone,
And hasten your Return. [*Exit Steward.*]
– No, no, my Lord,
This milky Gentleness and Course of yours,
Though I condemn not, yet under pardon
You are much more at task for want of Wisdom
Than prais'd for harmful Mildness.

ALBANY How far your Eyes may pierce I cannot tell;
Striving to better, oft we mar what's well.

GONERIL Nay then –

ALBANY Well, well, the 'vent. *Exeunt.*

Scene 5

Enter Lear, Kent, Gentleman, and Fool.

LEAR Go you before to Gloucester with these Letters; acquaint my Daughter no further with any thing you know than comes from her Demand out of the Letter. If your Diligence be not speedy, I shall be there afore you.

KENT I will not sleep, my Lord, till I have delivered your Letter. *Exit.*

FOOL If a Man's Brains were in's Heels, were't not in danger of Kybes?

LEAR I, Boy.

FOOL Then I prythee be merry, thy Wit shall not go Slip-shod.

LEAR Ha, ha, ha.

14–15 **use thee kindly** treat you with kindness. Compare I.iv.319–20.

16 **Crab** crab-apple. The Fool's point is that Lear's two daughters are apples of the same type (an observation Regan has made in I.i.70–71). He alludes to the teaching that 'by their fruits ye shall know them' (Matthew 7:20), which occurs in a passage where Jesus warns of 'false prophets, which come to you in sheep's clothing, but inwardly they are ravening wolves' (compare I.iv.322). The moral of the parable is that 'A good tree cannot bring forth evil fruit, neither can a corrupt tree bring forth good fruit' (Matthew 7:18). Whether it applies to the situations of Lear and Gloucester is yet to be seen.

tell (a) observe, (b) count, and (c) report. Compare I.i.211.

19 **taste** both (a) savour (compare I.iv.250–51), and (b) test, try (as in I.ii.48–49, and in the Book of Job). Compare I.ii.53.

24–25 **spy into** 'pierce' (I.iv.359). The Fool hints at the kind of 'Nose' that 'stands' (lines 20–21); see the notes to *Othello*, IV.i.144, and *Love's Labour's Lost*, V.ii.566, 567. He thus reminds Lear that men tend to be guided by their lusts (their prideful, upright 'I's', which are all too often in quest of a receptive female 'Eye' or 'Face' (line 21, echoed in IV.vi.118–20)) rather than by clear-sighted vision. Compare I.i.73. *Smell* recalls I.i.16.

30 **House** 'Shell' (line 27, echoing I.iv.214).

33 **Horns** both (a) virility, potency, and (b) exposed humiliation or weakness (the traits of a cuckold, whose horned brows signify that his 'Case' has been taken by males with better horns). For *case* as a term for the female genitalia, see *Romeo and Juliet*, II.iii.50–60; for the two senses of *horn*, see *The Two Gentlemen of Verona*, I.i.79. See the notes to I.i.140, 144.

37 **Thy . . . 'em** Your servants are fetching them. Compare I.iv.170–72.

38 **Seven Stars** the Pleiades, a group of stars in the constellation Taurus, so called because they were said to be the daughters of Atlas and Pleione. One star (the grieving Electra) is so dim that the Pleiades actually appear to be less than seven rather than 'moe' (more).

42 **take . . . perforce** seize my prerogatives by compulsion.

45 **beaten** disciplined. Compare I.iv.91, 119–21, 174–76, 183–86, 194–98, 268, 285, 305.

48 **Wise** ripe in understanding. See the notes to line 16 and V.ii.11.

FOOL Shalt see thy other Daughter will use thee kindly: for though she's as like this as a Crab's like an Apple, yet I can tell what I can tell.

LEAR What canst tell, Boy?

FOOL She will taste as like this as a Crab does to a Crab. Thou canst tell why one's Nose stands i'th' Middle on's Face?

LEAR No.

FOOL Why to keep one's Eyes of either side's Nose, that what a Man cannot smell out, he may spy into.

LEAR I did her wrong.

FOOL Canst tell how an Oyster makes his Shell?

LEAR No.

FOOL Nor I neither; but I can tell why a Snail has a House.

LEAR Why?

FOOL Why to put's Head in; not to give it away to his Daughters, and leave his Horns without a Case.

LEAR I will forget my Nature, so kind a Father? Be my Horses ready?

FOOL Thy Asses are gone about 'em. The Reason why the Seven Stars are no moe than Seven is a pretty Reason.

LEAR Because they are not Eight.

FOOL Yes indeed, thou wouldst make a good Fool.

LEAR – To take't again perforce: Monster Ingratitude!

FOOL If thou wert my Fool, Nuncle, I'd have thee beaten for being Old before thy Time.

LEAR How's that?

FOOL Thou shouldst not have been Old till thou hadst been Wise.

50 **in Temper** firm (like a sword) and stable ('not Mad'). Compare I.iv.318. The phrase 'not Mad' appears only in the Folio.

51 **How . . . ready?** Most editions delete 'Gentleman' from the stage direction that opens this scene; they then add '*Enter Gentleman*' just before this line.

54 **Maid** virgin, innocent.
Departure (a) leaving, (b) parting [of her thighs]. Compare the play on *part*, *parting*, and related notions in I.iv.78–79, 106–7, 162–63, 168–74, 200–2, 206–7, 214, 277, 280–83, 351; I.v.20–25, 32–34.

55 **Shall . . . shorter** shall lose her virginity soon [because she is too naive to be able to defend it properly], unless (a) time be abbreviated by events, or (b) male 'things' be 'cut shorter' so that they are incapable of threatening her maidenhead. See the notes to I.iv.106, 137, 201, 207, 214, 229, 332–33. *Shorter* echoes I.i.72–73, and it serves as a reminder that it is because Goneril's 'Deed of Love . . . comes too short' that Lear is now being 'cut shorter'. The King has been as trusting as a silly 'Maid', with the consequence that he will now be forced to learn what to make of the nothing to which his daughters are reducing him. In due course the equally dull-witted Gloucester will be 'cut shorter' in parallel fashion; and by the end of the play the same fate will befall a number of other characters, including those now actively engaged in cutting off others. Behind the imagery of this passage is the parable of stewardship in Luke 12:42–48. In the Geneva Bible of 1602, Jesus is quoted as saying, 'Who is a faithful steward and wise, whom the master shall make ruler over his household, to give them their portion of meat in season? Blessed is that servant, whom his master when he cometh, shall find so doing . . . But if that Servant say in his heart, My master doeth defer his coming, and shall begin to smite the servants and maidens, and to eat and drink and to be drunken, the master of that servant will come in a day when he thinketh not, and at an hour when he is not ware of, and will cut him off.' Compare IV.v.38 and IV.vi.259–66.

LEAR – O let me not be Mad, not Mad, sweet Heaven;
Keep me in Temper, I would not be Mad.
How now, are the Horses ready?

GENTLEMAN Ready, my Lord.

LEAR Come, Boy.

FOOL She that's a Maid now, and laughs at my Departure,
Shall not be a Maid long, unless things be cut shorter. *Exeunt.*

II.i This scene takes place inside the Earl of Gloucester's castle.

S.D. **severally** separately (through different stage entrances).

1 **Save** God preserve.

4 **Regan** This appears only in the Folio text.

6 **How comes** why is.

8 **abroad** now circulating.
ones items of news; reports.

9 **Ear-kissing Arguments** the kinds of tales that are whispered directly into a listener's ear. In time Curan's phrase will prove applicable to the Duchesses of Cornwall and Albany. See *Troilus and Cressida*, IV.v.26–29.

11 **toward** in the offing; impending. We have already seen indications of the conflict that has developed from Albany's disapproval of his wife's harsh behaviour towards her father (see I.iv.304, 325–26, 341–47, 354–61). This rumour suggests that Goneril's sister and her husband are also at odds with Albany; meanwhile it hints that other broils may be in the making as a consequence of Lear's 'Division of the Kingdom' (I.i.4).

14 **do** do so (hear such rumours).

16 **better best** even better than 'best'. Compare I.iv.104. Here as in I.i.290 and I.ii.24, *to night* carries ominous implications.

17 **perforce** whether it wills so or not. Compare I.iv.312 and I.v.42.

19 **queasy Question** dizzying (or nauseating) riskiness.

20 **act** enact, carry out. *Thing* recalls I.iv.201, 207.
Briefness haste, promptness.
work assist me.

22 **watches** 'hath set Guard' (line 18); is on the alert for you.
fly flee. The word 'Sir' appears only in the Folio.

23 **Intelligence is given** information has been provided about.

ACT II

Scene 1

Enter Bastard, and Curan, severally.

BASTARD Save thee, Curan.

CURAN And you, Sir. I have been with your Father, and given him notice that the Duke of Cornwall, and Regan his Duchess, will be here with him this Night.

BASTARD How comes that?

CURAN Nay I know not. You have heard of the News abroad, I mean the whisper'd ones, for they are yet but Ear-kissing Arguments.

BASTARD Not I; pray you what are they?

CURAN Have you heard of no likely Wars toward, 'twixt the Dukes of Cornwall and Albany?

BASTARD Not a word.

CURAN You may do then in time; fare you well, Sir. *Exit.*

BASTARD The Duke be here to night? The better best:
This weaves it self perforce into my Business.
My Father hath set Guard to take my Brother,
And I have one thing of a queasy Question
Which I must act. – Briefness and Fortune, work.
– Brother, a word, descend; Brother, I say.

Enter Edgar.

My Father watches. O Sir, fly this place,
Intelligence is given where you are hid;
You have now the good Advantage of the Night.
Have you not spoken 'gainst the Duke of Cornwall?

28 **Upon his Party** either (a) on behalf of his side, or (b) against his side (with *'gainst* meaning 'in anticipation of').

29 **Advise your self** (a) think carefully, and (b) take care.
on't of it.

31 **In cunning** as pretence [to keep them from figuring out that I am aiding you rather than trying to capture you]. The audience knows that Edmund's 'cunning' is actually of a very different kind. Compare I.ii.185, and see the note to I.i.20–21.

32 **quit you** acquit yourself; perform your part, and then quit (leave) this place. In lines 33–34 Edmund alternates voices and addresses in keeping with his adopted posture. See the notes to I.ii.154, 155.

35–36 **beget . . . Endeavour** reinforce the impression that I've fought valiantly [in trying to prevent Edgar's attempt to 'quit', escape].

40 **Mumbling . . . Charms** muttering demonic spells. Compare III.iv.43.
conjuring invoking, commanding.

41 **To . . . Mistress** to watch over him as his guardian. Here *stand's*, the Quarto reading, is substituted for the Folio's *stand*.

46 **revenging** justly punishing; here an allusion to Romans 12:19, itself a reference to Deuteronomy 32:35. In line 44 the word 'ho' appears only in the Folio.

47 **Parricides** father-murderers.
Thunder bend divine wrath direct. Edmund alludes to the traditional image of Zeus as the thunder-bearer (I.i.181); thunder is also associated with the God of Judaeo-Christian tradition: see Exodus 9:23, 19:16; Psalm 78:48; Revelation 4:5, 16:18. *Bend* (aim), a term from archery, echoes I.i.144.

48 **manifold** multiple; literally, with many folds (compare I.i.285).
Bond Edmund echoes I.i.94, I.ii.47–56, 122–23; *bound* recalls I.i.64.

50 **loathly opposite** abhorrently in opposition. Compare I.i.274–76.
stood maintained myself. Compare line 41, and I.v.20–25.

51 **fell** fierce.

52 **charges home** attacks.

He's coming hither, now i'th' Night, i'th' Haste,
And Regan with him. Have you nothing said
Upon his Party 'gainst the Duke of Albany?
Advise your self.

EDGAR I'm sure on't, not a Word.

BASTARD I hear my Father coming, pardon me:
In cunning I must draw my Sword upon you.
Draw, seem to defend your self. Now quit you well.
Yield, come before my Father. – Light ho, here.
– Fly, Brother. – Torches, Torches. – So
farewell. *Exit Edgar.*
– Some Blood drawn on me would beget Opinion
Of my more fierce Endeavour. I have seen Drunkards
Do more than this in Sport.

Enter Gloucester, and Servants with Torches.

– Father, Father,
Stop, stop, no help?

GLOUCESTER Now Edmund, where's the Villain?

BASTARD Here stood he in the Dark, his sharp Sword
out,
Mumbling of wicked Charms, conjuring the Moon
To stand's auspicious Mistress.

GLOUCESTER But where is he?

BASTARD Look, Sir, I bleed.

GLOUCESTER Where is the Villain,
Edmund?

BASTARD Fled this way, Sir, when by no means he could –

GLOUCESTER – Pursue him, ho; go after. [*Exeunt Servants.*]
– By no means what?

BASTARD Persuade me to the Murther of your Lordship,
But that I told him the revenging Gods
'Gainst Parricides did all the Thunder bend,
Spoke with how manifold and strong a Bond
The Child was bound to th' Father. Sir, in fine,
Seeing how loathly opposite I stood
To his unnatural Purpose, in fell Motion
With his prepared Sword he charges home

53 **unprovided** unprotected. Compare I.v.29–34.
latch'd caught; latched onto [with his sword].

54 **alarum'd** aroused; called to arms.

55 **Bold . . . Right** brave in defence of the right. Compare I.iv.255.

56 **gasted** frightened; made aghast.

59 **And . . . dispatch** and as soon as he is captured, he will be executed.

60 **Arch and Patron** leader and sponsor. *To night* echoes line 16.

63 **to the Stake** to captivity, where he will be tied to a stake and either tormented (as in a bear-baiting arena) or burned.

66 **pight** pitched; determined.

67 **discover** disclose, expose. Edmund's phrasing is apt; as a result of his plot, Edgar will emerge as a naked (dis-covered) beggar.

69 **stand** (a) stand up, (b) take the witness stand. Compare line 50. Also see I.i.200, 243–44, 278, and I.ii.22.
Reposal placement.

71 **faith'd** believed; accepted as delivered in good faith.

72 **I would, I** the second *I* (which appears only in the Quarto) can mean both (a) I, and (b) ay. Compare I.v.10.

73 **Character** handwriting (see I.ii.69–70). Edmund will 'produce' (bring forth) Edgar's true 'Character' in a more fundamental sense.

74 **Suggestion** prompting, urging; 'Practice' (plot).

77 **pregnant . . . Spirits** ready (fully prepared to emerge) and potent demons.

78 **strange and fast'ned** alien (unnatural) and indelibly resolved. 'I never got [begot] him' (line 79) occurs in the Quarto text only.

81 **Ports** exits; both (a) gates, and (b) seaports.

84 **due** proper. The word appears only in the Folio.

86 **capable** able to inherit my estate. Edmund has planted the idea for this outcome in line 68, where he has described himself as 'unpossessing' (unable to claim any of his father's property because he is not Gloucester's firstborn). The Earl pledges to rewrite his will. Gloucester's phrasing is inadvertently pertinent: *capable* derives from the Latin verb *capere*, 'to take or seize', and one of its meanings is 'capacious' (full, possessing to capacity). See the note to I.ii.21.

My unprovided Body, latch'd mine Arm,
And when he saw my best alarum'd Spirits,
Bold in the Quarrel's Right, rous'd to th' Encounter,
Or whether gasted by the Noise I made,
Full suddenly he fled.

GLOUCESTER Let him fly far;
Not in this Land shall he remain uncaught
And found; dispatch. – The Noble Duke my Master,
My worthy Arch and Patron, comes to night:
By his Authority I will proclaim it,
That he which finds him shall deserve our Thanks,
Bringing the murderous Coward to the Stake;
He that conceals him, Death.

BASTARD When I dissuaded him from his Intent
And found him pight to do it, with curst Speech
I threaten'd to discover him; he replied,
'Thou unpossessing Bastard, dost thou think,
If I would stand against thee, would the Reposal
Of any Trust, Virtue, or Worth in thee
Make thy Words faith'd? No, what should I deny
(As this I would, I, though thou didst produce
My very Character), I'd turn it all
To thy Suggestion, Plot, and damned Practice;
And thou must make a Dullard of the World
If they not thought the Profits of my Death
Were very pregnant and potential Spirits
To make thee seek it.' *Tucket within.*

GLOUCESTER O strange and fast'ned Villain,
Would he deny his Letter, said he? I never got him.
Hark, the Duke's Trumpets; I know not where he
comes;
All Ports I'll bar, the Villain shall not scape,
The Duke must grant me that; besides, his Picture
I will send far and near, that all the Kingdom
May have due Note of him; and of my Land,
Loyal and Natural Boy, I'll work the Means
To make thee capable.

88 **Strangeness** reports of incredible happenings. Most editions adopt the Quarto's 'strange news'; the Folio wording conveys a greater sense of astonishment.

89 **comes too short** is insufficient. See the note to I.v.55.

91 **crack'd** broken, split open. Compare I.ii.169, I.iv.183–86.

92 **my Father's Godson** Regan's phrasing implies that Lear was indirectly responsible for the behaviour Edmund has attributed to Edgar. Events will prove her words apt in a way she little suspects: Edgar will align himself with Lear, and meanwhile he will serve his own father as a 'Godson' in another sense (a son provided by the gods to aid him) and 'seek' his 'Life' and that of the King.

94 **Shame . . . hid** It shames me so to admit that my own flesh could do such a thing that I'd prefer to keep it secret. Gloucester's words anticipate the shameful nakedness with which Edgar will hide his identity to evade his would-be captors.

98 **of that Consort** a member of that company. Compare the derogatory sense *Consort* carries in *Romeo and Juliet*, III.i.47–52, 59–60.

99 **No . . . affected** it is not surprising, then, that he has lost his native affection for his father.

100 **put him on** urged him to. Compare I.iv.222–23.

101 **To . . . Revenues** so that they can share in the waste (dispersal) of Gloucester's estate. See Sonnet 129, lines 1–2.

107 **A Child-like Office** a demonstration of duty that shows you to be a true child. In fact Edmund has played on a child-like gullibility in Gloucester that resembles Lear's folly. See I.i.124–25; I.ii.79–83; I.iii.19–21; I.iv.109–11, 229–30, 253; I.v.54–55.

108 **bewray his Practice** expose his cunning. Compare lines 73–74.

112–13 **make . . . please** Choose the form of execution you prefer, and you can count on my power to effect it.

Enter Cornwall, Regan, and Attendants.

CORNWALL How now, my Noble Friend? Since I came hither
(Which I can call but now) I have heard Strangeness.
REGAN If it be true, all Vengeance comes too short
Which can pursue th' Offender; how dost, my Lord?
GLOUCESTER O Madam, my old Heart is crack'd, it's crack'd.
REGAN What, did my Father's Godson seek your Life?
He whom my Father nam'd, your Edgar?
GLOUCESTER O Lady, Lady, Shame would have it hid.
REGAN Was he not Companion with the riotous Knights
That tended upon my Father?
GLOUCESTER I know not, Madam.
'Tis too bad, too bad.
BASTARD Yes, Madam, he
Was of that Consort.
REGAN No Marvel then though he were ill affected;
'Tis they have put him on the Old Man's Death,
To have th' Expense and Waste of his Revenues.
I have this present Evening from my Sister
Been well inform'd of them, and with such Cautions,
That if they come to sojourn at my House
I'll not be there.
CORNWALL Nor I, assure thee, Regan.
– Edmund, I hear that you have shewn your Father
A Child-like Office.
BASTARD It was my Duty, Sir.
GLOUCESTER He did bewray his Practice, and receiv'd
This Hurt you see, striving to apprehend him.
CORNWALL Is he pursued?
GLOUCESTER Ay, my good Lord.
CORNWALL If he be taken, he shall never more
Be fear'd of doing Harm; make your own Purpose,
How in my Strength you please. – For you, Edmund,

114 **Instant** moment. Cornwall's word is doubly pertinent; it derives from the Latin word *stare* 'to stand' (compare lines 50, 69), and it serves as a reminder of the kind of standing up Edmund has sarcastically urged upon his 'Gods' in I.ii.22.

115 **ours** a member of my entourage. Compare *King John*, I.i.134–89.

116 **deep Trust** rooted loyalty. Cornwall is unaware of how 'deep' (hidden, penetrating) and 'dark-ey'd' (line 120) Edmund's 'Trust' ('Thrusting-on', I.ii.143) really is. In line 117 the word 'Sir' appears only in the Folio.

120 **out . . . Night** at an extraordinary hour [imposing on your hospitality in an 'unmannerly' fashion, I.i.146], when the eye of Night's needle is almost too dark to thread. Compare I.iv.359–61 and *King John*, V.iv.11. See the note on *to night* at I.ii.24.

121 **Prize** price, import. *Prize* can also mean *prise*, pry open or 'spy into' (I.v.24–25), a sense that consorts with Regan's eye-threading image. Before long Gloucester himself will be 'threading dark-ey'd Night'. By then the wanton-eyed Regan will be seeking the 'use' of a younger Gloucester's 'Advise' ('Counsail', line 128); compare *vice/vise* and their derivatives in *Othello*, II.iii.329 and III.iii.385, and in *Much Ado About Nothing*, V.ii.18–22.

122 **Advise** advice.

124 **Differences** disagreements. See the notes to I.iv.97, 146.

125 **answer . . . Home** respond to from a place other than our own castle.
several different, individual.

126 **attend Dispatch** are waiting to be dispatched (sent back with replies).

127 **Lay . . . Bosom** apply comforting bandages to your wounded heart.

129 **craves . . . Use** cry out for immediate attention. *Instant*, echoing line 114, is a reminder that Regan's 'Businesses' prompt her to stand up against her father and king. Before long the way she 'craves the Instant Use' will become more explicit. Compare line 17.

Whose Virtue and Obedience doth this Instant
So much commend it self, you shall be ours.
Natures of such deep Trust we shall much need:
You we first seize on.

BASTARD I shall serve you, Sir,
Truly, how ever else.

GLOUCESTER For him I thank your Grace.

CORNWALL You know not why we came to visit you?

REGAN Thus out of Season, threading dark-ey'd Night:
Occasions, Noble Gloucester, of some Prize,
Wherein we must have use of your Advise.
Our Father he hath writ, so hath our Sister,
Of Differences which I best thought it fit
To answer from our Home. The several Messengers
From hence attend Dispatch. Our good old Friend,
Lay Comforts to your Bosom, and bestow
Your needful Counsail to our Businesses,
Which craves the Instant Use.

GLOUCESTER I serve you, Madam,
Your Graces are right welcome. *Exeunt. Flourish.*

II.ii This scene takes place outside Gloucester's castle. In the opening stage direction *severally* appears only in the Folio text.

2 **I** both (a) I [I am who I am], and (b) ay. Compare II.i.72.
Mire dung-filled bog. Kent is calling the Steward a sow (see 2 Peter 2:22).

5 **Lipsbury Pinfold** the fold (pound for stray animals) for insolent upstarts from Liptown [who disregard the admonitions to servants in Ephesians 6:5–8]. *Care* recalls I.i.114.

9 **Broken Meats** partially eaten food; scraps. The play on *know* in line 8 recalls I.iv.175–76.

10 **Three-suited** owning only three suits (a servant's usual allotment). Compare III.iv.141–42.

11 **Woosted-stocking** worsted-stockinged (wearing coarse wool).

12 **Action-taking** given to invoking the Law rather than defending himself like a man (as will be shown in lines 37, 40).

12–13 **Glass-gazing** vain (preening in front of a mirror), 'Finical'.

13 **Super-serviceable** willing to do anything to please.

14 **Trunk-inheriting** inheriting or owning no more than a trunk (either a box of belongings or the Steward's own body). Compare I.i.180.

16 **Composition** sum, composite, mixture. *Mungril* (mongrel) echoes I.iv.53–54.

20 **Addition** titles just bestowed. Compare I.i.136–37, I.iv.158–59.

28 **Sop** a piece of floating toast (here one to soak up 'Moonshine'). Kent probably alludes to 'eggs in moonshine', fried eggs served with onions. The word 'yet' appears only in the Folio text.

Scene 2

Enter Kent, and Steward, severally.

STEWARD Good dawning to thee, Friend, art of this House?

KENT I.

STEWARD Where may we set our Horses?

KENT I'th' Mire.

STEWARD Prythee, if thou lov'st me, tell me.

KENT I love thee not.

STEWARD Why then I care not for thee.

KENT If I had thee in Lipsbury Pinfold, I would make thee care for me.

STEWARD Why dost thou use me thus? I know thee not.

KENT Fellow, I know thee.

STEWARD What dost thou know me for?

KENT A Knave, a Rascal, an Eater of Broken Meats; a Base, Proud, Shallow, Beggarly, Three-suited, Hundred-pound, Filthy Woosted-stocking Knave; a Lily-livered, Action-taking, Whoreson, Glass-glazing Super-serviceable, Finical Rogue; one Trunk-inheriting Slave; one that wouldst be a Bawd in way of good Service, and art nothing but the Composition of a Knave, Beggar, Coward, Pandar, and the Son and Heir of a Mungril Bitch; one whom I will beat into Clamours whining if thou deni'st the least Syllable of thy Addition.

STEWARD Why, what a Monstrous Fellow art thou, thus to rail on one that is neither known of thee nor knows thee?

KENT What a Brazen-fac'd Varlet art thou, to deny thou knowest me? Is it Two Days since I tripp'd up thy Heels, and beat thee before the King? Draw, you Rogue, for though it be Night, yet the Moon shines. I'll make a Sop o'th'

29 **cullionly** ball-sized, base. *Cullions* are testicles.

30 **Barber-monger** pretty boy (frequent patron of barbershops).

35 **carbonado your Shanks** score (slash) your hindquarters, like meat to be grilled. *Part* (line 34) recalls I.iv.106–7, 277, 351; II.i.28. Here as elsewhere, the genital suggestiveness of the phrasing is apt.

36 **come your ways** come on now.

39 **neat** fastidious, prim; sissy.

S.D. **(with his Rapier drawn)** This information derives from the Quarto text.

42 **Goodman Boy** pretty youth. Both terms are insulting here. *Goodman* was another term for 'yeoman', a householder below the rank of gentleman.

43 **flesh ye** initiate you into manhood (giving you your first taste of blood). See the notes to *1 Henry VI*, IV.vi.36, and *Macbeth*, V.vii.71.

45 **Keep Peace** Cornwall's orders would have been familiar to an audience in Shakespeare's time; private duelling was forbidden, in accordance with Romans 12:17–13:7.

49 **Difference** quarrel, dispute. Compare II.i.123–25.

51 **bestirr'd your Valour** activated your courage. Kent's sarcasm recalls the exchanges with Oswald in I.iv.83–99; and *bestirr'd* echoes *Stirrility*, I.iv.292.

52 **disclaims in thee** disinherits you; refuses to claim any part of you.

54 **Strange** odd, quirky. Compare II.i.88.

57 **ill** both (a) ineptly, poorly, and (b) evil, vicious.

60 **ancient** aged.

61 **at . . . Grey-beard** because of his grey beard's pleadings.

62 **Zed** the letter Z.
Unnecessary Letter superfluous member of the alphabet (because *s* can serve the same purposes). Compare I.iv.207, where the Fool calls Lear 'an O without a Figure'.

Moonshine of you, you whoreson cullionly Barber-monger, draw.

STEWARD Away, I have nothing to do with thee.

KENT Draw, you Rascal; you come with Letters against the King, and take Vanity the Puppet's part against the Royalty of her Father. Draw, you Rogue, or I'll so carbonado your Shanks – Draw, you Rascal, come your ways.

STEWARD Help, ho, Murther, help.

KENT Strike, you Slave: stand, Rogue, stand, you neat Slave, strike.

STEWARD Help, ho, Murther, Murther.

Enter Bastard (with his Rapier drawn), Cornwall, Regan, Gloucester, Servants.

BASTARD How now, what's the matter? Part.

KENT With you, Goodman Boy; if you please, come, I'll flesh ye; come on, young Master.

GLOUCESTER Weapons? Arms? What's the matter here?

CORNWALL Keep Peace, upon your Lives; he dies that strikes again. What is the matter?

REGAN The Messengers from our Sister and the King?

CORNWALL What is your Difference? Speak.

STEWARD I am scarce in Breath, my Lord.

KENT No marvel, you have so bestirr'd your Valour, you cowardly Rascal. Nature disclaims in thee: a Tailor made thee.

CORNWALL Thou art a Strange Fellow: a Tailor make a Man?

KENT A Tailor, Sir: a Stone-cutter, or a Painter, could not have made him so ill, though they had been but Two Years o'th' Trade.

CORNWALL Speak yet, how grew your Quarrel?

STEWARD This ancient Ruffian, Sir, whose Life I have spar'd at Suit of his Grey-beard –

KENT Thou whoreson Zed, thou Unnecessary Letter.

64 **unboulted** (a) unsifted (like lumpy lime that has to be pulverized before it can be mixed into mortar), and (b) unbolted (unhinged).

65 **daub . . . Jakes** plaster or caulk a privy. *Wagtail* refers to the fluttering tail feathers of a shaking bird.

69 **Anger . . . Privilege** righteous indignation can be excused.

73 **bite . . . twain** chew through the ties that bind human beings in sacred harmony; here a metaphor for the bonds of matrimony, family, and society. See Ephesians 4:3, 6:1–9. Compare I.i.94.

74 **Which . . . intrince** which are to be untied. *Intrince* is related to *intricate*, entangled. *Unloose* means 'loosen'.
smooth massage; soothe, flatter.

77 **Revenge** urge their Lords to vengeance (see the note to line 45). Most editors follow the Quarto and print *renege*.
Halcyon Beaks weathervane-like beaks (like those of the kingfisher).

78 **Gall and Vary** irritation (the Quarto prints *gale*) and variation.

81 **Smoile you** do you smile at. *Epileptic* suggests that Oswald trembles.

82 **Sarum Plain** the plain near Salisbury, sometimes thought to be the site of Camelot, where the legendary King Arthur had his court.

87 **likes** pleases. *Countenance* (cheek) plays on *cunnus* (see I.i.20–21) and *Fault*.

89 **my . . . Plain** my profession to speak directly. Compare I.i.130, 150, 161–62, 201, 242–44; I.iv.12–22, 34–39.

91 **stands** both (a) rests, and (b) stands up insolently. This word and *Instant* (line 92) echo II.i.114.

93 **affect** adopt as an affectation ('Garb'). See the note to I.i.285.

94 **saucy Roughness** impudent abrasiveness. Compare I.i.21–25, I.ii.146–69.
constrains the Garb forces his manner (here likened to a costume). Like Lear, Cornwall accuses Kent of 'strain'd Pride' (I.i.172). See the note on *Gate* at I.iv.285.

– My Lord, if you will give me leave, I will
tread this unboulted Villain into Mortar and
daub the Wall of a Jakes with him. – Spare my
Grey-beard, you Wagtail?

CORNWALL Peace, Sirrah,
You beastly Knave, know you no Reverence?

KENT Yes Sir, but Anger hath a Privilege.

CORNWALL Why art thou angry?

KENT That such a Slave as this should wear a Sword,
Who wears no Honesty. Such smiling Rogues as these
Like Rats oft bite the holy Cords a' twain
Which are t' intrince, t' unloose; smooth every Passion
That in the Natures of their Lords rebel,
Being Oil to Fire, Snow to the Colder Moods;
Revenge, affirm, and turn their Halcyon Beaks
With every Gall and Vary of their Masters,
Knowing naught (like Dogs) but Following.
– A Plague upon your Epileptic Visage,
Smoile you my Speeches as I were a Fool?
Goose, if I had you upon Sarum Plain,
I'd drive ye cackling home to Camelot.

CORNWALL What art thou Mad, Old Fellow?

GLOUCESTER How fell you out?
Say that.

KENT No Contraries hold more Antipathy
Than I and such a Knave.

CORNWALL Why dost thou call him Knave?
What is his Fault?

KENT His Countenance likes me not.

CORNWALL No more, perchance, does mine, nor his,
nor hers.

KENT Sir, 'tis my Occupation to be Plain:
I have seen better Faces in my Time
Than stands on any Shoulder that I see
Before me at this Instant.

CORNWALL This is some Fellow
Who, having been prais'd for Bluntness, doth affect
A saucy Roughness, and constrains the Garb

95 **Quite . . . Nature** in a way that goes against his normal behaviour.

97 **And . . . so** if they (his listeners) will receive it as such.

99 **Craft** cunning; the opposite of honest 'Plainness'.
corrupter Ends dishonourable purposes. Cornwall's phrasing hints at the kind of rudeness implied in line 94, as opposed to the behaviour of cajoling courtiers who 'stretch their Duties nicely' (line 101). *Stretch* anticipates IV.ii.22–23 and V.iii.310–12.

100 **Silly-ducking Observants** foolish, bowing sycophants.

103 **Under . . . Aspect** with the permission of your great countenance. Kent mocks the obsequious rhetoric of flatterers.

105 **flicking . . . Front** the forehead of the flickering Sun god. Kent is pretending to worship the royal Cornwall. See the note to I.ii.117. Compare *flicking* to the phrasing in *Romeo and Juliet*, II.i.230–33, II.ii.1–4.

108 **beguil'd** deceived; with wordplay on *gilded*, 'gold-plated'.

114 **very late** recently.

115 **upon his Misconstruction** when he (the King) misconstrued my standoffish manner as offensive. See I.iv.83–99.

116 **he . . . Displeasure** Kent, as part of a plot ('compact') to humour and encourage the King's irritability.

117–22 **being . . . again** while I was down, insulted and scorned me and affected a fierce manliness that made him appear worthy in the eyes of the King, won the King's praises for challenging a man who was on the ground only because he had fallen, and in the flush of confidence inspired by this brave act (requiring as much courage as it takes to assault a corpse), he drew his sword upon me here again. The Quarto reads *dread* in line 121. *Fleshment* (fleshing) echoes line 43.

Quite from his Nature. He cannot flatter, he;
An Honest Mind and Plain, he must speak Truth,
And they will take it so; if not, he's Plain.
These kind of Knaves I know, which in this Plainness
Harbour more Craft and more corrupter Ends
Than twenty Silly-ducking Observants
That stretch their Duties nicely.

KENT Sir, in good Faith, in sincere Verity,
Under th' Allowance of your great Aspect,
Whose Influence, like the Wreath of radiant Fire
On flicking Phoebus' Front –

CORNWALL What mean'st by this?

KENT To go out of my Dialect, which you discommend so much; I know, Sir, I am no Flatterer; he that beguil'd you in a Plain Accent was a Plain Knave, which for my part I will not be, though I should win your Displeasure to entreat me to't.

CORNWALL What was th' Offence you gave him?

STEWARD I never gave him any.
It pleas'd the King his Master very late
To strike at me upon his Misconstruction,
When he, compact and flattering his Displeasure,
Tripp'd me behind; being down, insulted, rail'd,
And put upon him such a deal of Man
That worthied him, got Praises of the King
For him attempting who was self-subdued,
And in the Fleshment of this dead Exploit
Drew on me here again.

123 **Aiax . . . Fool** Ajax pales in comparison with them for folly and braggadocio. Kent is probably alluding to the incident in which the Homeric warrior, feeling insulted by the Greek leaders' refusal to award him the armour of the slain Achilles, went mad and slaughtered an 'army' of cows and sheep. Shakespeare depicts Aiax as a stupid braggart in *Troilus and Cressida*. Here as elsewhere, *Aiax* plays on 'a Jakes' (compare line 65).

there both (a) in their place (compare I.iv.146–60) and (b) their (the word in the Quarto, substituted for the Folio's *there* in most modern editions). To a theatre audience, hearing this line spoken, the meanings of both *there* and *their* are applicable.

Stocks a wooden frame in which an offender's ankles (and sometimes his wrists) were locked to punish him.

124 **reverent** aged, dignified (probably meant sarcastically, since Kent is being anything but reverent to Cornwall).

127 **On whose Employment** in whose service.

128 **do small Respects** show little respect. *Bold* echoes II.i.55. *Respects* recalls I.i.252–54.

134 **You . . . so** you should treat me with more courtesy.

being his Knave since you are his knave (a word meaning both 'servant' and 'villain'). Compare I.iv.47, 86.

135 **Colour** livery, quality. Cornwall likens Kent to the 'riotous Knights' (II.i.95) that Regan has warned him against.

136 **away** forward [to a more central position on the stage].

138 **Fault** offence. See I.iv.280–81. Lines 138–41 and 147 ('For . . . Legs.') occur in the Quarto only.

139 **check** rebuke, discipline.

Your . . . Correction the demeaning punishment you intend.

140 **'temnest** contemnest; most contemptible.

Pilferings minor acts of thievery.

142 **take it ill** be insulted. Compare lines 56–57.

143 **so . . . Messenger** treated so slightingly by the way his messenger is punished. See the note to I.v.55.

144 **answer that** respond to that charge. Compare I.iii.11.

147 **following her Affairs** acting on her instructions. See the note on *follow* at I.iv.44–45.

148 CORNWALL This speech heading appears only in the Folio. In the Quarto, line 148 concludes Regan's speech.

150 **Disposition** temperament.

KENT None of these Rogues and Cowards
But Aiax is there Fool.
CORNWALL Fetch forth the Stocks!
– You stubborn ancient Knave, you reverent Braggart,
We'll teach you.
KENT Sir, I am too Old to learn.
Call not your Stocks for me, I serve the King,
On whose Employment I was sent to you.
You shall do small Respects, show too bold Malice
Against the Grace and Person of my Master,
Stocking his Messenger.
CORNWALL Fetch forth the Stocks;
As I have Life and Honour, there shall he sit till Noon.
REGAN Till Noon? Till Night, my Lord, and all Night
too.
KENT Why Madam, if I were your Father's Dog,
You should not use me so.
REGAN Sir, being his Knave, I will.
CORNWALL This is a Fellow of the self same Colour
Our Sister speaks of. Come, bring away the
Stocks. *Stocks brought out.*
GLOUCESTER Let me beseech your Grace not to do so.
His Fault is much, and the good King his Maister
Will check him for't. Your purpos'd low Correction
Is such as basest and 'temnest Wretches for Pilferings
And most common Trespasses are punish'd with.
The King his Master needs must take it ill
That he, so slightly valu'd in his Messenger,
Should have him thus restrain'd.
CORNWALL I'll answer that.
REGAN My Sister may receive it much more worse
To have her Gentleman abus'd, assaulted
For following her Affairs. Put in his Legs.
CORNWALL Come, my Lord, away.
Exit [followed by all but Gloucester and Kent].
GLOUCESTER I am sorry for thee, Friend; 'tis the Duke's
pleasure,
Whose Disposition all the World well knows

151 **rubb'd** diverted. In the game of bowls, a rub was any impediment on the lawn that interfered with the course of the ball as it curved towards its destination. Compare I.ii.125–26.

152 **watch'd and travail'd** stayed awake and laboured in my travels. *Travail* and *travel* are interchangeable words in Shakespeare's plays. See the note on *Watchers* in *Macbeth*, II.ii.70.

154 **A . . . Heels** Kent's heels are protruding. Compare I.v.8–12.

155 **too blame** too blameworthy.

157 **approve . . . Saw** prove true the well-known proverb. Compare I.i.187.

158–59 **Thou . . . Sun** you have departed from Heaven's shelter to the excessive heat of 'the warm Sun'. Kent's phrasing also hints that the King will eventually benefit from 'comfortable Beams' (line 161).

160 **thou . . . Globe** the rising Sun, which lights the Globe beneath it. Kent's words also suggest (a) the King, whose light and warmth are greatly missed at the moment, and (b) the Globe players, whose fortunes depend on both kinds of 'Beacon' (King and Sun). See the notes to line 105 and to I.ii.117.

162–63 **Nothing . . . Misery** Being 'obscured', reduced to 'Nothing' (see I.iv.200–2), gives one a special perspective on 'Miracles' (signs of grace). *Misery* echoes I.i.111.

164–66 **Time . . . Remedies** a time to mend the ills of this rank nation (swollen with infection). *Time* recalls I.i.285.

166 **o'er-watch'd** (a) overworked from 'watching'; (b) watched over from above. Compare line 152.

167 **Vantage** advantage (playing on 'viewpoint'). The stage direction at line 169 ('*Sleeps*') derives from the Quarto text.

171 **No . . . free** no means of escape is unguarded (II.i.81). The appearance of a second 'shameful' victim provides an on-stage answer to Kent's prayer that Fortune once more turn her 'Wheel' (line 169). Most modern editions add new scene divisions to mark Kent's sleep and the entrance and exit of Edgar, with II.iii commencing with what is Edgar's half of line 169 here, and II.iv. commencing with what is line 190 in this edition.

173 **attend my Taking** wait to capture me.

Will not be rubb'd nor stopp'd. I'll entreat for thee.
KENT Pray do not, Sir; I have watch'd and travail'd hard;
Some time I shall sleep out, the rest I'll whistle.
A Good Man's Fortune may grow out at Heels;
Give you good morrow.
GLOUCESTER The Duke's too blame in this:
'Twill be ill taken. *Exit.*
KENT Good King, that must approve the common Saw,
Thou out of Heaven's Benediction com'st
To the warm Sun.
– Approach, thou Beacon to this under Globe,
That by thy comfortable Beams I may
Peruse this Letter. Nothing almost sees Miracles
But Misery. I know 'tis from Cordelia,
Who hath most fortunately been inform'd
Of my obscured Course, and shall find Time
From this enormous State, seeking to give
Losses their Remedies. All weary and o'er-watch'd,
Take Vantage, heavy Eyes, not to behold
This shameful Lodging. – Fortune goodnight; smile
Once more, turn thy Wheel. *Sleeps.*

Enter Edgar.

EDGAR I heard my self proclaim'd,
And by the happy Hollow of a Tree
Escap'd the Hunt. No Port is free, no place
That Guard and most unus'al Vigilance
Does not attend my Taking. Whiles I may scape

174–77 **bethought . . . Beast** of a mind to assume the most abject 'Shape' (compare I.iv.323–24) that contemptuous Poverty ever imposed to reduce 'Man' to beastliness. Compare lines 139–41 and I.iv.10–12.

178 **Loins** crotch, privates.
elf tie in elf-locks (matted and tangled 'Knots').

179 **presented** (a) openly displayed, and (b) represented, acted.
out-face face down; stand up to and overcome.

181 **Proof and President** example and precedent.

182 **Bedlam Beggars** insane vagabonds. *Bedlam* recalls I.ii.153–54.

183 **mortified** deadened, 'numb'd'. The word *bare* is here inserted from the Quarto text.

184 **Wodden-pricks** the wooden pins that wodden (insane) beggars stick into their flesh. Compare *wodde* (mad) in *A Midsummer Night's Dream*, II.i.192; and see line 199 for another use of *Wodden*.

185 **Object** appearance, self-presentation. Compare I.i.217.

186 **pelting** both (a) paltry, and (b) stone-throwing.
Sheep-cotes sheepfolds. Compare line 5.

187 **Lunatic Bans** crazed curses.

188 **Inforce their Charity** compel people to aid them.
Turlygod the god of a sect of naked Parisian beggars.

189 **Edgar . . . am** If I try to retain my former identity as Edgar, I will be reduced to 'nothing' indeed (compare lines 162–63). Like Kent, Edgar has 'raz'd' his 'Likeness' (I.iv.4).

196 **Cruel Garters** The Fool puns on *crewel* ('Woosted', line 11), the spelling in the Quarto. He points to Kent's wooden 'Garters' (the stocks).

199 **Overlusty at Legs** too active with his legs (as with a vagabond, who has run away from his assigned post). The Fool's words also apply to *Legs* in the sense that equates with *Loins*. See *Troilus and Cressida*, I.ii.15–17.
Wodden both (a) crazy (compare line 110), and (b) wooden.

200 **Nether-stocks** stockings (as opposed to 'overstocks', breeches), punning on *Stocks*.

201 **thy Place** your social standing (as the King's servant). Compare lines 125–29, 137–44, 212.

I will preserve my self, and am bethought
To take the Basest and most Poorest Shape
That ever Penury in contempt of Man
Brought near to Beast. My Face I'll grime with Filth,
Blanket my Loins, elf all my Hairs in Knots,
And with presented Nakedness out-face
The Winds and Persecutions of the Sky.
The Country gives me Proof and President
Of Bedlam Beggars, who with roaring Voices
Strike in their numb'd and mortified bare Arms
Pins, Wodden-pricks, Nails, Sprigs of Rosemary;
And with this Horrible Object, from low Farms,
Poor pelting Villages, Sheep-cotes, and Mills,
Sometimes with Lunatic Bans, sometime with Prayers,
Inforce their Charity. Poor Turlygod, Poor Tom,
That's something yet: Edgar I nothing am. *Exit.*

Enter Lear, Fool, and Gentleman.

LEAR 'Tis strange that they should so depart from
Home,
And not send back my Messengers.
GENTLEMAN As I learn'd,
The Night before there was no Purpose in them
Of this Remove.
KENT Hail to thee, Noble Master.
LEAR Ha?
Mak'st thou this Shame thy Pastime?
KENT No, my Lord.
FOOL Ha, ha, he wears Cruel Garters. Horses are
tied by the Heads, Dogs and Bears by th' Neck,
Monkeys by th' Loins, and Men by th' Legs. When
a Man's Overlusty at Legs, then he wears Wodden
Nether-stocks.
LEAR What's he that hath so much thy Place mistook
To set thee here?
KENT It is both he and she:
Your Son and Daughter.

206 **swear I** swear ay (with the Folio's upright *I* serving as a reminder that Kent is standing up to Lear in the name of Jupiter's wife, just as Lear's two daughters are asserting their wills against any superior who opposes them). Compare I.i.73, 106; I.ii.21; I.v.10, 23–26; II.i.72–73; II.ii.2, 90–92. And see the note to I.iv.229. The Lear and Kent exchanges in lines 204–5 ('No . . . have.') are here inserted from the Quarto text. Kent's half of line 206 appears only in the Folio.

208 **Respect** both (a) a person who should be respected, and (b) Respect (reverence, proper behaviour) itself. Compare I.i.242–44 and II.ii.128.

209 **Resolve . . . Haste** explain to me with all due speed.

210–11 **Usage . . . us** treatment, given the fact that you came from me.

214 **reeking** both (a) sweating, and (b) perfumed. Compare I.iv.120–22.

215 **painting** both (a) panting (the Quarto word), and (b) painting (speaking in cosmetic rhetoric, with flattering flourishes).

217 **spight of Intermission** despite interrupting my presentation.

218 **presently** immediately.

218–19 **on . . . Meiny** on the basis of what those letters contained, they called forth their menials (household servants).

220–21 **attend . . . Answer** wait until they had leisure to reply. *Answer* recalls line 144.

224–25 **Being . . . Highness** seeing that he was the same knave who recently acted so insolently towards you. Compare line 94.

226 **Man** (a) manliness (courage), (b) frailty (passion ungoverned by reason), and (c) fidelity as your 'man' (see the note to I.iv.12).

228 **found** judged. Compare I.iv.175–76.

230 **wil'd** both (a) will'd (meaning 'wilful') and (b) wild (a word closely associated with *willed* in Shakespeare's time). Compare line 489.

232 **wear Rags** are impoverished. The Fool likens Lear to his stocked servant (and, without realizing it, to the 'Poor Tom' who just entered and left the stage in rags). This speech (lines 230–40) appears only in the Folio.

LEAR No.
KENT Yes.
LEAR No, I say.
KENT I say yea.
LEAR No, no, they would not.
KENT Yes
They have.
LEAR By Jupiter I swear no.
KENT By Juno I swear I.
LEAR They durst not do't,
They could not, would not do't: 'tis worse than Murther
To do upon Respect such violent Outrage.
Resolve me with all modest Haste which way
Thou might'st deserve, or they impose, this Usage,
Coming from us.
KENT My Lord, when at their Home
I did commend your Highness' Letters to them,
Ere I was risen from the place that shewed
My Duty kneeling, came there a reeking Post,
Stew'd in his Haste, half Breathless, painting forth
From Goneril his Mistress Salutations;
Deliver'd Letters, spight of Intermission,
Which presently they read; on those Contents
They summon'd up their Meiny, straight took Horse,
Commanded me to follow and attend
The Leisure of their Answer, gave me Cold Looks;
And meeting here the other Messenger,
Whose Welcome I perceiv'd had poison'd mine,
Being the very Fellow which of late
Display'd so saucily against your Highness,
Having more Man that Wit about me, drew;
He rais'd the House with loud and coward Cries;
Your Son and Daughter found this Trespass worth
The Shame which here it suffers.
FOOL Winter's not gone yet if the wil'd Geese fly
that way.
Fathers that wear Rags

234 **bear Bags** carry moneybags. The Fool's phrase is also a reminder of the genital bags that symbolize virility (see the notes to I.iv.136, 214, and I.v.55).

235 **see . . . Kind** discover that their children treat them with kind respect. *Kind* recalls I.v.14–15.

237 **turns the Key** opens the latch.

239 **Dolours** pains, with wordplay on *dollars*.
tell both (a) count, and (b) recount, tell about. Compare I.v.16–17.

241 **Mother** a name for *hysterica passio* (line 242), a choking pain that climbs up from its clime ('Element') in the womb (*hystera* in Greek). The Folio's *Historica* spelling relates Lear's passion to his recent history. *Oh*, the Folio spelling, is here retained as a way of distinguishing between a vocative (*O*) and a groan or sigh (*Oh*).

244 **here** This word appears only in the Folio.

247 **small a Number** few knights. *Number* recalls the riddles in I.iv. See the notes to I.iv.201, 207, 214, 229, I.v.55.

248 **And** if.

251 **set . . . Ant** let an ant be your teacher. See I.i.298–99, I.iii.20–21, and I.iv.191–92.

253 **follow their Noses** walk straight. Compare I.v.24–25 and II.i.120. *Stinking* (line 255) recalls line 214.

256 **least** lest. Compare I.i.95–96.

257 **Following** both (a) holding on and taking the same path, and (b) being a faithful servant. Compare lines 79, 146–47, and I.i.141–42, I.iv.44, 111–12. Kent will follow till he breaks (V.iii.216–17); see the note to lines 44–45.

258 **draw thee after** pull you up with him. *Draw* recalls I.i.86–87, 144.

259–60 **give . . . again** return mine to me. *Counsel* echoes I.iv.149 and II.i.121–29.

261 **Fool** both (a) unwise man (here one who fails to look out for number one), and (b) professional fool. Lines 260–61 echo I.iv.327.

263 **for Form** (a) to conform to propriety, (b) as a pretence. *Gain* recalls *King John*, II.i.596–97.

Do make their Children Blind,
But Fathers that bear Bags
Shall see their Children Kind.
Fortune, that arrant Whore,
Ne'er turns the Key to the Poor.

But for all this, thou shalt have as many Dolours for thy Daughters as thou canst tell in a Year.

LEAR Oh how this Mother swells up toward my Heart!
– *Historica passio*, down, thou climing Sorrow:
Thy Element's below. – Where is this Daughter?

KENT With the Earl, Sir, here within.

LEAR Follow me not, stay here.
Exit.

GENTLEMAN Made you no more Offence but what you speak of?

KENT None.
How chance the King comes with so small a Number?

FOOL And thou hadst been set i'th' Stocks for that Question, thou'dst well deserv'd it.

KENT Why, Fool?

FOOL We'll set thee to School to an Ant, to teach thee there's no Labouring i'th' Winter. All that follow their Noses are led by their Eyes but Blind Men, and there's not a Nose among Twenty but can smell him that's Stinking. Let go thy Hold, when a Great Wheel runs down a Hill, least it break thy Neck with Following; but the Great One that goes upward, let him draw thee after. When a Wise Man gives thee better Counsel, give me mine again: I would have none but Knaves follow it, since a Fool gives it.

That Sir which serves and seeks for Gain,
And follows but for Form,

264 **pack** (a) conspire, 'Revolt', and (b) pack up, flee (line 273).

269 **perdie** for sure; from the French *pardieu*, 'by God'.

271 **Deny** refuse.
Weary This word recalls line 167 and I.iii.13, I.iv.72.

272 **travail'd** travelled laboriously. Compare line 152.
Fetches deceptive ruses. In line 274 Lear plays on another sense of *fetch* (obtain). Compare *Hamlet*, II.i.38.

273 **The . . . off** the indications of betrayal and desertion.

275 **Fiery Quality** irascible disposition (dominated by Choler, the humour that results from an excess of the element Fire). See I.i.303–5, where the same condition is ascribed to Lear, and I.i.314, where Goneril and Regan vow to act 'i'th' Heat'. Compare line 135 (where *Colour* plays on *choler*), and I.ii.11–12, 23, 146–47 (dragons were proverbially associated with fire), 180–84; I.iii.5.

276 **Unremoveable** immovable, inflexible, 'Fix'd'. Compare I.iv.282–83.

277 **Course** chosen path. This word echoes lines 164–65, and I.i.133, 190; I.ii.92–93; I.iii.26–27; I.iv.222, 355.

283 **I** both (a) I [do], and (b) ay. Compare line 206. The exchanges that precede this reply (lines 281–82) appear only in the Folio; so also with line 286 below.

285 **tends Service** awaits their attendance (attention to his 'commands').

289–90 **Infirmity . . . bound** sickness always fails to perform the duties that require strong health. Compare I.i.205.

291 **Nature, being oppress'd** our human natures, being burdened with infirmities.

Will pack when it begins to Rain
And leave thee in the Storm.
But I will tarry, the Fool will stay,
And let the Wise Man fly;
The Knave turns Fool that runs away,
The Fool no Knave perdie.

KENT Where learn'd you this, Fool?

FOOL Not i'th' Stocks, Fool.

Enter Lear and Gloucester.

LEAR Deny to speak with me? They are Sick, they are Weary,
They have travail'd all the Night? Mere Fetches,
The Images of Revolt and Flying off.
Fetch me a better Answer.

GLOUCESTER My dear Lord,
You know the Fiery Quality of the Duke,
How Unremoveable and Fix'd he is
In his own Course.

LEAR Vengeance, Plague, Death, Confusion.
Fiery? What Quality? Why Gloucester, Gloucester,
I'd speak with the Duke of Cornwall and his Wife.

GLOUCESTER Well, my good Lord, I have inform'd them so.

LEAR 'Inform'd them'? Dost thou understand me, Man?

GLOUCESTER I, my good Lord.

LEAR The King would speak with Cornwall, the dear Father
Would with his Daughter speak; commands, tends Service:
Are they 'inform'd' of this? My Breath and Blood:
'Fiery'? The 'fiery' Duke, tell the hot Duke that –
No, but not yet, may be he is not Well.
Infirmity doth still neglect all Office,
Whereto our Health is bound, we are not our selves,
When Nature, being oppress'd, commands the Mind

292 **forbear** bear up patiently; forgo my demands for the moment. Compare I.ii.180.

293 **fallen . . . Will** at odds with [trying to suppress] my unruly Will. Compare line 230.

294–95 **To . . . Man** to mistake a hallucinatory flare-up (the result of fever) for a manifestation of the man's normal behaviour.

295 **Death . . . State** [on second thoughts,] to the grave with my rebuke of 'headier Will'; my newly calm 'State' is ill-founded. *State* echoes line 165; it also recalls I.i.51, 151, and I.ii.111–12.

295–96 **wherefore . . . here?** why should my man be in these stocks?

297 **Remotion** 'Removal' (line 194, echoed by line 276), here meaning both (a) being away from their own castle, and (b) remoteness (as signalled by their cold refusal to see Lear).

298 **Practice** pretence; a device. Compare I.ii.203; II.i.73–74, 108. In line 300 *presently* means 'now'. The word 'Go' in line 299 appears only in the Folio text.

303 **rising Heart** Lear refers once again to his *hysterica passio*.

304 **Cockney** London cook, here a pampered, naive one such as the maid referred to in I.v.54–55. Her 'Brother' (lines 307–9) is equally simple, buttering (greasing) his hay and thereby making his horse refuse it. Cheating ostlers (stablehands) used this 'Practice' on others' horses to economize on provender.

305 **Eels** The Fool is no doubt referring to more than one kind of wanton (frisky, disobedient) creature. See *Pericles*, IV.iii.153–54. *Paste* carries the same genital implications as *Pye* (a piece of pie) in *Henry VIII*, I.i.52.

306 **knapp'd . . . Coxcombs** rapped them on the noggin. Like *Cockney*, *Coxcomb* hints at the male member, and in conjunction with *Stick* it suggests a Fool's 'bauble' (see *Romeo and Juliet*, II.iii.98–100, and see the note to I.iv.164).

S.D. **Kent . . . liberty** This stage direction appears only in the Folio.

315 **Sepulchring an Adultress** on the assumption that an adulterous liaison with another man resulted in your birth.

Free released from the stocks. Lear addresses Kent. It may be that Kent exits after Lear says 'Some other Time for that.' On the other hand, he may stay beside Lear until he and the Fool exit after line 468.

To suffer with the Body. I'll forbear
And am fallen out with my more headier Will,
To take the Indispos'd and Sickly Fit
For the Sound Man. Death on my State: wherefore
Should he sit here? This Act persuades me
That this Remotion of the Duke and her
Is Practice only. Give me my Servant forth;
Go tell the Duke and's Wife I'd speak with them;
Now, presently; bid them come forth and hear me,
Or at their Chamber Door I'll beat the Drum
Till it cry Sleep to Death.

GLOUCESTER I would have all well betwixt you.
Exit.

LEAR Oh me, my Heart! My rising Heart! But down.

FOOL Cry to it, Nuncle, as the Cockney did to
the Eels, when she put 'em i'th' Paste alive,
she knapp'd 'em o'th' Coxcombs with a Stick and
cried 'Down, Wantons, down.' 'Twas her Brother
that in pure Kindness to his Horse buttered his
Hay.

Enter Cornwall, Regan, Gloucester, Servants.

LEAR Good morrow to you both.

CORNWALL Hail to your Grace.
Kent here set at liberty.

REGAN I am glad to see your Highness.

LEAR Regan, I think you are. I know what Reason
I have to think so; if thou should'st not be glad,
I would divorce me from thy Mother's Tomb,
Sepulchring an Adultress. – O are you Free?
Some other Time for that. – Beloved Regan,

317 **Naught** naughty, wicked; 'Nothing' (see I.iv.137).
Oh Here and elsewhere, this edition follows the spelling in the original texts when the context suggests a groaning *oh* rather than a vocative O.

317–18 **she . . . here** Pointing to his breast, Lear likens himself to Prometheus, whom Zeus chained to a rock in the Caucasus so that vultures could gnaw for ever at his innards. Compare lines 232–35 and I.iv.273–75, 281–84, 301–3.

321 **take Patience** apply patience to your hysteria.

322 **value her Desert** put a price on her deservings.

323 **scant her Duty** be stingy in meeting her 'Obligation'. Compare I.i.283.

326 **restrained the Riots** controlled the unruliness. Compare lines 142–44. Like Lear's half of line 323, this speech (lines 324–28) appears only in the Folio text.

331 **his Confine** its bounds (lifetime). Compare IV.vi.26.

332 **Discretion . . . State** judgement that understands your condition.

336 **mark . . . House** note how this would present our household. See the note to line 481. The word 'but' appears only in the Folio.

338 **Age is Unnecessary** old people are superfluous. Compare line 62.

339 **vouchsafe** grant.

340 **unsightly Tricks** pranks too unbecoming to be watched.

342 **abated . . . Train** deprived me of half my entourage.

343 **Look'd . . . me** glared at me like 'dark-ey'd Night' (II.i.120).
strook me struck (darted at) me [like a poisonous snake]. *Serpent* (line 344) recalls line 223 and I.iv.301–3.

346 **ingrateful Top** ungrateful head.

347 **taking** infecting, cursing.

350 **Fen** marshy land. *Pow'rful* (spelled *powrefull* in the Quarto, and *powrfull* in a crowded line in the Folio) may involve a pun on *power* and *pour* similar to those in *Macbeth*, I.v.28, IV.i.18. *Sun* recalls line 105.

Thy Sister's Naught; Oh Regan, she hath tied
Sharp-tooth'd Unkindness like a Vulture here.
I can scarce speak to thee; thou'lt not believe
With how deprav'd a Quality – Oh Regan.

REGAN I pray you, Sir, take Patience; I have hope
You less know how to value her Desert
Than she to scant her Duty.

LEAR Say? How is that?

REGAN I cannot think my Sister in the least
Would fail her Obligation. If, Sir, perchance
She have restrained the Riots of your Followers,
'Tis on such Ground, and to such wholesome End,
As clears her from all Blame.

LEAR My Curses on her.

REGAN O Sir, you are Old;
Nature in you stands on the very Verge
Of his Confine. You should be rul'd, and led
By some Discretion that discerns your State
Better than you your self. Therefore I pray you
That to our Sister you do make Return,
Say you have wrong'd her.

LEAR Ask her Forgiveness?
Do you but mark how this becomes the House?
'Dear Daughter, I confess that I am Old;
Age is Unnecessary: on my Knees I beg
That you'll vouchsafe me Raiment, Bed, and Food.'

REGAN Good Sir, no more: these are unsightly Tricks.
Return you to my Sister.

LEAR Never, Regan:
She hath abated me of Half my Train,
Look'd black upon me, strook me with her Tongue
Most Serpent-like, upon the very Heart.
All the stor'd Vengeances of Heaven fall
On her ingrateful Top. – Strike her young Bones,
You taking Airs, with Lameness.

CORNWALL Fie, Sir, fie.

LEAR You nimble Lightnings, dart your blinding Flames
Into her scornful Eyes: infect her Beauty,
You Fen-suck'd Fogs, drawn by the pow'rful Sun,

351 **fall and blister** decline into a patchwork of blisters. Lear is probably thinking of one of the symptoms of venereal disease.

352 **Rash Mood** irrational fury.

354 **Tender-hefted** heaved (moved) by tenderness. Compare I.i.92–93.

356 **comfort . . . burn** bring warmth without excessive heat. Compare lines 157–62.

358 **scant my Sizes** reduce my numbers. Compare lines 247, 321–23. *Bandy* recalls I.iv.90.

359 **oppose the Bolt** lock the door; an echo of lines 236–37.

361 **Offices** duties ('Dues', line 362), obligations. *Bond* recalls II.i.48.

362 **Effects of Curtesy** manifestations of courtesy. The Folio spelling hints at wordplay on *cur*; see *The Merchant of Venice*, I.iii.129–30, and *Julius Caesar*, III.i.42–46.

366 **approves her Letter** proves her letter true. See line 157.

368 **easy borrowed Pride** easily-usurped haughtiness. *Pride* can also refer to 'Proud Array' (III.iv.85), costly, ostentatious garments (compare lines 39, 52–53, 94–95).

369 **Dwells . . . follows** is nurtured by the corrupt favour of the mistress he serves. *Follows* echoes lines 257, 260–63.
fickly fickle (the word in the Quarto, which most editions adopt).

370 **Varlet** base peasant, 'Slave' (line 368).

372 **on't** of it.

373 **sweet Sway** benign rule. *Sway* recalls I.ii.55–56.

374 **Allow Obedience** is well disposed to those who obey you. *Allow* echoes lines 102–3 and I.iv.222–23. The word 'you' appears only in the Folio.

375 **Make . . . Cause** take on my case as one in which you too have an interest. *Cause* and *case* both derive from the Latin word *causa*. Compare I.iv.316.
take my Part both (a) side with me, and (b) be my attorneys. *Part* recalls lines 33–34, 109, and I.i.139, I.iv.170–72, 277, and anticipates III.ii.72–73. Lear's plea for divine assistance would have struck theologically sophisticated members of Shakespeare's audience as an ironic echo of Matthew 7:11, where Jesus says, 'If ye then, being evil, know how to give good gifts unto your children, how much more shall your Father which is in heaven give good things to them that ask him?' Compare the Fool's remarks in lines 232–37.

To fall and blister.
REGAN O the blest Gods! So will
You wish on me when the Rash Mood is on.
LEAR No, Regan, thou shalt never have my Curse:
Thy Tender-hefted Nature shall not give
Thee o'er to Harshness. Her Eyes are fierce, but thine
Do comfort and not burn. 'Tis not in thee
To grudge my Pleasures, to cut off my Train,
To bandy Hasty Words, to scant my Sizes,
And in conclusion to oppose the Bolt
Against my coming in. Thou better know'st
The Offices of Nature, Bond of Childhood,
Effects of Curtesy, Dues of Gratitude.
Thy Half o'th' Kingdom hast thou not forgot,
Wherein I thee endow'd.
REGAN Good Sir, to th' Purpose.
LEAR Who put my Man i'th' Stocks? *Tucket within.*
CORNWALL What Trumpet's that?
REGAN I know't, my Sister's: this approves her Letter,
That she would soon be here.

Enter Steward.

– Is your Lady come?
LEAR This is a Slave whose easy borrowed Pride
Dwells in the fickly Grace of her he follows.
– Out, Varlet, from my Sight.
CORNWALL What means your Grace?
LEAR Who stock'd my Servant? Regan, I have good
hope
Thou didst not know on't.

Enter Goneril.

Who comes here? – O Heavens!
If you do love Old Men, if your sweet Sway
Allow Obedience, if you your selves are Old,
Make it your Cause; send down and take my Part.

379 **Indiscretion** lack of judgement. Compare lines 331–32.

380 **Dotage** senility, folly. Compare I.iv.42–43, 306–7, 339.

383 **much less Advancement** a less exalted promotion (alluding sardonically to Kent's placement on an elevated platform, the stocks); that is, a much more severe punishment. In line 382 'Sir' appears only in the Folio.

385 **Expiration . . . Month** conclusion of your month of residence with Goneril. Regan's phrasing suggests that Lear is just as moody as the 'weaker vessels' (1 Peter 3:7) who undergo menstrual cycles. See the note to line 234. *Seem* (line 384) echoes I.i.3, 201, and I.iv.14.

391 **abjure** forswear; reject.

392 **wage against** take arms against; with a reminder that Lear is now a man whose own wages have been cut in half.
Enmity . . . Air hostility of 'taking Airs' (line 347). *Air* is a reminder that Lear's problems derive from the enmity of the *heirs* to whom he has bequeathed his estate.

394 **Necessity's sharp Pinch** the painful constraints imposed by our basic physical needs, by 'Base Life' (line 398). Lear's phrasing echoes line 318. *Necessity* also recalls lines 62 and 338 and I.ii.138.

395 **hot-bloodied** angry, choleric. Compare line 275.

397 **Squire-like** like a knight's attendant.

398 **a foot** afoot (on foot, upright).

399 **Sumpter** load-carrying horse or groom (stablehand).

406 **Bile** boil; here pronounced to echo *vile*.

407 **imbossed Carbuncle** rank 'Plague-sore' (swollen to a head).

408 **corrupted** infected. Lear's imagery relates to syphilis.
chide scold.

409 **call it** invoke it (as a curse).

Art not asham'd to look upon this Beard?
– O Regan, will you take her by the Hand?

GONERIL Why not by th' Hand, Sir? How have I offended?
All's not Offence that Indiscretion finds
And Dotage terms so.

LEAR – O Sides, you are too tough!
Will you yet hold? – How came my Man i'th' Stocks?

CORNWALL I set him there, Sir; but his own Disorders
Deserv'd much less Advancement.

LEAR You? Did you?

REGAN I pray you, Father, being Weak, seem so.
If till the Expiration of your Month
You will return and sojourn with my Sister,
Dismissing half your Train, come then to me.
I am now from Home, and out of that Provision
Which shall be needful for your Entertainment.

LEAR Return to her? And Fifty Men dismiss'd?
No, rather I abjure all Roofs, and choose
To wage against the Enmity o'th' Air,
To be a Comrade with the Wolf and Owl:
Necessity's sharp Pinch. Return with her?
Why the hot-bloodied France, that Dowerless took
Our Youngest borne, I could as well be brought
To knee his Throne, and Squire-like Pension beg,
To keep Base Life a foot. Return with her?
Persuade me rather to be Slave and Sumpter
To this detested Groom.

GONERIL At your Choice, Sir,

LEAR I prythee, Daughter, do not make me Mad.
I will not trouble thee, my Child; farewell,
We'll no more meet, no more see one another.
But yet thou art my Flesh, my Blood, my Daughter,
Or rather a Disease that's in my Flesh,
Which I must needs call mine. Thou art a Bile,
A Plague-sore or imbossed Carbuncle,
In my corrupted Blood. But I'll not chide thee;
Let Shame come when it will, I do not call it,

410 **Thunder-bearer** Zeus, 'Jove' (line 411). Compare lines 205–6 and I.i.181, II.i.46–47.

412 **Mend** heal. Compare I.i.95.
at thy Leisure in your own good time. *Leisure* echoes lines 219–21.

413 **Patient** passive, submissive, calm of mind.

415 **look'd . . . yet** didn't expect your arrival this early. Compare I.iv.90, 203–4, II.ii.343.

416 **fit** proper. This word echoes lines 294–95 and I.iv.347, II.i.124–25. It anticipates III.ii.76. Here, as in line 382, 'Sir' is a Folio addition.

417 **mingle** mix (qualifying your 'Passion' by diluting it with 'Reason'). See the notes to I.i.243–44 and I.ii.181.

419 **well spoken** spoken with full awareness and deliberation.

421 **well** sufficient.

422 **Charge** expense.

425 **Hold Amity** maintain friendly relations. Regan's words echo Mark 3:25, where Jesus says that 'if a house be divided against itself, that house cannot stand'. Compare line 336, and see the note to line 481. What Lear has yet to recognize is that he himself has divided, and thereby undone, his own 'house' (both family and realm). See I.iv.165–202.

426–27 **receive Attendance / From** be served by.

428 **slack** neglect. This word echoes I.iii.10–11.

429 **comptrol** control; both (a) supervise, and (b) discipline.

430 **spy a Danger** perceive a risk I hadn't fully registered before. *Spy* recalls I.v.23–25.

432 **Place or Notice** room, position, or recognition. *Place* echoes lines 202–3.

433 **in Good Time** just in the nick of time. See lines 329–31, and compare I.i.300–5, 314.

434 **Depositaries** trustees; stewards over my holdings.

435 **Reservation** both (a) exception to (exemption from) what I had bequeathed you, and (b) reserve (a provision for my own use during my remaining lifetime). Compare I.i.133–36. *Followed* echoes lines 256–57 and anticipates lines 445–46.

I do not bid the Thunder-bearer shoot,
Nor tell Tales of thee to high-judging Jove.
Mend when thou canst, be better at thy Leisure;
I can be Patient, I can stay with Regan,
I and my Hundred Knights.

REGAN Not altogether so.
I look'd not for you yet, nor am provided
For your fit Welcome. Give Ear, Sir, to my Sister;
For those that mingle Reason with your Passion
Must be content to think you Old, and so –
But she knows what she does.

LEAR Is this well spoken?

REGAN I dare avouch it, Sir. What, Fifty Followers?
Is it not well? What should you need of more?
Yea, or so many? Sith that both Charge and Danger
Speak 'gainst so great a Number? How in one House
Should many People, under two Commands,
Hold Amity? 'Tis hard, almost impossible.

GONERIL Why might not you, my Lord, receive
Attendance
From those that she calls Servants, or from mine?

REGAN Why not, my Lord? If then they chanc'd to slack
ye,
We could comptrol them. If you will come to me
(For now I spy a Danger), I entreat you
To bring but Five and Twenty; to no more
Will I give Place or Notice.

LEAR I gave you All.

REGAN And in Good Time you gave it.

LEAR Made you my Guardians, my Depositaries,
But kept a Reservation to be followed
With such a Number. What, must I come to you
With Five and Twenty? Regan, said you so?

REGAN And speak 't again, my Lord: no more with me.

439 **well favour'd** attractive; with handsome favours (faces, features).

441 **Stands . . . Praise** holds at least some position in the hierarchy of things worthy of praise. *Stands* recalls lines 90–92.

443 **thou . . . Love** Lear's exercise in quantification recalls the love competition (I.i) that got him into this predicament.

445 **follow** be assigned to you. This word echoes lines 252–53.

447 **reason . . . Need** don't bother calculating the necessity.

448 **Poorest Thing** least possession. Compare lines 175–78.

451 **onely** solely (one-ly). See the notes to I.i.73, II.ii.206.
were gorgeous were all one needed to be accounted beautiful.

453 **scarcely . . . warm** only barely performs its necessary function, if indeed it does even that.

456 **Grief** both (a) grievance (a sense of having been treated unjustly), and (b) griefs (disappointments, agonies, and sorrows).

457 **stirs** both (a) moves, and (b) mixes (compare lines 51, 417).

458 **fool . . . much** don't victimize me so much (make me such a fool) as.

459 **tamely** obediently; meekly. At this point Lear has no desire to be a patient Job or a cheek-turning Christian disciple. Compare Matthew 5:5, 38–48.
touch me with instil in me; empower me with. Lear's phrasing suggests a form of mending (compare line 412) or healing, as in Luke 8:40–48. He wants to be restored to the manhood he has put off.
Noble Anger the righteous indignation that is the earthly embodiment of divine wrath.

467 **Flaws** faults, cracks (line 138 and I.iv.280); here, splinters.

468 **Or ere** before.

LEAR – Those Wicked Creatures yet do look well favour'd
When others are more Wicked: not being the Worst
Stands in some Rank of Praise. – I'll go with thee:
Thy Fifty yet doth double Five and Twenty,
And thou art Twice her Love.

GONERIL Hear me, my Lord:
What need you Five and Twenty? Ten? Or Five?
To follow in a House where twice so many
Have a Command to tend you?

REGAN What need One?

LEAR O reason not the Need. Our basest Beggars
Are in the Poorest Thing superfluous.
Allow not Nature more than Nature needs:
Man's Life is cheap as Beast's. Thou art a Lady;
If onely to go warm were gorgeous,
Why Nature needs not what thou gorgeous wear'st,
Which scarcely keeps thee warm; but for true Need –
– You Heavens, give me that Patience, Patience I need;
You see me here, you Gods, a poor Old Man,
As full of Grief as Age, wretched in both;
If it be you that stirs these Daughters' Hearts
Against their Father, fool me not so much
To bear it tamely; touch me with Noble Anger,
And let not Women's Weapons, Water Drops,
Stain my Man's Cheeks. – No, you unnatural Hags,
I will have such Revenges on you both
That all the World shall – I will do such things,
What they are yet I know not, but they shall be
The Terrors of the Earth! You think I'll weep;
No, I'll not weep. I have full Cause of Weeping,
But this Heart shall break into a hundred thousand Flaws *Storm and Tempest.*
Or ere I'll weep. – O Fool, I shall go Mad.

Exeunt [*leaving Cornwall, Regan, and Goneril*].

CORNWALL Let us withdraw, 'twill be a Storm.

REGAN This House

471 **Blame** fault, blameworthiness. Compare lines 155 and I.ii.44–45. *Rest* recalls I.i.124–25.

472 **taste** both (a) test, make trial of, and (b) consume. See I.v.19–20.

472–73 **For his / Particular** as for his own person. Compare line 375 and I.iv.351.

474 **purpos'd** resolved.

478 **calls to Horse** demands a horse.

Whether where, whither. Here the Folio spelling reinforces our awareness of the weather Lear's 'will' is creating within himself on this 'Wil'd Night' (line 489). Like Cornwall's half of line 478, the clause 'He . . . Horse' appears only in the Folio.

479 **give him way** give him his head (like a horse whose rider allows him to gallop unchecked).

480 **stay** remain here. But *stay* can also mean 'halt', and that sense is also pertinent.

481 **high** Assuming that *high* is an erroneous scribal or compositorial echo of line 477, most editors adopt the Quarto's *bleak* here. But Shakespeare may well have wanted to reinforce the correspondence between Lear's 'high Rage' (the King's internal 'Storm', lines 469, 490) and the 'Winds' that Lear has decided to 'wage against' (line 392). Lear's situation recalls that of the foolish man depicted in Matthew 7:24–27, who 'built his house upon the sand; and the rain descended, and the floods came, and the winds blew, and beat upon that house; and it fell: and great was the fall of it'. Compare lines 336, 423–25.

482 **sorely ruffle** grievously bustle.

484 **procure** purchase, obtain. Regan goes on to suggest that Lear's 'Injuries' will help 'cure' him (care for him and mend him). See the second note to line 459.

485 **Schoolmasters** teachers (proverbial in Shakespeare's time for their stern disciplinary rods). Compare lines 251–52 and I.iii.20–21. Compare *Macbeth*, I.vii.1–12.

486 **desperate** dangerous (so hopeless that they have nothing to lose by resorting to violence).

487 **incense** enflame, incite. See the note to line 275.

488 **abus'd** both (a) deceived, and (b) misled, misused.

489 **Wil'd** both (a) strong-willed, and (b) wild. Compare lines 230, 292–93.

Is little: the Old Man and's People cannot be well
Bestow'd.
GONERIL 'Tis his own Blame hath put himself
From Rest, and must needs taste his Folly.
REGAN For his
Particular, I'll receive him gladly, but not
One Follower.
GONERIL So am I purpos'd. Where is
My Lord of Gloucester?
CORNWALL Followed the Old Man forth.

Enter Gloucester.

He is return'd.
GLOUCESTER The King is in high Rage.
CORNWALL Whether is he going?
GLOUCESTER He calls to Horse, but will I know not
whether.
CORNWALL 'Tis best to give him way, he leads himself.
GONERIL My Lord, entreat him by no means to stay.
GLOUCESTER Alack, the Night comes on, and the high
Winds
Do sorely ruffle; for many Miles about
There's scarce a Bush.
REGAN O Sir, to Wilful Men
The Injuries that they themselves procure
Must be their Schoolmasters. Shut up your Doors:
He is attended with a desperate Train,
And what they may incense him to, being apt,
To have his Ear abus'd, Wisdom bids fear.
CORNWALL Shut up your Doors, my Lord: 'tis a Wil'd
Night.
My Regan counsels well: come out o'th' Storm.
Exeunt.

III.i This scene takes place on a barren heath (II.ii.482–83) near Gloucester's castle. Kent and the Gentleman enter 'severally' (from separate doors). And as often happens in Shakespeare, the dialogue begins in mid-line, here immediately after an offstage rumbling to indicate 'Storm still' (the unremitting sounds of wind and thunder).

2 **minded like** in the same mental and emotional state as. See the note to II.ii.481.

4 **Contending . . . Elements** both (a) fighting against and (b) making alliance with the moody weather.

6 **curled** billowing, wavy.
Main both (a) the sea, and (b) the mainland.

7 **change** degenerate. The passage from 'tears' (line 7) to 'all' (line 15) occurs only in the Quarto. It appears to have been cut from the text eventually published in the Folio; so also with lines 30–41. Lines 4–7 parallel *Macbeth*, V.v.48–49, where Macbeth wishes 'th' Estate o'th' World were now undone'.

8 **Eyeless Rage** blind [or blinding] fury. Compare 'dark-ey'd Night' (II.i.120) and 'high Rage' (II.ii.477).

9 **make Nothing of** obliterate; treat as if they were no obstacle. The Gentleman's phrasing echoes such previous passages as I.i.91 and I.iv.137–42, 206–10.

10 **his . . . Man** the microcosm ('Little World') of his own body and mind. Compare *Julius Caesar*, II.i.60–68.
outscorn 'out-face' (II.ii.180), defy.

12 **Cub-drawn Bear** mother bear drained of milk by her suckling cub (and thus dangerously 'desperate', II.ii.486, like the 'Belly-pinched' and therefore ravenous 'Wolf', line 13). *Drawn* echoes II.ii.258.
couch seek refuge, crouching in a sheltered place.

16 **out-jest** another means of 'Contending with the fretful Elements' (line 4). Compare lines 10–11.

17 **Heart-strook** heart-rending. Compare II.ii.467.

18 **Warrant . . . Note** assurance provided by my knowledge.

19 **Commend . . . thing** commit a precious secret.

21 **Cunning** indirection (as in *Hamlet*, II.i.63), pretence. See the note to II.i.11.

ACT III

Scene 1

Storm still. Enter Kent, and a Gentleman, severally.

KENT Who's there besides
Foul Weather?
GENTLEMAN One minded like the Weather, most
Unquietly.
KENT I know you. Where's the King?
GENTLEMAN Contending with the fretful Elements:
Bids the Wind blow the Earth into the Sea,
Or swell the curled Waters 'bove the Main,
That things might change or cease; tears his white Hair,
Which the impetuous Blasts with Eyeless Rage
Catch in their Fury and make Nothing of,
Strives in his Little World of Man to outscorn
The to-and-fro-conflicting Wind and Rain.
This Night, wherein the Cub-drawn Bear would couch,
The Lion and the Belly-pinched Wolf
Keep their Fur dry, unbonneted he runs,
And bids what will take all.
KENT But who is with him?
GENTLEMAN None but the Fool, who labours to out-jest
His Heart-strook Injuries.
KENT Sir, I do know you,
And dare upon the Warrant of my Note
Commend a dear thing to you. There is Division
(Although as yet the Face of it is cover'd
With mutual Cunning) 'twixt Albany and Cornwall,

22–23 **that . . . high** whose guiding stars have put them in high positions. Lines 22–29 occur only in the Folio, where they appear to replace the lines (30–42) from the Quarto version of the play which the Folio text omits. Many scholars regard the two passages as incompatible, and they therefore argue that to combine them is to disregard the evidence that whoever revised this scene for the Folio version of *King Lear* – Shakespeare himself, in the view of most interpreters – wished to substitute new material for old, not add new material to old.

23 **seem no less** appear to be nothing other than faithful servants.

24 **Speculations** eyes, 'Spies'.

26 **Snuffs and Packings** disagreements and plottings. See II.ii.264.

27 **hard Rein** difficult riding [driving the King to madness]. *Rein* plays on both *reign* and *rain* (compare I.iv.310–18; II.ii.262–68, 454–68, and see the note to II.ii.481).

29 **Furnishings** either (a) outward signs, or (b) decoys.

32 **Wise . . . Negligence** aware of our political and military disarray. Lines 30–42 occur only in the Quarto printing of the play.

37 **making just Report** [for your] giving a reliable testimony.

38 **bemadding** insanity-inducing.

39 **plain** complain of. But *cause to plain* can also mean 'reason to become plain over'. Lear is about to learn that it is his 'Occupation to be Plain' (II.ii.89): simple, direct, unadorned. Compare II.ii.189–90, 447–53.

40 **Blood and Breeding** nobility, ancestry. Compare I.iii.25.

42 **Office** responsibility.

45 **Out-wall** exterior appearance. In line 44 the word 'am' appears only in the Folio text.

48 **Fellow** here, both (a) base peasant, and (b) fellow member of the King's court.

49 **Fie** curses.

53 **Effect** bring to pass.

54 **your . . . this** you labour in that way [with *way* meaning both 'direction' and 'manner'], I in this.

54 **holla** holler to.

Who have (as who have not that their great Stars
Thron'd and set high?) Servants, who seem no less,
Which are to France the Spies and Speculations
Intelligent of our State. What hath been seen,
Either in Snuffs and Packings of the Dukes
Or the hard Rein which both of them hath borne
Against the old kind King, or something deeper
Whereof (perchance) these are but Furnishings –
But true it is, from France there comes a Power
Into this scattered Kingdom, who already
(Wise in our Negligence) have secret Feet
In some of our best Ports and are at point
To shew their open Banner. Now to you,
If on my Credit you dare build so far
To make your Speed to Dover, you shall find
Some that will thank you, making just Report
Of how unnatural and bemadding Sorrow
The King hath cause to plain.
I am a Gentleman of Blood and Breeding,
And from some Knowledge and Assurance, offer
This Office to you.

GENTLEMAN I will talk further with you.

KENT No, do not:
For Confirmation that I am much more
Than my Out-wall, open this Purse and take
What it contains. If you shall see Cordelia
(As fear not but you shall), shew her this Ring,
And she will tell you who that Fellow is
That yet you do not know. Fie on this Storm,
I will go seek the King.

GENTLEMAN Give me your Hand;
Have you no more to say?

KENT Few Words, but to
Effect more than all yet: that when we have found
The King (in which your pain that way, I'll this),
He that first lights on him holla the other.

Exeunt.

III.ii The scene remains on the stormy heath.

1 **crack** break open. *Cheeks* recalls II.ii.459–61.

2 **Cataracts** floodgates of the skies ('the windows of heaven' in the description of Noah's Flood in Genesis 7:11).
Hurricanoes waterspouts.

3 **Cocks** weathercocks. This line echoes II.ii.304–7.

4 **Sulph'rous** brimstone-fuelled. Lear is alluding to Hell-fire.
Thought-executing curse-fulfilling.

5 **Vaunt-curriors** both (a) vanguards, precursors, couriers, and (b) vaunt-carriers (ministers of vengeance).
Oak-cleaving trunk-splitting. This line recalls II.ii.410. Compare *Coriolanus*, V.iii.151–53.

6 **all-shaking** omnipotent. *Shaking* recalls I.iv.311.

7 **Rotundity** roundness.

8 **Germains** germens; the seeds ('Moulds') of human germination.

10 **Court Holy-water** the perfume of royal flattery.

12 **ask . . . Blessing** plead for your daughters' (or daughter's) grace. The Fool is begging Lear to disregard the normal order of things, where patriarchs bless their children (as in Genesis 27–28, where the blind Isaac is tricked into blessing Jacob rather than his older brother Esau). Compare I.iv.110–11, and see the notes to I.i.124–25, 206, 209, 255–56. In IV.vii.55–57 Lear will attempt to do as the Fool advises.

16 **tax** task, accuse.

18 **Subscription** debt, obligation (literally, 'underwriting').

21 **Servile Ministers** obsequiously slavish agents.

23 **high-engender'd Battailes** high-born battalions. Here *high* means (a) sky-borne, (b) righteous, and (c) divine.

25 **House** dwelling, either (a) a man-made house (such as Gloucester's castle), or (b) a shelter or 'Head-piece' provided by Nature (such as the protection referred to in I.v.27–34). See the note to II.ii.481. In line 24 'ho' appears only in the Folio.

Scene 2

Storm still. Enter Lear and Fool.

LEAR Blow, Winds, and crack your Cheeks; rage, blow,
You Cataracts; and Hurricanoes, spout
Till you have drench'd our Steeples; drown the Cocks.
You Sulph'rous and Thought-executing Fires,
Vaunt-curriors of Oak-cleaving Thunderbolts,
Singe my White Head. And thou all-shaking Thunder,
Strike flat the thick Rotundity o'th' World,
Crack Nature's Moulds, all Germains spill at once
That makes ingrateful Man.

FOOL O Nuncle, Court Holy-water in a dry House is better than this Rain-water out o' Door. Good Nuncle, in, ask thy Daughters Blessing: here's a Night pities neither Wise Men nor Fools.

LEAR Rumble thy Belly full: spit, Fire; spout, Rain.
Nor Rain, Wind, Thunder, Fire are my Daughters;
I tax not you, you Elements, with Unkindness;
I never gave you Kingdom, call'd you Children;
You owe me no Subscription. Then let fall
Your horrible Pleasure. Here I stand your Slave,
A poor, infirm, weak, and despis'd Old Man.
But yet I call you Servile Ministers,
That will with two pernicious Daughters join
Your high-engender'd Battailes 'gainst a Head
So Old and White as this. O ho! 'tis Foul.

FOOL He that has a House to put's Head in has a good Head-piece.

27–34 **The . . . Wake** The man who concentrates on lodging his 'Codpiece' (see I.iv.198), his genital 'Toe', rather than attending to his 'Head', his 'Heart', shall lose everything to lice (become diseased and beggarly). *Beggars* refers both to whores and to those who 'marry' them (even figuratively, as in I.i.9–25). *Corn* can refer to (a) a hard, thick growth on the toe, (b) a syphilitic sore on the 'Toe', (c) a horn (Latin *cornus*) on the brow of the *cornuto* (Italian for 'cuckold', as noted in I.i.140), or (d) the harvest corn (wheat) or fruit of 'Bastardizing' (I.ii.151). Whatever its nature, a corn can disturb a man's sleep (as Gloucester will find when his 'Corn' makes him 'cry woe'). *Toe* recalls I.v.8–12.

36 **made . . . Glass** rehearsed her vanity in a mirror. *Made* can also refer to begetting and to the new 'Mouths' it produces. Meanwhile *Glass* can refer to a 'weaker vessel' that is easily cracked, see the note to I.i.16, and compare *Pericles*, IV.vii.156.

40 **Grace** Like 'Wise Man', this word should refer to Lear. But despite his costume, which features a large 'Codpiece', the Fool has more 'Grace' (spiritual insight) than the King whose 'Toe' (passion) has ruled his 'Heart' (reason).

44 **Gallow** intimidate (put the fear of the gallows into).
Wanderers . . . Dark night-prowlers (beasts of prey, and perhaps even demonic spirits). Compare I.i.37, II.i.120.

45 **Since . . . Man** since I attained full manhood (maturity).

48 **carry** bear up under. Kent's phrasing echoes I.iv.170–74.

49 **Affliction** physical buffeting. Compare I.iv.305.

50 **dreadful Pudder** frightening tumult.

51 **Find . . . now** discover who their enemies (lawbreakers) really are.

52–53 **undivulged . . . Justice** undisclosed and unpunished offences.

54 **Perjur'd** liar (here one who has broken vows or given false testimony under oath).
Simular of Virtue apparently virtuous man (one who only simulates true integrity).

55 **Caitiff** villain; literally, a 'captive' (man possessed by evil).

56–57 **That . . . Life** who in an underhanded manner has taken advantage of some fitting cover to plot homicide.

57 **Close pent-up** tightly closeted.

The Codpiece that will house
Before the Head has any,
The Head and he shall louse;
So Beggars marry many.
The Man that makes his Toe
What he his Heart should make
Shall of a Corn cry woe
And turn his Sleep to Wake.
For there was never yet Fair Woman but she made Mouths in a Glass.

Enter Kent.

LEAR No, I will be the Pattern of all Patience,
I will say nothing.
KENT Who's there?
FOOL Marry here's Grace and a Codpiece: that's a Wise Man and a Fool.
KENT Alas, Sir, are you here? Things that love Night
Love not such Nights as these. The wrathful Skies
Gallow the very Wanderers of the Dark
And make them keep their Caves. Since I was Man,
Such Sheets of Fire, such Bursts of horrid Thunder,
Such Groans of roaring Wind and Rain, I never
Remember to have heard. Man's Nature cannot carry
Th' Affliction, nor the Fear.
LEAR Let the great Gods
That keep this dreadful Pudder o'er our Heads
Find out their Enemies now. Tremble, thou Wretch
That hast within thee undivulged Crimes
Unwhipp'd of Justice. Hide thee, thou Bloody Hand,
Thou Perjur'd, and thou Simular of Virtue
That art Incestuous. Caitiff, to Pieces shake,
That under covert and convenient Seeming
Has practis'd on Man's Life. Close pent-up Guilts,

58–59 **Rive . . . Grace** split open your containers (guilty consciences) and beg mercy of these fearful ministers of justice.

61 **hard . . . Hovel** near here is a crude hut. *Hard* anticipates the additional senses the word acquires in lines 63–64 (unfeeling, inflexible, unpitying). *House* echoes line 25.

64 **whereof 'tis rais'd** of which it has been erected. *Rais'd* is a reminder that this house is now ruled by those whom Lear has raised: both (a) reared, and (b) elevated to power.

65 **demanding after you** when I asked where you were.

66–67 **force . . . Curtesy** compel them to offer the hospitality they have withheld. *Scanted* recalls I.i.283 and II.ii.358.

67 **turn** 'change' (yielding to madness), III.i.7.

70 **The . . . strange** the skill our needs impose on us can astonish us. *Necessities* echoes II.ii.394, 447.

71 **vild** vile, base (such as the 'Straw' meant for farm animals).

74 **tyne** tiny.

76 **make . . . fit** content himself with the lot that Fortune fits him with (bearing in mind that it may be fitting in some way). The Fool's verse alludes to Matthew 7:24–27; see the note to II.ii.481.

79 **Brave . . . Curtizan** a night severe enough to cool the lusts of even a courtesan. This speech (lines 79–96) appears only in the Folio.

82 **mar their Malt** dilute their alcoholic brew. See II.ii.417.

83 **are . . . Tutors** know more about fashion than professional tailors do. Compare II.ii.485.

84 **Heretics** Here *burn'd* alludes to venereal inflammations.

88 **Cut-purses . . . Throngs** pickpockets come to where crowds gather.

89 **Usurers . . . Field** moneylenders count (and report) their fortunes openly. *Tell* recalls II.ii.238–40.

91 **Albion** England.

Rive your concealing Continents, and cry
These dreadful Summoners Grace. I am a Man
More sinn'd against than sinning.

KENT Alack, Bare-headed?
Gracious my Lord, hard by here is a Hovel;
Some Friendship will it lend you 'gainst the Tempest.
Repose you there, while I to this hard House
(More harder than the Stones whereof 'tis rais'd,
Which even but now, demanding after you,
Deni'd me to come in) return, and force
Their scanted Curtesy.

LEAR My Wits begin to turn.
Come on, my Boy. How dost, my Boy? Art Cold?
I am Cold my self. – Where is this Straw, my Fellow?
The Art of our Necessities is strange
And can make vild things precious. Come, your Hovel.
Poor Fool and Knave, I have one part in my Heart
That's sorry yet for thee.

FOOL He that has and a little-tyne Wit
With heigh-ho, the Wind and the Rain,
Must make content with his Fortunes fit,
Though the Rain it raineth every Day.

LEAR True, Boy. Come bring us to this Hovel. *Exit.*

FOOL This is a Brave Night to cool a Curtizan.
I'll speak a Prophecy ere I go:
When Priests are more in Word than Matter;
When Brewers mar their Malt with Water,
When Nobles are their Tailors' Tutors,
No Heretics burn'd, but Wenches' Suitors,
When every Case in Law is Right,
No Squire in Debt, nor no Poor Knight,
When Slanders do not live in Tongues,
Nor Cut-purses come not to Throngs,
When Usurers tell their Gold i'th' Field,
And Bawds and Whores do Churches build,
Then shall the Realm of Albion

92 **Confusion** both (a) bewilderment, and (b) devastation. The literal meaning of *confusion* is 'fuse (pour or mix) together', and the Fool's prophecy is itself an illustration of the principle to which it refers. Lines 81–84 describe manifest instances of corruption; lines 85–90 describe what appear to be signs of a utopian society in which evil has been replaced by good and even pimps and their prostitutes have become exemplary pillars of the Faith. Some editions place lines 91–92 after line 83.

94 **Going . . . Feet** (a) travelling shall be done on foot (rather than in luxurious coaches), and (b) *Going* shall refer only to 'walking' rather than to 'copulation' (see the note to I.iv.130). Compare the Fool's remarks on 'Toe' (lines 31–34) and 'Heels' (I.v.8–12).

95 **Merlin** the seer in the Camelot of King Arthur. In the chronicles Shakespeare drew from, Lear's 'Time' was well before Merlin's.

III.iii This scene takes place inside Gloucester's castle; the phrase '*with Lights*' derives from the Quarto.

2 **Unnatural** against Nature; unkind. See the note to I.iv.64.

2–3 **leave . . . him** permission to aid Lear.

4 **on pain of** on penalty of (at the risk of).

12 **Closet** either (a) private chamber, or (b) desk cabinet.

14 **Power already footed** army already landed.
incline to join with; give assistance to.

15 **privily** privately, secretly.

17 **Charity** both (a) relief of the needy, and (b) Christian compassion (*caritas* in Latin, *agape* in Greek).

20–21 **There . . . toward** Unusual things are in the offing (as in II.i.11). As soon as Gloucester leaves, we see that he has no inkling of the 'strange things' in store for him. *Strange* can mean 'foreign' (here a reminder of the invading French forces); but it can also mean 'alien' (estranging), and in due course that sense will apply to the product of Gloucester's own 'strange things' (the illicit activities that resulted in the birth of a son willing to treat his own father as a stranger). See the note to III.ii.27–34. And compare the references to strangeness in I.i.116, 216–21, 259–60; I.ii.133; II.i.78, 87–88; II.ii.54; III.ii.70–71.

Come to great Confusion;
Then comes the Time, who lives to see't,
That Going shall be us'd with Feet.

This Prophecy Merlin shall make, for I live before his Time. *Exit.*

Scene 3

Enter Gloucester and Edmund, with Lights.

GLOUCESTER Alack, alack, Edmund, I like not this Unnatural Dealing. When I desired their leave that I might pity him, they took from me the Use of mine own House, charg'd me on pain of perpetual Displeasure neither to speak of him, entreat for him, or any way sustain him.

BASTARD Most Savage and Unnatural.

GLOUCESTER Go to; say you nothing. There is Division between the Dukes, and a worse matter than that. I have received a Letter this Night, 'tis dangerous to be spoken; I have lock'd the Letter in my Closet. These Injuries the King now bears will be revenged home; there is part of a Power already footed. We must incline to the King. I will look him, and privily relieve him. Go you and maintain talk with the Duke, that my Charity be not of him perceived. If he ask for me, I am ill, and gone to Bed; if I die for it (as no less is threat'ned me), the King my old Master must be relieved. There is strange things toward, Edmund: pray you be careful. *Exit.*

23 **Curtesy** display of 'Charity' (line 17). *Curtesy* recalls III.ii.66–67 (and echoes *Curtizan*, III.ii.79); compare II.ii.362.

25 **draw me** attract to me. *Draw* recalls III.i.12.

26 **looses** both (a) releases, discharges (as in procreation), and (b) loses (compare I.i.266, I.iv.317). Lines 25–27 reverberate with the phallic imagery of II.i.50, II.ii.206, 304–6, and other passages. *All* recalls II.ii.432

III.iv This scene returns us to the hovel near Gloucester's castle.

2 **The . . . rough** the cruel oppression of the unsheltered storm is too severe. The stage direction in line 3 appears only in the Folio, which adds the same stage direction in lines 63, 104 and 167. The Folio is also the sole source for the word 'here' in lines 4 and 22.

8 **fix'd** both (a) implanted, and (b) the focus of attention. This word recalls I.iv.283.

9 **shun** avoid; flee from. So also in line 21, where Lear implicitly relates 'Madness' to the mouths of his bear-like daughters (lines 11, 15) or to 'the roaring Sea' of despair (compare IV.vi.1–80).

11 **meet . . . Mouth** confront the bear at his most dangerous. *Mouth* echoes I.i.92–93 and III.ii.35–36 and anticipates line 15.

Free free of its own agony or disease. Compare II.ii.172.

12 **Tempest . . . Mind** Compare II.ii.477–82; III.i.2–11.

14 **Save what beats** except for what pulsates or hammers as on a forge. *Beats* echoes I.iv.285–86 and II.ii.301–2.

15 **as** as if.

16 **punish home** revenge my injuries. Compare II.i.52, III.iii.12–13. Lines 17–18 (from 'In' to 'endure') appear only in the Folio; so also with lines 26–27.

20 **Frank** free, liberal, open; generous. Line 20 echoes II.ii.432, III.iii.26.

BASTARD This Curtesy, forbid thee, shall the Duke
Instantly know, and of that Letter too.
This seems a Fair Deserving, and must draw me
That which my Father looses: no less than all.
The Younger rises when the Old doth fall. *Exit.*

Scene 4

Enter Lear, Kent, and Fool.

KENT Here is the place, my Lord; good my Lord, enter.
The Tyranny of the open Night's too rough
For Nature to endure. *Storm still.*
LEAR Let me alone.
KENT Good my Lord, enter here.
LEAR Wilt break my Heart?
KENT I had rather break mine own; good my Lord,
enter.
LEAR Thou think'st 'tis much that this contentious
Storm
Invades us to the Skin so; 'tis to thee,
But where the Greater Malady is fix'd,
The Lesser is scarce felt. Thou'dst shun a Bear,
But if thy Flight lay toward the roaring Sea
Thou'dst meet the Bear i'th' Mouth. When the Mind's
Free,
The Body's Delicate: the Tempest in my Mind
Doth from my Senses take all Feeling else
Save what beats there, Filial Ingratitude.
Is it not as this Mouth should tear this Hand
For lifting Food to't? But I will punish home;
No, I will weep no more. In such a Night
To shut me out? Pour on, I will endure.
In such a Night as this? – O Regan, Goneril,
Your old kind Father, whose Frank Heart gave all –
O that way Madness lies, let me shun that,

26 **Houseless Poverty** homeless beggar. Lear addresses the Fool. *Houseless* recalls III.ii.25, 63.

29 **bide the Pelting** endure the buffeting pellets. Compare II.ii.187.

30 **Unfed Sides** exposed ribs (compare II.ii.380); 'window'd Raggedness' (both open and latticed).

31 **lop'd** (a) looped (loopholed, open), (b) lopped off (ragged), and (c) loping. *Raggedness* recalls II.ii.232–35.

32–33 **O . . . this** I have concerned myself too little with this. *Care* echoes I.i.40, 51, 103, 114; I.iv.206; II.ii.4–6.

33 **Take Physic, Pomp** (a) submit yourself to medical care, Luxury, and (b) be healed, Kingship. Compare I.i.166–67, II.ii.321.

35 **shake . . . them** cast off everything that gives you more shelter from the elements than beggars enjoy. *Shake* recalls I.iv.311 and III.ii.6, 55; *Superflux* (superfluity, excess) echoes II.ii.447–48.

36 **shew . . . Just** prove the skies to be more just (treating all creatures equally) than are pomp-biased human courts.

37 **Fathom and Half** Edgar utters a sailor's cry, probably to indicate that he believes the storm water to be nine feet deep. This line and the stage direction that precedes it appear only in the Folio; so also with 'through Flame' in lines 51–52.

38 **Spirit** The Fool probably means 'evil spirit'.

45 **follows me** (a) pursues me, (b) attends me. Compare II.ii.255–57. In line 46 'Humh' appears only in the Folio.

54 **Halters . . . Pue** hangman's nooses in the pew (the gallery outside his window), to tempt Poor Tom to submit to despair and commit suicide. *Pue* derives from the Old French *puye*, a parapet, balustrade, or balcony.

No more of that.
KENT Good my Lord, enter here.
LEAR Prythee go in thy self, seek thine own Ease.
This Tempest will not give me leave to ponder
On things would hurt me more. But I'll go in.
– In, Boy, go first. You Houseless Poverty,
Nay get thee in; I'll pray, and then I'll sleep. *Exit* [*Fool*].
– Poor naked Wretches, where so e'er you are
That bide the Pelting of this pitiless Storm,
How shall your Houseless Heads and Unfed Sides,
Your lop'd and window'd Raggedness, defend you
From Seasons such as these? O I have ta'en
Too little Care of this. – Take Physic, Pomp:
Expose thy self to feel what Wretches feel,
That thou mayst shake the Superflux to them
And shew the Heavens more Just.

Enter Edgar, and Fool.

EDGAR Fathom and Half, Fathom and Half. Poor Tom.
FOOL Come not in here, Nuncle; here's a Spirit, help me, help me.
KENT Give me thy Hand, who's there?
FOOL A Spirit, a Spirit; he says his name's Poor Tom.
KENT What art thou that dost grumble there i'th' Straw? Come forth.
EDGAR Away, the foul Fiend follows me, through the sharp Hawthorne blow the Winds. Humh, go to thy Bed and warm thee.
LEAR Didst thou give all to thy Daughters? And art thou come to this?
EDGAR Who gives any thing to Poor Tom? Whom the foul Fiend hath led through Fire, and through Flame, through Sword and Whirlpool, o'er Bog and Quagmire; that hath laid Knives under his Pillow, and Halters in his Pue, set Rats-bane by his Porridge, made him Proud of Heart, to

57–58 **course . . . Traitor** chase his shadow, thinking it treacherous. *Bay* (line 56) means 'reddish brown'.

58 **Bliss** bless (a dialectal pronunciation that suggests 'Heaven').

60 **Star-blasting** baleful planetary influences, 'Taking' (compare I.iv.106–7; II.ii.172–74, 346–47).

61 **Charity** kindness, deed of love. Compare III.iii.17.

62–63 **There . . . there** These lines are probably to be accompanied by lunging attempts to catch the 'foul Fiend'.

64 **Pass** state, situation. Compare *Trespass* in II.ii.228.

65 **save** preserve. *Nothing* recalls III.i.9; *all* echoes II.ii.433.

68 **sham'd** shocked, embarrassed by his nakedness.

69 **pendulous** overhanging.

70 **fated . . . Faults** prepared to punish men's crimes.
light alight, land.

75 **Should . . . Flesh** are expected to afflict their bodies this way [because their own flesh (offspring) spurned them].

76 **Judicious** both (a) wise, and (b) just.

77 **Pelican** Lear's adjective derives from the belief that a mother pelican, unable to find food for her voracious young, would feed them the blood of her own heart.

78–79 **Pillicock . . . loo** Edgar sings about a lover sitting on his hill. His name, suggested by 'Pelican', carries implications similar to those of 'Coxcomb' and 'Cockney' in II.ii.304–6.

84 **commit . . . Spouse** Do not commit adultery (Exodus 20:14). Tom's other exhortations paraphrase additional commandments in the Mosaic Decalogue.

85 **Proud Array** gaudy, costly clothing. Edgar alludes to the commandment against covetousness (Exodus 20:17); but his words also recall 1 Timothy 2:9, where (in the 1560 Geneva Bible's rendering of the passage) the Apostle Paul exhorts women to 'aray them selves in comely apparell, with shamefastness and modestie, not with . . . costly apparell'. Compare II.ii.450–53. *Sweet-heart* can mean either (a) sweet heart, or (b) sweetheart (lover).

88 **wore . . . Cap** displayed my mistress's favours. *Proud in Heart* echoes Proverbs 16:5, 'Every one that is proud in heart is an abomination to the Lord.'

ride on a Bay Trotting Horse, over four-incht
Bridges, to course his own Shadow for a
Traitor. Bliss thy five Wits, Tom's a cold.
O do de, do de, do de, bliss thee from
Whirlwinds, Star-blasting, and Taking; do
Poor Tom some Charity, whom the foul Fiend
vexes. There could I have him now, and there,
and there again, and there. *Storm still.*

LEAR Has his Daughters brought him to this Pass?
– Couldst thou save nothing? Wouldst thou give
'em all?

FOOL Nay, he reserv'd a Blanket, else we had been
all sham'd.

LEAR Now all the Plagues that in the pendulous Air
Hang fated o'er Men's Faults light on thy Daughters.

KENT He hath no Daughters, Sir.

LEAR Death, Traitor, nothing could have subdu'd
Nature
To such a Lowness but his Unkind Daughters.
Is it the Fashion that Discarded Fathers
Should have thus little Mercy on their Flesh?
Judicious Punishment: 'twas this Flesh begot
Those Pelican Daughters.

EDGAR Pillicock sat on Pillicock Hill, alow;
alow, loo, loo.

FOOL This Cold Night will turn us all to Fools
and Madmen.

EDGAR Take heed o'th' foul Fiend, obey thy
Parents, keep thy Word's Justice, swear not,
commit not with Man's sworn Spouse: set not
thy Sweet-heart on Proud Array. Tom's a cold.

LEAR What hast thou been?

EDGAR A Servingman? Proud in Heart, and Mind; that
curl'd my Hair, wore Gloves in my Cap; serv'd
the Lust of my Mistress' Heart, and did the Act
of Darkness with her. Swore as many Oaths as I

91 **broke** (a) forswore, and (b) exploded foul wind in Heaven's 'sweet Face' (compare *The Comedy of Errors*, III.i.76).

92–93 **slept . . . Lust** plotted lustful schemes in his dreams.

94–95 **out-Paramour'd the Turk** enjoyed larger harems than the Sultan.

95 **Light of Ear** (a) easily tempted, and (b) heedless of conscience ('the Disease of Not Listening', 2 *Henry IV*, I.ii.134–35).

97–99 **Let . . . Woman** Do not allow yourself to be seduced.

100 **Plackets** openings in skirts (symbolic of other openings).

101 **Lenders' Books** moneylenders' account books. See III.ii.89. *Pen* can refer to more than one kind of authorial implement. See *The Merchant of Venice*, V.i.236–37, where 'the Clark's Pen' is threatened with castration.

103 **suum, mum, nonny** either (a) nonsense syllables to imitate the 'Cold Wind', or (b) fragments of a lyric.

104 **Sesey** This word probably means 'cease, let him alone'. Compare *The Taming of the Shrew*, Induction, i.6.

105 **answer** meet, face. Compare I.i.153; I.iii.11; II.i.124–25; II.ii.144, 220–21, 274.

107 **Is . . . this?** Lear's words recall Psalm 8:4–6, whose question 'What is man, that thou art mindful of him?' is quoted in Hebrews 2:6–8.

110 **on's are Sophisticated** of us are garbed in sophistry (clothing, cosmetics, and courtly manners) to hide our true natures.

111 **Unaccommodated** (a) uncovered, (b) unsheltered, (c) unfurnished with the trappings of civilization, and (d) unsupplied with women (see 2 *Henry IV*, III.ii.87); in short, Man in 'Extremity' (line 106). *Forked* (line 112) recalls I.i.144.

113 **Lendings** borrowed accommodations (as defined in lines 108–9 and in the note to line 111). Lear's gesture will prove prophetic; compare V.iii.306.

119 **Walking Fire** (a) moving will-o'-the-wisp, and (b) torch-bearing 'old Lecher's Heart'. In light of lines 116–18, Gloucester's appearance at this moment is apt; see the notes to III.ii.27–34, 44.

120 **Flibbertigibbet** a dancing devil. Shakespeare drew this and other devils' names from Samuel Harsnett's *Declaration of Egregious Popish Impostors* (1603).

spake Words, and broke them in the sweet Face of Heaven. One that slept in the contriving of Lust, and wak'd to do it. Wine lov'd I deeply, Dice dearly; and in Woman, out-Paramour'd the Turk. False of Heart, Light of Ear, Bloody of Hand; Hog in Sloth, Fox in Stealth, Wolf in Greediness, Dog in Madness, Lion in Prey. Let not the Creaking of Shoes, nor the Rustling of Silks betray thy poor Heart to Woman. Keep thy Foot out of Brothels, thy Hand out of Plackets, thy Pen from Lenders' Books, and defy the foul Fiend. Still through the Hawthorne blows the Cold Wind. Says suum, mum, nonny, Dolphin my Boy, Boy Sesey; let him trot by. *Storm still.*

LEAR Thou wert better in a Grave, then to answer with thy Uncover'd Body this Extremity of the Skies. Is Man no more than this? Consider him well. Thou ow'st the Worm no Silk, the Beast no Hide, the Sheep no Wool, the Cat no Perfume. Ha? Here's three on's are Sophisticated; thou art the thing it self. Unaccommodated Man is no more but such a poor, bare forked Animal as thou art. – Off, off, you Lendings: come, unbutton here.

Enter Gloucester, with a Torch.

FOOL Prythee Nuncle, be contented; 'tis a Naughty Night to swim in. Now a little Fire in a wild Field were like an old Lecher's Heart: a small Spark, all the rest on's Body cold.
Look, here comes a Walking Fire.

EDGAR This is the foul Flibbertigibbet; he begins

121 **Curfew** nine o'clock (when fires were to be covered).
First Cock midnight.

122 **the . . . Pin** the cataract, which 'squints the Eye', impairing sight. Compare *The Winter's Tale*, I.ii.287.

125 **Swithold** Saint Withold (or Swithun), an English saint who exorcized evil spirits and protected people from 'the Night-mare' (an incubus who took possession of sleeping bodies) and her nine imps.

128 **Troth-plight** betrothed (possibly a reference to 'her Nine-fold'). Compare I.i.102–3, 285. Many editions follow the Quarto here, which includes no hyphen; that version of the passage yields the meaning 'faith pledge'.

129 **aroint** begone (a dialectal corruption of 'avaunt').

135 **Wall-newt** the kind of newt (lizard) that lives on walls (as opposed to the *Water*, water-newt). *Tod-pole* means 'tadpole'.

137 **Sallets** salads.

140 **from . . . Tithing** from one ten-family parish to another.

144 **Dear** the Folio's spelling for *deer*, game animals.

146 **Smulkin** another demonic 'Follower' named in Harsnett.

149 **Prince of Darkness** chief of the devils, Satan.

151 **vild** vile (wild, foul).

152 **gets** begets, conceives. Compare II.i.79.

153 **my . . . suffer** my duty to my Sovereign [and my obligations as a host] cannot permit me.

154 **hard** inflexible, inhumane. Compare III.ii.61–64.

156 **tyrannous** tyrannically cruel. The metrical position of this word (calling for it to be pronounced 'tyr'nnous') and the phrasing ('take hold upon you') suggest wordplay on *tyre*, 'tear and devour'. Compare lines 2–3.

at Curfew, and walks at First Cock; he gives the Web and the Pin, squints the Eye, and makes the Hare-lip; mildews the white Wheat, and hurts the poor Creature of Earth.

Swithold footed thrice the old,
He met the Night-mare and her Nine-fold;
Bid her alight,
And her Troth-plight,
And aroint thee, Witch, aroint thee.

KENT How fares your Grace?

LEAR What's he?

KENT Who's there? What is't you seek?

GLOUCESTER What are you there? Your Names?

EDGAR Poor Tom, that eats the swimming Frog, the Toad, the Tod-pole, the Wall-newt and the Water; that in the Fury of his Heart, when the foul Fiend rages, eats Cow-dung for Sallets; swallows the old Rat, and the Ditch-dog; drinks the green Mantle of the standing Pool; who is whipp'd from Tithing to Tithing, and stock'd, punish'd, and imprison'd; who hath three Suits to his Back, six Shirts to his Body.

Horse to ride, and Weapon to wear;
But Mice, and Rats, and such small Dear
Have been Tom's Food for seven long Year.

Beware my Follower. – Peace, Smulkin; peace, thou Fiend.

GLOUCESTER What, hath your Grace no better Company?

EDGAR The Prince of Darkness is a Gentleman.
Modo he's call'd, and Mahu.

GLOUCESTER Our Flesh and Blood, my Lord, is grown so vild
That it doth hate what gets it.

EDGAR Poor Tom's a cold.

GLOUCESTER Go in with me; my Duty cannot suffer
T' obey in all your Daughters' hard Commands.
Though their Injunction be to bar my Doors
And let this tyrannous Night take hold upon you,

157 **ventured** risked my life.

159 **Philosopher** Lear means 'natural philosopher' (scientist); but by now Edgar has also evolved into a 'lover of wisdom' (the original Greek sense of the word) who can contemplate 'the Cause of Thunder' (line 160) from a perspective that combines metaphysics, theology, and ethics. *Thunder* echoes II.i.47 and II.ii.410.

162 **learned Theban** Lear may be thinking of Tiresias, the blind seer who explains the cause of the divine displeasure against Thebes and pushes Oedipus towards an 'Eyeless Rage' (III.i.8) in Sophocles' *Oedipus Tyrannus*. See line 122 and the note to I.i.163.

163 **prevent the Fiend** thwart the workings of the Devil [and save myself from damnation]. Compare line 82, and see the note to I.iv.316.

166 **Importune** urge. Here, as is often true in Shakespeare, the original Latin sense is pertinent: 'demand entrance to a portal'. The words 'once more' appear only in the Folio; so also with the stage direction following line 167.

172 **out-law'd . . . Blood** legally disinherited. See the note to II.i.86.

173 **But . . . late** only recently, a very short while ago.

175 **craz'd** cracked, flawed. Compare I.i.16, III.ii.467, III.ii.1.

176 **cry you mercy** please forgive me. Lear asks pardon for another delay while he turns back to Poor Tom. In view of what will soon happen to Gloucester for extending 'mercy', the old King's words are grimly ironic.

182 **soothe him** humour him; flatter his whim.

185 **good Athenian** Lear is probably using another Greek name for his 'Noble Philosopher'. But his words could also apply to Gloucester, linking the old man's torch to the lantern with which Diogenes the Cynic sought the face of an honest man. Compare *Othello*, V.i.64.

Yet have I ventured to come seek you out
And bring you where both Fire and Food is ready.
LEAR First let me talk with this Philosopher.
– What is the Cause of Thunder?
KENT Good my Lord,
Take his Offer: go into th' House.
LEAR I'll talk a Word with this same learned Theban:
What is your Study?
EDGAR How to prevent the Fiend,
And to kill Vermin.
LEAR Let me ask you one word in private.
KENT Importune him once more to go, my Lord.
His Wits begin t' unsettle.
GLOUCESTER Canst thou blame him?
Storm still.
His Daughters seek his Death: ah, that Good Kent,
He said it would be thus, poor Banish'd Man.
Thou sayest the King grows Mad; I'll tell thee, Friend,
I am almost Mad my self. I had a Son,
Now out-law'd from my Blood: he sought my Life
But lately, very late. I lov'd him, Friend,
No Father his Son dearer: true to tell thee,
The Grief hath craz'd my Wits. What a Night's this?
– I do beseech your Grace –
LEAR O cry you mercy, Sir.
– Noble Philosopher, your company.
EDGAR Tom's a cold.
GLOUCESTER In, Fellow, there, into th' Hovel; keep thee warm.
LEAR Come, let's in all.
KENT This way, my Lord.
LEAR With him:
I will keep still with my Philosopher.
KENT Good my Lord, soothe him: let him take the Fellow.
GLOUCESTER Take him you on.
KENT Sirrah, come on; go along with us.
LEAR Come, good Athenian.

187 **Child Rowland** Edgar's verses probably refer to the young knight Roland, nephew of the legendary Charlemagne and protagonist of the French epic *Chanson de Roland*. The spelling of the name in the original texts suggests wordplay on the need to row over flooded land. Edgar has entered with the phrase 'Fathom and Half' (line 37); he now exits with a reminder of what the Fool has just called 'a Naughty Night to swim in' (lines 115–16). The 'Dark Tower' is Poor Tom's equivalent of Noah's Ark. 'Rowland' is here called a 'Child' because he has not yet attained the knighthood for which he strives. The 'Dark Tower' Edgar refers to recalls the 'hard House' (III.ii.63) from which 'Rowland' and his companions have been excluded.

189 **British** The traditional nursery rhyme ('Jack the Giant Killer') has *English* here; Shakespeare's variation is a reminder that *King Lear* is set in pre-Christian Britain.

III.v This scene takes place inside Gloucester's castle.

3 **censured** judged. Compare III.v.3.

4 **Nature . . . Loyalty** my natural inclination [to love and protect my father] yields to patriotic loyalty [to my ruler]. Edmund's remarks recall I.ii.1–22, where he has invoked what Tennyson would refer to in *In Memoriam A.H.H.* as 'Nature, red in tooth and claw' (the law of the jungle, where cunning and might make right).

4–5 **something fears** somewhat frightens.

8–9 **a . . . himself** a reprehensible evil streak in Gloucester that provoked Edgar with good reason [to do what he did].

12 **approves** proves (as in II.ii.366).
Intelligent both (a) knowing, and (b) spying, fully cooperating partisan ('Party'). Compare II.i.23, III.i.24–25.

14 **were not** did not exist.

16 **the Duchess** Regan, Cornwall's wife.

19 **True or false** whether it proves 'certain' or not. It doesn't occur to Cornwall that his phrase can also refer to whether Edmund is 'true or false' (honest and loyal or not).

21 **Apprehension** arrest, trial, and punishment.

GLOUCESTER No Words, no Words: hush.

EDGAR Child Rowland to the Dark Tower came;
His Word was still 'Fie, Foh, and Fum,
I smell the Blood of a British Man.' *Exeunt.*

Scene 5

Enter Cornwall and Edmund.

CORNWALL I will have my Revenge ere I depart his House.

BASTARD How, my Lord, I may be censured, that Nature thus gives way to Loyalty, something fears me to think of.

CORNWALL I now perceive it was not altogether your Brother's Evil Disposition made him seek his Death, but a provoking Merit set a-work by a reprovable Badness in himself.

BASTARD How Malicious is my Fortune, that I must repent to be Just? This is the Letter which he spoke of, which approves him an Intelligent Party to the Advantages of France. O Heavens! that this Treason were not, or not I the Detector.

CORNWALL Go with me to the Duchess.

BASTARD If the Matter of this Paper be certain, you have Mighty Business in hand.

CORNWALL True or false, it hath made thee Earl of Gloucester. Seek out where thy Father is, that he may be ready for our Apprehension.

22 **comforting the King** giving aid and comfort to the enemy (as Edmund and his patrons will construe Gloucester's humane efforts to relieve the King's distress). Many editions mark lines 22–23 ('If . . . fully.') as an aside. But it may well be that Edmund speaks these words to Cornwall rather than to himself.

23 **stuff . . . fully** provide even fuller evidence of his guilt. Shakespeare frequently uses *stuff* in a copulative sense (see *Timon of Athens*, IV.iii.269–70); here that implication is another reminder of the 'reprovable Badness' in Gloucester that produced the Bastard who now plots to undo him.

25 **Blood** Edmund's implied meaning is 'filial ties'. But since *Blood* can also refer to the passion that makes a man 'stand up' (I.ii.22), it recalls both the circumstances of Edmund's conception and the 'Composition' he drew from them (I.ii.11–15). *Blood* echoes III.iv.188–89.

27 **dear Father** Cornwall offers himself as Edmund's surrogate father; compare II.i.113–17, where Cornwall seizes on the Bastard's first display of a 'Child-like Office' (II.i.106–7).

III.vi This scene returns us to the hovel outside Gloucester's castle.

2 **piece out** augment. Compare I.i.95, 202. Line 1 echoes III.iv.2.

3 **Addition** further furnishings. Compare II.ii.18–20.

6 **Impatience** inability to endure his torments without protest.

7 **Frateretto** another of the devils mentioned in Harsnett.

7–8 **Nero . . . Darkness** the tyrannical Emperor Nero is a fisherman in the lake of fire in Hades. Edgar may be alluding to Nero's murder of his mother Agrippina, whose womb he slit open, according to Chaucer's 'Monk's Tale', to see 'Wher he conceyved was'. Soon Lear will be seeking to 'anatomize Regan' (line 76); in IV.vi.111–31 his mind will return to 'the Sulphurous Pit'.

11 **Yeoman** a property-owning man below the rank of gentleman. The Fool's riddle plays on the distinction between a madman and a 'made man', one who has risen above his allotted station in society; compare *A Midsummer Night's Dream*, IV.ii.17–18. Lines 13–15 appear only in the Folio text.

BASTARD If I find him comforting the King, it will stuff his Suspicion more fully. I will persever in my Course of Loyalty, though the Conflict be between that and my Blood.

CORNWALL I will lay Trust upon thee; and thou shalt find a dear Father in my Love. *Exeunt.*

Scene 6

Enter Kent and Gloucester.

GLOUCESTER Here is better than the Open Air, take it thankfully. I will piece out the Comfort with what Addition I can; I will not be long from you.

KENT All the powre of his Wits have given way to his Impatience: the Gods reward your Kindness.

Exit [*Gloucester*].

Enter Lear, Edgar, and Fool.

EDGAR Frateretto calls me, and tells me Nero is an Angler in the Lake of Darkness. Pray, Innocent, and beware the foul Fiend.

FOOL Prythee Nuncle, tell me, whether a Madman be a Gentleman or a Yeoman.

LEAR A King, a King.

FOOL No, he's a Yeoman, that has a Gentleman to

14–15 **sees . . . him** watches his son become elevated to a gentleman's status before his father rises to that level of dignity. *Mad* puns on *made* ('arrived'), and in this context it reminds us that Edmund has just been 'made' the 'Earl of Gloucester' (III.v.19–20) and is 'before' (more important than) his father, who will soon be verging on a madness parallel to that of his King.

16 **burning Spits** sharp spits (here used to refer to swift swords) 'hizzing' (hissing) from the fireplace.

20 **Boy's Love** the affection and loyalty of either (a) a page, or (b) a son (such as Gloucester's). Lines 18–56 occur only in the Quarto.

22 **arraign them straight** bring them to trial immediately.

24 **Sapient Sir** wise gentleman.

25 **glars** dialect for 'glares' (looks blank, 'amaz'd', line 35).

25–26 **Wanst . . . Eyes?** Do you lack eyes to see? Compare the reference to defective ears in III.iv.95 and IV.ii.81–83.

27 **Come . . . me** Edgar quotes from a song about coming over a boorn (bourn, brook); by altering *boorn* to *Broom*, he suggests that 'Bessy' is a witch who resists (line 24) crossing the courtroom bar to stand trial.

32 **Hoppedance** another devil.

36 **Cushings** cushions.

38 **robbed** Most editions emend to *robed*, which Lear probably means; but *robbed* applies to all the participants in this scene.

41 **deal justly** both (a) be honest in our dealings with others, and (b) give the defendants a fair trial. Poor Tom is assuming his role as a 'Yokefellow of Equity' (member of the 'Bench' or 'Commission', the panel of justices). He goes on to quote a pastoral ballad about a neglectful shepherd who has allowed his flock to wander into a wheatfield; if the shepherd will blow his horn to call them back, the sheep will be unharmed. *Corn* (line 43) recalls III.ii.27–34, and reminds us that Gloucester is about to suffer 'Harm' for what he did as a 'jolly Shepherd'. Line 42 echoes I.ii.15 and III.iv.92–93.

44 **Minikin** dainty, pretty. *Mouth* recalls III.iv.11.

46 **Pur the Cat** a witch's familiar (attendant spirit).

his Son: for he's a Mad Yeoman that sees his
Son a Gentleman before him.

LEAR To have a Thousand with red burning Spits
Come hizzing in upon 'em.

EDGAR The foul Fiend bites my Back.

FOOL He's Mad that trusts in the Tameness of a
Wolf, a Horse's Health, a Boy's Love, or a
Whore's Oath.

LEAR It shall be done, I will arraign them straight.
– Come sit thou here, most learned Justice.
Thou Sapient Sir, sit here. – No, you
She-Foxes –

EDGAR Look where he stands and glars. – Wanst
thou Eyes? – At Trial, Madam.
Come o'er the Broom, Bessy, to me.

FOOL Her Boat hath a Leak,
And she must not speak,
Why she dares not come over to thee.

EDGAR The foul Fiend haunts poor Tom in the
Voice of a Nightingale. Hoppedance cries in
Tom's Belly for two white Herring. – Croak
not, black Angel, I have no Food for thee.

KENT How do you, Sir? Stand you not so amaz'd;
will you lie down and rest upon the Cushings?

LEAR I'll see their Trial first, bring in their
Evidence.
– Thou robbed Man of Justice, take thy Place.
– And thou his Yokefellow of Equity,
Bench by his side. You are o'th' Commission,
Sit you too.

EDGAR Let us deal justly.
– Sleepest or wakest thou, jolly Shepherd?
Thy Sheep be in the Corn,
And for one Blast of thy Minikin Mouth,
Thy Sheep shall take no Harm.
Pur the Cat is grey.

LEAR Arraign her first: 'tis Goneril, I here take

52 **Cry you mercy** pardon me. Compare III.iv.176.
Join-stool joined stool (a low stool made by a joiner), in this case a stand-in for a 'forked Animal' (III.iv.112).

53 **Warp'd Looks** 'frowns' (I.iv.204), here those of a piece of wood.

54 **What . . . an** what stuff her heart is made on (of).

55 **Corruption . . . Place!** Lear assumes that the defendant escapes because she has bribed a justice (line 56). But *Place* can also refer to Goneril's 'most precious Square of Sense' (I.i.75).

61 **mar my Counterfeiting** spoil my acting. *Mar* recalls I.iv.36, 360; III.ii.82. Edgar speaks this as an aside.

62 **Trey, Blanch** Three, White (the names of the dogs Lear imagines).

67 **Mastiff** a fierce dog often used to bait bulls and bears.

68 **Brach or Hym** female (see I.iv.121) or male (him).

69 **Bobtail tight** stiff curtail (docked tail). Most editions adopt the Quarto's *tike*, 'cur'.
Troudle-tail a Folio variant of the Quarto's *trundle-tail*, a long-tailed dog.

72 **leapt the Hatch** jumped over the lower half of a divided door.

73 **Do de, de de** Poor Tom is probably making the sounds that accompany shivering; so also in III.iv.59.
sese cease. Compare III.iv.104.

74 **Wakes** parish festivals.

75 **thy . . . Dry** your animal horn (cup) is empty. Edgar is imitating a beggar's cry, possibly with the implication that he is running out of inspiration for his 'Counterfeiting' (line 61).

76 **Then . . . Regan** [since the dogs 'are fled',] let them chew up Regan and dissect her till only a skeleton (*anatomy*) remains.

77 **breeds** both (a) resides, and (b) reproduces. Compare III.i.39–40.

78 **Hard-hearts** impenetrably impenitent consciences. Lear's imagery recalls III.ii.61–67. It also recalls such biblical passages as Exodus 7:1–4, Isaiah 63:17, and John 12:40.

my Oath before this honourable Assembly, kick'd the poor King her Father.

FOOL Come hither, Mistress, is your name Goneril?

LEAR She cannot deny it.

FOOL Cry you mercy, I took you for a Join-stool.

LEAR And here's another, whose Warp'd Looks proclaim
What Store her Heart is made an. Stop her there;
Arms, Arms; Sword, Fire! Corruption in the Place!
– False Justicer, why hast thou let her scape?

EDGAR Bless thy five Wits.

KENT O pity: Sir, where is the Patience now
That you so oft have boasted to retain?

EDGAR – My Tears begin to take his part so much
They mar my Counterfeiting.

LEAR The little Dogs
And all, Trey, Blanch, and Sweetheart: see, they bark
At me.

EDGAR Tom will throw his Head at them.
– Avaunt, you Curs:
Be thy Mouth or Black or White,
Tooth that poisons if it bite;
Mastiff, Greyhound, Mongril, Grim,
Hound or Spaniel, Brach or Hym;
Or Bobtail tight or Troudle-tail,
Tom will make him weep and wail;
For with throwing thus my Head
Dogs leapt the Hatch and all are fled.
Do de, de de, sese:
Come, march to Wakes and Friars and Market-towns.
Poor Tom, thy Horn is Dry.

LEAR Then let them anatomize Regan: see what breeds about her Heart. Is there any Cause in Nature that make these Hard-hearts? – You, Sir, I entertain for one of my Hundred; only I do not like the Fashion of your Garments. You

81 **Persian** synonymous with 'gorgeous' (II.ii.451–52), but also associated with unalterability. In Daniel 6:8 we read: 'Now, O King, establish the decree, and sign the writing, that it be not changed, according to the law of the Medes and Persians, which altereth not.' Lear is probably addressing his 'learned Theban' (III.iv.162), Poor Tom.

87 **And . . . Noon** The Fool names a bedtime that is as 'out of Season' (II.i.120) as Lear's suppertime (lines 85–86). These turn out to be the Fool's last words in the play. They appear only in the Folio text.

97 **Stand . . . Loss** are certain to be forfeited.

99 **Oppressed** overwhelmed, pressed beyond endurance. Compare II.ii.291. Except for 'Come, come away' (line 103), lines 99–117 ('KENT . . . lurk') occur only in the Quarto. *Follow* recalls the biblical passages cited at I.iv.44–45.

100 **balm'd . . . Sinews** soothed (healed) your injured nerves and joints.

101–2 **if . . . Cure** if an opportunity for relief is not permitted soon, are in a state that will be hard to restore. The literal meaning of *Convenience* is 'coming together', and here it signifies a balm for what is 'broken'. *Hard* echoes III.ii.61–64, and the phrase 'Stand in hard Cure' epitomizes the central moral of this Job-like play: endure patiently the afflictions sent to purge you of the flaws that derive from too much ease and comfort.

104 **bearing our Woes** both (a) suffering 'Miseries' like our own, and (b) taking our woes onto their own backs (like the greatest of 'our Betters' when he bore the Cross). Compare II.ii.162–63, and see the note to I.iv.44–45. Line 104 suggests that Gloucester (Edgar's 'Better') is assisting Kent (and perhaps the Fool) in what Edgar will shortly refer to as 'Bearing Fellowship' (as they carry Lear off stage).

107 **Leaving . . . behind** abandoning all thoughts that are free of pain and all illusions of happiness. Compare III.iv.6–14.

108 **Sufferance** both (a) suffering, and (b) endurance, 'Bearing'.

110 **Portable** tolerable; able to be ported (carried).

will say they are Persian; but let them be
chang'd.

Enter Gloucester.

KENT Now good my Lord, lie here and rest awhile.
LEAR Make no Noise, make no Noise, draw the
Curtains: so, so, we'll go to Supper i'th'
Morning.
FOOL And I'll go to Bed at Noon.
GLOUCESTER Come hither, Friend: where is the King
my Master?
KENT Here, Sir, but trouble him not, his Wits are gone.
GLOUCESTER Good Friend, I prythee take him in thy
Arms;
I have o'er-heard a Plot of Death upon him.
There is a Litter ready: lay him in't
And drive toward Dover, Friend, where thou shalt meet
Both Welcome and Protection. Take up thy Master:
If thou shouldst dally Half an Hour, his Life
With thine, and all that offer to defend him,
Stand in assured Loss. Take up, take up,
And follow me, that will to some Provision
Give thee quick Conduct.
KENT Oppressed Nature sleeps.
– This Rest might yet have balm'd thy broken Sinews,
Which, if Convenience will not allow,
Stand in hard Cure. – Come help to bear thy Maister,
Thou must not stay behind.
GLOUCESTER Come, come away.
[*Exeunt all but Edgar.*]
EDGAR When we our Betters see bearing our Woes,
We scarcely think our Miseries our Foes.
Who alone suffers suffers most i'th' Mind,
Leaving Free Things and Happy Shows behind;
But then the Mind much Sufferance doth o'er-skip
When Grief hath Mates, and Bearing Fellowship.
How Light and Portable my Pain seems now

111 **bow** bow low, curtsy. Compare I.i.144, 148–49.

112 **He . . . fathered** His children have treated him as my father has 'fathered' me.

113–15 **Mark . . . thee** Pay heed to sounds that signal danger, and reveal yourself only when fickle Opinion, whose unjust views sully your reputation now, welcomes you back and recognizes your true virtue.

116 **What . . . King** Whatever else happens tonight, may the King safely escape. *To night* recalls II.i.60.

117 **Lurk** stay under cover [for the time being].

III.vii This scene takes us back to Gloucester's castle.

3 **seek . . . Gloucester** Most editions insert a stage direction after this line to indicate that several servants leave. But it may be that they await more detailed orders and depart after line 23.

6 **keep . . . company** escort Goneril to Albany's castle.

8 **fit** suitable. Cornwall little knows how 'fit' such actions are for Edmund's 'Beholding'. Compare II.ii.416, III.ii.76.

9 **festivate** pleasant [because of our confidence that we will be victorious]. The Quarto prints *festuant.* The Second Folio (1632) emends the First Folio's *festiuate* to *festinate* (speedy, from the Latin *festinus*), and most of today's editions follow suit. It is quite possible that the First Folio reading derives either from a misreading of the manuscript or from an erroneous *n/u* substitution (which is very common in the early texts) but it is equally possible that *festivate* is a Shakespearean coinage, designed to combine *fast* and *festive* (with wordplay on *Displeasure*, line 5) and to accentuate the hubris that will soon prove to be Cornwall's undoing.

11 **intelligent** equipped with up-to-date information. Compare III.v.11–13.

13 **Lord of Gloucester** Edmund's second promotion is now an accomplished fact (see III.v.19–21, 26–27, where Cornwall creates a new Earl of Gloucester and adopts the Bastard as his son).

17 **Hot . . . him** seeking him with utmost fervour.

18 **Dependants** attendants.

When that which makes me bend makes the King bow.
He childed as I fathered. – Tom, away:
Mark the high Noises, and thy self bewray
When False Opinion, whose Wrong Thoughts defile
thee,
In thy Just Proof repeals and reconciles thee.
What will hap more to night, safe scape the King;
Lurk, lurk. [*Exit.*]

Scene 7

Enter Cornwall, Regan, Goneril, Bastard, and Servants.

CORNWALL Post speedily to my Lord your Husband, shew him this Letter. The Army of France is landed: seek out the Traitor Gloucester.

REGAN Hang him instantly.

GONERIL Pluck out his Eyes.

CORNWALL Leave him to my Displeasure. – Edmund, keep you our Sister company: the Revenges we are bound to take upon your traitorous Father are not fit for your Beholding. Advise the Duke where you are going, to a most festivate Preparation; we are bound to the like. Our Posts shall be swift and intelligent betwixt us. – Farewell, dear Sister. – Farewell, my Lord of Gloucester.

Enter Steward.

– How now? Where's the King?

STEWARD My Lord of Gloucester hath convey'd him
hence;
Some five or six and thirty of his Knights,
Hot Questrists after him, met him at Gate,
Who, with some other of the Lord's Dependants,

23 **Pinion . . . Thief** bind his arms as if he were no better than a common thief. Gloucester will be accorded the same dignity that Kent and Lear have received.

24 **pass . . . Life** pass judgement on his life (sentence him to death). The word 'well' appears only in the Folio.

25 **Form of Justice** Cornwall means 'due process' (normal judicial procedure). But his phrasing is a reminder that what is going on here lacks even the appearance of 'Justice'. Compare the 'Form of Justice' in the preceding scene (III.vi.22–86).

25–26 **our . . . Wrath** our executive authority shall bow (defer with obsequious politeness) to our anger. *Curt'sy* recalls II.ii.362, III.ii.66–67, and III.iii.23–24.

27 **comptrol** control; both (a) prevent, and (b) rebuke. Compare II.ii.429. The Quarto stage direction following this line tells us that Gloucester is 'brought in by two or three'.

29 **corky** dry and withered; ineffectual because of their age.
What . . . Graces? both (a) What is the meaning of this? and (b) What are you intending to do?

30 **consider . . . Guests** bear in mind the obligations that guests have to their hosts. Gloucester reminds Cornwall of one of the most sacred bonds ('ancient Amities', I.ii.165) of human society. Compare *Macbeth*, I.vii.12–16.

31 **Foul Play** wanton violation of justice.

32 **Hard** tight. Regan's adverb recalls III.vi.101–2.

33 **are** are a 'Traitor' yourself (one who betrays justice and humanity).

35 **Ignobly** lacking in nobility, due courtesy.

36 **White** old. Compare the references to Lear's white hair in III.i.7 and III.ii.23–24.
Naughty wicked (a much stronger word in Shakespeare's time than it tends to be now). Compare III.iv.115–16.

37 **ravish** steal, rape.

38 **quicken** return to life.

40 **ruffle** beat down, bully. Compare II.ii.481–82.

Are gone with him toward Dover, where they boast
To have well-armed Friends.

CORNWALL Get Horses for
Your Mistress.

GONERIL Farewell sweet Lord, and Sister.

CORNWALL Edmund, farewell.
[*Exeunt Edmund, Goneril, and Steward.*]
– Go seek the Traitor Gloucester,
Pinion him like a Thief, bring him before us.
[*Exeunt Servants.*]
– Though well we may not pass upon his Life
Without the Form of Justice, yet our Power
Shall do a Curt'sy to our Wrath, which Men
May blame but not comptrol.

Enter Gloucester, and Servants.

– Who's there? The Traitor?

REGAN Ingrateful Fox, 'tis he.

CORNWALL Bind fast his corky Arms.

GLOUCESTER What means your Graces?
Good my Friends, consider you are my Guests:
Do me no Foul Play, Friends.

CORNWALL Bind him, I say.

REGAN Hard, hard. – O filthy Traitor.

GLOUCESTER Unmerciful Lady,
As you are, I am none.

CORNWALL To this Chair bind him.
– Villain, thou shalt find –

GLOUCESTER By the kind Gods, 'tis most
Ignobly done to pluck me by the Beard.

REGAN So White, and such a Traitor?

GLOUCESTER Naughty Lady,
These Hairs which thou dost ravish from my Chin
Will quicken and accuse thee. I am your Host:
With Robbers' Hands my hospitable Favours
You should not ruffle thus. What will you do?

42 **Be simple answer'd** both (a) reply briefly and 'to th' Purpose' (II.ii.364), and (b) give a simple (honest, direct) reply.

43 **Confederacy** friendship, collaboration.

44 **Late footed** who have recently set foot. *Footed* echoes III.i.32–33 and III.iv.125; it anticipates line 66.

46 **I . . . down** I have in my possession a letter composed by one who guessed at where my loyalties might lie. Gloucester has told Edmund about this letter in III.iii.10–12.

49 **Wherefore** why.

50 **charg'd at peril** See II.ii.480, 485, 489; III.iii.2–6.

52 **I . . . Course** Gloucester compares himself to a bear in a baiting arena, surrounded by baying mastiffs. Against overwhelming odds, he must 'stand the Course' (endure the onslaughts of his enemies). Gloucester's phrasing echoes the Apostle Paul's reference to fighting 'a good fight', finishing the 'course', and keeping 'the faith' in 2 Timothy 4:7. *Stand* recalls II.ii.440–41, III.ii.19, III.vi.95–97.

56 **Anointed** sanctified as God's deputy – in a coronation ceremony that derives from Hebrew tradition (see Psalm 23:5).

Boarish Fangs the sharp teeth and tusks of a wild boar. Most editions adopt the Quarto's *rash* (strike slashingly) rather than the Folio's *stick*. *Boarish* echoes I.iv.171.

58 **buoy'd up** risen in response.

59 **stelled Fires** Gloucester probably means 'stars' (*stellae* in Latin), but it is also possible that he is referring to lightning flashes.

60 **holp** helped.

61 **stern** hard, unyielding. The Quarto has *dearn* (dire, dreadful), a reading most editions adopt.

62 **turn the Key** open the door. Compare II.ii.236–37.

63 **All . . . subscribe** Every other creature, however cruel, acknowledges the need for pity. *Subscribe* recalls III.ii.18.

64 **winged Vengeance** swift, harpy-like embodiments of divine retribution.

CORNWALL Come, Sir, what Letters had you late from France?
REGAN Be simple answer'd, for we know the Truth.
CORNWALL And what Confederacy have you with the Traitors
Late footed in the Kingdom?
REGAN To whose Hands
You have sent the Lunatic King. Speak.
GLOUCESTER I have a Letter guessingly set down
Which came from one that's of a Neutral Heart
And not from one oppos'd.
CORNWALL Cunning.
REGAN And False.
CORNWALL Where has thou sent the King?
GLOUCESTER To Dover.
REGAN Wherefore
To Dover? Wast thou not charg'd at peril –
CORNWALL Wherefore to Dover? Let him answer that.
GLOUCESTER I am tied to th' Stake, and I must stand the Course.
REGAN Wherefore to Dover?
GLOUCESTER Because I would not see thy cruel Nails
Pluck out his poor old Eyes, nor thy fierce Sister
In his Anointed Flesh stick Boarish Fangs.
The Sea, with such a Storm as his bare Head
In Hell-black Night endur'd, would have buoy'd up
And quench'd the stelled Fires:
Yet poor old Heart, he holp the Heavens to rain.
If Wolves had at thy Gate howl'd that stern Time,
Thou shouldst have said 'Good Porter, turn the Key.'
All Cruels else subscribe: but I shall see
The winged Vengeance overtake such Children.
CORNWALL See't shalt thou never. – Fellows, hold the Chair.
– Upon these Eyes of thine I'll set my Foot.
GLOUCESTER He that will think to live till he be Old,
Give me some Help. – O cruel! – O you Gods.
REGAN One Side will mock another: th' other too.

75 **shake . . . Quarrel** make it shake over this dispute. *Shake* recalls III.iv.35.
mean intend to do. Compare line 29.

77 **take . . . Anger** both (a) take your chances against my fury, and (b) put yourself at risk because of your own wrath. A nobleman was not required to respond to a challenge from a man below his rank; here Cornwall not only fights, he draws first. Compare V.iii.141–54.

78 **A Peasant . . . thus?** In a scene that is filled with disruptions of normal order, the Servant's defiance of his master and mistress is an indication of how badly Lear's kingdom has degenerated since its head of state abdicated his responsibilities.

S.D. **She . . . behind** Like 'Draw and fight' above, this stage direction occurs only in the Quarto.

80 **see . . . him** be sure that some injury is inflicted on him.

81 **vild Jelly** vile gelatinous fluid.

82 **Lustre** both (a) beauty [to look at, as with a lustrous pearl], and (b) light [as perceived].

85 **quit** requite; answer.
Out out upon thee; curses on you.

87 **made . . . us** disclosed your treacherous designs to us.

91 **out at Gates** out of doors. Compare I.iv.285.
smell Regan's taunt (reminding Gloucester that he will never see with his eyes again) recalls I.i.16, I.v.20–25, II.ii.252–53, III.iv.189.

94 **Eyeless Villain** Cornwall's terms for Gloucester echoes, and gives ironic foreshadowing to, lines 54–56, 63–65, and such previous passages as I.i.161–62; I.iv.315–18; I.v.20–25; II.i.120; II.ii.152, 162–63, 167–69, 252–55; III.i.8; III.iv.119, 162; III.vi.14–16, 25–27.

95 **Dunghill** refuse heap (where dung and other garbage was deposited).
apace freely.

97–98 **I'll . . . Good** I'll know that there is no cosmic justice (no divine punishment of evil) if this man comes to a good end. Lines 97–105 occur only in the Quarto text. In the Quarto the speech heading for line 97 is simply '*Servant*'. Most of today's editions rename these characters '2 Servant' and '3 Servant'; meanwhile they designate as '1 Servant' the 'Servant' who has died defending Gloucester earlier in the scene.

CORNWALL If you see Vengeance –
SERVANT Hold your Hand, my Lord:
I have serv'd you ever since I was a Child,
But better Service have I never done you
Than now to bid you hold.
REGAN How now, you Dog?
SERVANT If you did wear a Beard upon your Chin,
I'd shake it on this Quarrel. What do you mean?
CORNWALL My Villain? *Draw and fight.*
SERVANT Nay then come on, and take the Chance of Anger.
REGAN – Give me thy Sword. A Peasant stand up thus?
She takes a Sword and runs at him behind. Kills him.
SERVANT Oh I am slain. – My Lord, you have one Eye left
To see some Mischief on him. Oh. [*Dies.*]
CORNWALL Lest it see more, prevent it. – Out vild Jelly:
Where is thy Lustre now?
GLOUCESTER All Dark and Comfortless? Where's my Son Edmund?
– Edmund, enkindle all the Sparks of Nature
To quit this Horrid Act.
REGAN Out, treacherous Villain,
Thou call'st on him that hates thee. It was he
That made the Overture of thy Treasons to us,
Who is too Good to pity thee.
GLOUCESTER O my Follies! Then Edgar was abus'd.
– Kind Gods, forgive me that, and prosper him.
REGAN Go thrust him out at Gates, and let him smell
His way to Dover. *Exit [a Servant] with Gloucester.*
– How is't, my Lord? How look you?
CORNWALL I have receiv'd a Hurt: follow me, Lady.
– Turn out that Eyeless Villain; throw this Slave
Upon the Dunghill. – Regan, I bleed apace;
Untimely comes this Hurt. Give me your Arm.
Exeunt [all but two Servants].
1 SERVANT I'll never care what Wickedness I do
If this Man come to Good.

99 **meet . . . Death** encounter death in the traditional fashion (at a ripe old age).

101 **the Bedlam** Poor Tom (Edgar, disguised as a lunatic).

102–3 **roguish . . . thing** vagabondish insanity will permit him to be led or guided anywhere.

104 **Flax . . . Eggs** ingredients for a plaster to salve and cover Gloucester's bloody eye-sockets. As Lewis Theobald noted in his editions in the eighteenth century, the dialogue suggests that the two Servants exit in different directions ('severally', as in the stage direction that opens III.i).

2 SERVANT If she live long,
And in the end meet the Old Course of Death,
Women will all turn Monsters.
1 SERVANT Let's follow the old Earl, and get the Bedlam
To lead him where he would: his roguish Madness
Allows it self to any thing.
2 SERVANT Go thou, I'll fetch some Flax and Whites of Eggs
To apply to his bleeding Face. Now Heaven help him. *Exeunt.*

IV.i This scene returns us to the heath, on the way to Dover.

1 **contemn'd** despised, held in contempt. Compare II.ii.4–7.

3 **dejected** both (a) cast off, and (b) downcast.

4 **Stands . . . Esperance** is a state that still offers reason for hope ('Esperance', from the Latin *sperare*). *Stands* echoes III.vii.52.
lives . . . Fear has no fear of losing what it has obtained.

6 **Laughter** happiness, fulfilment, triumph (compare I.iv.301, I.v.54–55). Edgar's imagery derives from the proverbial figure of Fortune as a turning wheel. The Fool has alluded to the same notion in II.ii.255–69, and Lear has hinted at it in I.iv.280–84 and II.ii.289–90 (where 'bound' picks up on what the Fool has said in lines 255–58).

7 **unsubstantial** both (a) immaterial, (b) inconstant, and (c) unaccommodating (see III.iv.111–13). *Air* recalls II.ii.346–47, 391–92; III.iv.69–70; and III.vi.1. Here again it reminds us of the 'insubstantial' (empty-hearted) heirs that both Lear and Gloucester have embraced; as a result true heirs such as Edgar and Cordelia have been rendered insubstantial (turned into 'little seeming Substance', I.i.201.)

9 **Blasts** gusts (compare I.iv.313). Edgar's sentiments echo Duke Senior's reflections on 'The Seasons Difference, as the Icy Fang / And churlish Chiding of the Winter's Wind, / Which when it bites and blows upon my Body / Even till I shrink with Cold, I smile and say / "This is no Flattery: these are Counsellors / That feelingly persuade me what I am." / Sweet are the Uses of Adversity' (*As You Like It*, II.i.6–12). This sentence ('Welcome . . . Blasts', lines 6–9) appears only in the Folio text of *King Lear*.

10 **poorly led** (a) led like a poor (pitiable) beggar, (b) led by an impoverished old man, and (c) ineptly guided. In this line the earliest version of the First Quarto reads 'poorlie, leed'; the revised version reads 'parti, eyd'. On the hypothesis that the Folio printers were here relying upon a copy of Q1 with this passage in its uncorrected state, some editors emend line 10 to read: 'My father parti-ey'd?' In the Quarto the preceding stage direction reads '*led by*' rather than '*and*' as in the Folio. Since the Folio version of this passage makes adequate sense, and may well be the playscript reading, there is no compelling reason to alter it.

ACT IV

Scene 1

Enter Edgar.

EDGAR Yet better thus, and known to be contemn'd,
Than, still contemn'd and flatter'd, to be worst:
The lowest and most dejected thing of Fortune
Stands still in Esperance, lives not in Fear:
The Lamentable Change is from the Best,
The Worst returns to Laughter. – Welcome, then,
Thou unsubstantial Air that I embrace:
The Wretch that thou hast blown unto the Worst
Owes Nothing to thy Blasts.

Enter Gloucester and an Old Man.

But who comes here?
My Father poorly led? World, World, O World!

11–12 **But . . . Age** If the extraordinary changes you bring to our fortunes didn't make us detest you, life would be unwilling to give itself over to death when we reach old age. Edgar is attempting to justify worldly suffering on the grounds that (a) it makes us distrust Fortune and the vices she breeds (see II.ii.255–69), and (b) it makes us yearn for a better 'Life' in the next world.

18 **Way** (a) path, (b) destination, (c) reason to travel further.
want both (a) lack (need), and (b) desire.

20–21 **Our . . . Commodities** our accommodations give us a false sense of well-being, and our very deprivations turn out to be our most precious possessions. See Matthew 5:27–30 and 18:9, where Jesus says 'if thine eye offend thee, pluck it out' (echoed by Lear in I.iv.316–18). And compare II.ii.162–63, 180–81, 483–85; III.ii.27–34, 74–77; III.iv.32–36, 110–14.

22 **The . . . Wrath** who unwillingly fuelled your deceived and misused father's choleric anger. See the note to II.ii.275.

23 **see . . . Touch** feel you in my hands. *Touch* echoes II.ii.459.

26 **ere** both (a) ere (before), and (b) e'er (ever).

31 **He . . . Reason** Gloucester means 'he possesses some reasoning powers; he's not completely mad'. But his words can also be intepreted in other ways: (a) there is some cause for his situation (compare Lear's first reaction to Poor Tom in III.iv.48–49, 64–73), and (b) he has some reason to keep living (some 'Way', line 18).

36 **wanton** carefree, unfeeling. By comparing men to flies, Gloucester reduces humanity to an even baser level than a 'Worm' (line 33), an image that probably derives from Job 25:4–6, 'How then can man be justified with God? or how can he be clean that is born of a woman? Behold even to the moon, and it shineth not; yea, the stars are not pure in his sight. How much less man, that is a worm? and the son of man, which is a worm?' *Sport* recalls II.i.37.

37 **How . . . be?** How has this state of affairs come about?

38 **Bad . . . Sorrow** it's a rotten job to be required to cheer up those who are suffering. Edgar now assumes the function of the Fool (see III.i.16–17, and compare *Love's Labour's Lost*, V.ii.839–47).

But that thy strange Mutations make us hate thee,
Life would not yield to Age.
OLD MAN O my good Lord, I have been your Tenant,
And your Father's Tenant, these Fourscore Years.
GLOUCESTER Away, get thee away: good friend be
gone,
Thy Comforts can do me no Good at all,
Thee they may hurt.
OLD MAN You cannot see your Way.
GLOUCESTER I have no Way, and therefore want no
Eyes;
I stumbled when I saw. Full oft 'tis seen
Our Means secure us, and our mere Defects
Prove our Commodities. – Oh dear Son Edgar,
The Food of thy abused Father's Wrath,
Might I but live to see thee in my Touch
I'd say I had Eyes again.
OLD MAN How now? Who's there?
EDGAR – O Gods! Who is't can say 'I am at the
Worst'?
I am worse than ere I was.
OLD MAN 'Tis poor mad Tom.
EDGAR – And worse I may be yet: the Worst is not
So long as we can say 'This is the Worst.'
OLD MAN Fellow, where goest?
GLOUCESTER Is it a Beggar-man?
OLD MAN Madman, and Beggar too.
GLOUCESTER He has some Reason, else he could not
beg.
I'th' last night's Storm I such a Fellow saw,
Which made me think a Man a Worm. My Son
Came then into my Mind, and yet my Mind
Was then scarce Friends with him; I have heard more
since.
As Flies to wanton Boys are we to th' Gods:
They kill us for their Sport.
EDGAR – How should this be?
Bad is the Trade that must play Fool to Sorrow,

42 **twain** two. Compare II.ii.73–74 and IV.vi.202–4.

43 **for ancient Love** (a) for the sake of the love we've shown each other in the past, (b) out of respect for the elderly, and (c) in keeping with time-honoured traditions of charity.

44 **which** whom.

46 **'Tis . . . Plague** it shows how diseased our age is.

50 **on't** of it. *Best* recalls line 5, and II.i.16, 54, 124, II.ii.479.

51 **daub it** plaster over (hide) my true self. Compare II.ii.63–65.

52 **– And . . . must** This sentence appears only in the Folio text.

54 **Style** both (a) stile (a set of steps over a fence or wall), and (b) manner (another sense of 'Horseway').
Gate both (a) gateway (opening), and (b) gait.

55 **scarr'd** both (a) injured, buffeted, and (b) scared.

56 **Bless . . . Fiend** May God protect you, yeoman's son, from the Devil. Compare III.iv.58, 163.

58 **as Obidicut** for example, Obidicut (the first of another series of demons). Lines 57–62 occur in the Quarto only.

59 **Dumbness** muteness; an inability to speak.

60 **Stiberdigebit** a variant of *Flibberdigibbet*, III.iv.120.
Mobing mobbing, acting riotously and unruly. Most editions emend this line to read 'of mopping and mowing' (making faces); but the Quarto phrasing suggests that *Mobing* is a demon.

64 **humbled . . . Strokes** Gloucester means 'scarr'd out of [your] good Wits' (line 55). But his words could also mean 'humbled through affliction' (purged of pride, so that you are able to bear any affliction). Compare lines 8–9, 20–21.

65 **Makes . . . Happier** is to your advantage (because you are benefiting from my 'Distribution' of unneeded 'Means', lines 69, 20).

66 **Superfluous . . . Man** over-accommodated and luxury-indulged man. Compare III.iv.35, 111.

Ang'ring it self and others. – Bless thee, Master.
GLOUCESTER – Is that the Naked Fellow?
OLD MAN Ay, my Lord.
GLOUCESTER Get thee away. If for my sake thou wilt
O'er-take us hence a Mile or twain i'th' Way
Toward Dover, do it for ancient Love; and bring
Some Covering for this Naked Soul, which I'll
Intreat to lead me.
OLD MAN Alack, Sir, he is Mad.
GLOUCESTER 'Tis the Time's Plague when Madmen
lead the Blind.
Do as I bid thee, or rather do thy Pleasure;
Above the rest, be gone.
OLD MAN I'll bring him the best 'Parel that I have,
Come on't what will. *Exit.*
GLOUCESTER – Sirrah, Naked Fellow.
EDGAR Poor Tom's a cold – I cannot daub it further.
GLOUCESTER Come hither, Fellow.
EDGAR – And yet I must. – Bless thy
Sweet Eyes, they bleed.
GLOUCESTER Know'st thou the Way to Dover?
EDGAR Both Style and Gate, Horseway and Footpath.
Poor Tom hath been scarr'd out of his good Wits.
Bless thee, Goodman's Son, from the foul Fiend.
Five Fiends have been in Poor Tom at once: of
Lust, as Obidicut; Hobbididence, Prince of
Dumbness; Mahu, of Stealing; Modo, of Murder;
Stiberdigebit, of Mobing; and Mohing, who since
possesses Chambermaids and Waiting Women. So
bless thee, Master.
GLOUCESTER Here take this Purse, thou whom the
Heavens' Plagues
Have humbled to all Strokes. That I am Wretched
Makes thee the Happier. Heavens deal so still.
Let the Superfluous and Lust-dieted Man,

67 **slaves your Ordinance** treats your laws with contempt.

67–68 **that will . . . feel** whose perceiving powers are so daubed over by 'Excess' (line 69) that he is prevented from feeling the 'Blasts' (line 9) that would make him 'see' reality. Compare III.vi.25–26. *Powre* (power) recalls II.ii.350, and it reminds us of the pouring rain that Gloucester, like Lear, has brought upon himself by building his house on sand. See the note to II.ii.481. For him, as for his King, the 'Heavens' are afflicting him with cleansing 'Strokes'.

71 **I** both 'I' and 'Ay'. Compare II.ii.283.

IV.ii This scene takes place on the approach to Albany's residence. Goneril, accompanied by Edmund, is met by Oswald.

1–2 **I . . . Way** I am shocked that my unmanly and unmannerly husband didn't come out to greet us himself. *Mild* recalls I.iv.354–58. It may be that this sentence, like the one that follows it, is spoken to Oswald.

7 **loyal . . . Son** Oswald refers to the 'Loyalty' with which Edmund has incriminated his father (see III.v.22–25). But his words are an unintended reminder of the genuine 'loyal Service' that Poor Tom has undertaken in the previous scene.

10–11 **What . . . Offensive** From the Steward's point of view, it is Albany who has 'turn'd the Wrong Side out' (line 9). The Duke's reaction to events is the very opposite of what worldly self-regard would seem to dictate. Albany has become the kind of 'Sot' (fool) defined in II.ii.251–69, a man who declines to be a knave who 'serves and seeks for Gain'.

12 **Cowish Terror** the cow-like meekness (I.iv.355–57) that permits itself to be 'humbled to all Strokes' (IV.i.64).

13 **undertake** take up challenges to his honour; assume any part that calls for courage. Goneril is speaking to Edmund.

13–14 **he'll . . . Answer** he is insensitive to insults and injuries that require a real man to stand up for himself. Goneril's phrasing echoes (while contrasting with) IV.i.66–68. *Answer* recalls III.iv.105–7, III.vii.42; and *tie* harks back to III.vii.52.

14 **Our . . . Way** the hopes we expressed while travelling here.

That slaves your Ordinance, that will not see
Because he does not feel, feel your Powre quickly:
So Distribution should undo Excess,
And each Man have enough. Dost thou know Dover?

EDGAR I, Master.

GLOUCESTER There is a Cliff, whose high and bending Head
Looks fearfully in the confined Deep:
Bring me but to the very Brim of it,
And I'll repair the Misery thou dost bear
With something Rich about me. From that Place
I shall no Leading need.

EDGAR Give me thy Arm:
Poor Tom shall lead thee. *Exeunt.*

Scene 2

Enter Goneril, Bastard, and Steward.

GONERIL Welcome, my Lord. I marvel our Mild Husband
Not met us on the way. Now where's your Master?

STEWARD Madam within, but never Man so chang'd.
I told him of the Army that was landed;
He smil'd at it. I told him you were coming;
His Answer was 'the Worse'. Of Gloucester's Treachery,
And of the loyal Service of his Son,
When I inform'd him, then he call'd me Sot
And told me I had turn'd the Wrong Side out.
What most he should dislike seems Pleasant to him;
What like, Offensive.

GONERIL – Then shall you go no further.
It is the Cowish Terror of his Spirit
That dares not undertake: he'll not feel Wrongs
Which tie him to an Answer. Our Wishes on the way

17–18 **I . . . Hands** I must exchange 'Names' (titles and roles) with my husband and let him become the lady of the house. The *Distaff* (the rod on which flax or wool was wound for spinning) was a symbol of woman's work. Goneril plans to turn Albany into 'an O without a Figure' (I.iv.207).

19 **like** likely.

21–22 **spare . . . Head** don't protest, lower your head [while I give you 'this' – evidently a love token for Edmund's neck or cap]. Goneril is offering 'Ear-kissing Arguments' (II.i.9) for an alliance between Edmund and herself.

24 **Conceive** both (a) think venturous thoughts, and (b) look forward to an opportunity to 'conceive' privately in response to 'a Mistress's Command'. *Conceive* echoes I.i.12–13 and I.iv.71–72; it thus reminds us that Edmund's stretchable 'Spirits' derive from those of the 'Lust-dieted Man' (IV.i.66) who has just lost his eyes.

25 **Yours . . . Death** I will be your faithful knight (and 'die' in your rank embrace) in the most death-defying situations. Edmund's words will prove prophetic. For the erotic sense of *Death*, compare *Much Ado About Nothing*, V.ii.110–12. Line 26 appears only in the Folio.

27 **my Fool** my ineffectual husband. See the note to lines 10–11.

29 **I . . . Whistle** Goneril alludes to the proverb 'It is a poor dog that is not worth the whistling' (a warm welcome). The '*Exit*' preceding Albany's entrance derives from the Quarto printing.

31–36 **I . . . Use** I worry about your 'Nature', since a branch that disdains its source and isolates itself within its own borders cannot survive; she who cuts herself off from her nourishing roots and trunk must dry up, die, and be cast on the hearth for the 'Use' reserved for firewood. See Matthew 7:18–20, and the notes to I.i.98, I.ii.165, I.iv.17, II.ii.425, 481.

32 **it** its (so also in line 33). In Shakespeare's time *it* and *his* were the usual forms for the neuter possessive singular pronoun.

36 **Text** Scripture you allude to. In addition to the passages noted in connection with lines 31–36, Goneril's words also recall John 15:6, 'If a man abide not in me, he is cast forth as a branch, and is withered; and men gather them, and cast them into the fire, and they are burned.'

41 **Head-lugg'd Bear** bear being dragged by the head. Lines 31–48 ('I . . . Deep') appear only in the Quarto.

43 **suffer** permit, tolerate. Compare III.vi.108–9.

May prove Effects. Back, Edmund, to my Brother;
Hasten his Musters and conduct his Powres.
I must change Names at Home, and give the Distaff
Into my Husband's Hands. This trusty Servant
Shall pass between us: ere long you are like to hear
(If you dare venture in your own behalf)
A Mistress's Command. Wear this; spare Speech,
Decline your Head. This Kiss, if it durst speak,
Would stretch thy Spirits up into the Air:
Conceive, and fare thee well.

BASTARD Yours in the Ranks of Death.

GONERIL My most dear Gloucester.

Exit [*Edmund*].

Oh the Difference of Man and Man. To thee
A Woman's Services are due; my Fool
Usurps my Body.

STEWARD Madam, here comes my Lord. *Exit.*

Enter Albany.

GONERIL I have been worth the Whistle.

ALBANY Oh Goneril,
You are not worth the Dust which the rude Wind
Blows in your Face. I fear your Disposition;
That Nature which contemns it Origin
Cannot be bordered certain in it self;
She that her self will sliver and disbranch
From her Material Sap perforce must wither
And come to Deadly Use.

GONERIL No more: the Text is Foolish.

ALBANY Wisdom and Goodness to the Vild seem Vild;
Filths savour but themselves. What have you done?
Tigers, not Daughters, what have you perform'd?
A Father and a gracious Aged Man,
Whose Reverence even the Head-lugg'd Bear would
lick,
Most barbarous, most degenerate, have you madded.
Could my good Brother suffer you to do it?

44 **by . . . benefited** who has received so many gifts from Lear.

45 **visible** manifest (like lightning). Compare III.vii.63–64.

47 **perforce** of necessity.

48 **Monsters . . . Deep** This phrase recalls I.iv.273–75 and III.vii.98–100.

50 **That . . . Blows** who turns his other cheek when struck (Matthew 5:38–39). Compare II.ii.458–59, III.i.1, and III.vi.104–5.
a . . . Wrongs a head to carry horns, not as the fierce 'Brows' of a bold warrior (see *Hamlet*, III.iii.5–7), but as trophies of your lack of male readiness. See I.v.32–34, 55.

51–52 **an . . . Suffering** an eye to tell you that 'Honour' suffers (tolerates) no 'Wrongs'.

52–54 **that . . . Mischief** who is unaware that even fools consider pitiful those base slaves who are already being 'punish'd' (by their own 'Suffering') even before they receive further 'Mischief', let alone before they do 'Mischief' in retaliation. Lines 52–58 ('that . . . so?') occur only in the Quarto text.

56–58 **thy . . . so?'** your state (both condition and 'Land') depends upon (*begins* with) your not being 'Noiseless', but you only quietly complain.

59 **seems** appears. Most editions adopt the Quarto's *shews*.

59–60 **Proper . . . Woman** Deformity is less horrid when it displays itself in the Devil than in Woman [since one *expects* the Fiend to be monstrous]. Lines 61–66 occur only in the Quarto.

61 **Changed** both (a) transformed, and (b) exchanged (because possessed by a fiend, line 65). Compare lines 3, 17.
Self-cover'd Thing monster wearing the cover ('Feature', 'shield') of a woman who now looks like the monster she is.

62 **my Fitness** fit for me (compare III.vii.6–8); my nature.

64 **dislecate** dislocate; rend.

66 **Marry . . . mew** [yes] indeed, keep your manhood under restraint (mewed up, like a caged falcon). *Marry* (an adverb that derived from an oath referring to the Virgin Mary) here plays on the matrimonial sense. *Mew* reinforces the implication that Albany is no more frightening than a meowing cat.

70 **thrill'd with Remorse** pierced with pity [for Gloucester].

A Man, a Prince, by him so benefited –
If that the Heavens do not their visible Spirits
Send quickly down to tame the vild Offences,
It will come Humanity must perforce
Prey on it self like Monsters of the Deep.

GONERIL Milk-liver'd Man,
That bear'st a Cheek for Blows, a head for Wrongs,
Who hast not in thy Brows an Eye discerning
Thine Honour from thy Suffering, that not know'st
Fools do those Villains pity who are punish'd
Ere they have done their Mischief, where's thy Drum?
France spreads his Banners in our Noiseless Land
With plumed Helm; thy State begins thereat,
Whilst thou, a Moral Fool, sits still and cries
'Alack, why does he so?'

ALBANY See thy self Divel:
Proper Deformity seems not in the Fiend
So Horrid as in Woman.

GONERIL Oh vain Fool.

ALBANY Thou Changed and Self-cover'd Thing, for shame
Be-Monster not thy Feature. Were't my Fitness
To let these Hands obey my Blood, they are apt
Enough to dislecate and tear thy Flesh and Bones.
How e'er thou art a Fiend, a Woman's Shape
Doth shield thee.

GONERIL Marry your Manhood mew –

Enter a Messenger.

ALBANY – What News?

MESSENGER Oh my good Lord, the Duke of Cornwall's Dead,
Slain by his Servant, going to put out
The other Eye of Gloucester.

ALBANY Gloucester's Eyes.

MESSENGER A Servant that he bred, thrill'd with Remorse,

71 **bending** directing. The incident described occurs in III.vii.70–77.

72 **Threat enrag'd** infuriated by this defiance. Most editions follow the Quarto and print *thereat*. The metrical position of the word indicates a disyllabic pronunciation ('thuh-rét'), so there would probably be little distinction to a theatre audience. *Stroke* (line 74) recalls IV.i.63–64. *Pluck'd* (line 75) recalls I.iv.316.

76 **Justices** 'winged Vengeance' (III.vii.64); compare III.vi.56.
nether both (a) earthly, and (b) base, vile. Compare II.ii.199–201.

79 **craves** calls for.

80 **One . . . well** a part of me is pleased with this news of Cornwall's death [since it removes one obstacle to my advancement to sole power].

81–83 **But . . . Life** But now that she is a widow, and one with Edmund at her side for the moment, the erotic fantasies I've erected may turn out to be a structure that falls upon my own hated (and hate-full) existence. Goneril's imagery hints at the fate of the impious Philistines who invited Samson into their temple to taunt him (see Judges 16:23–30). Goneril's 'Fancy' also suggests Jesus' parable about those who fail to heed his 'Text' (line 36). According to Matthew 7:26–27, 'every one that heareth these sayings of mine, and doeth them not, shall be likened unto a foolish man, which built his house upon the sand: And the rain descended, and the floods came, and the winds blew, and beat upon that house; and it fell: and great was the fall of it.' This passage lies behind much of the action of *King Lear* (see the notes to II.ii.481 and III.vi.25–26); for another treatment of it see 2 *Henry IV*, I.iii.36–62. And for *Building* as a metaphor for fleshly lusts, see *Measure for Measure*, II.iv.95. Compare *Misconstruction* in II.ii.115 of *King Lear*.

84 **I'll . . . answer** In the Quarto this sentence is followed by an '*Exit*.' The absence of such a stage direction in the Folio may be an oversight, but it may also be an indication that Shakespeare (or the playwright's acting company) decided to alter this moment and keep Goneril on stage to the end of the scene.

87 **back again** on his way back to Regan at Gloucester's castle.

89 **inform'd** gave evidence. Compare I.iv.351; II.i.102–3; II.ii.163–65, 281–86; and IV.ii.8.
quit left

Oppos'd against the Act, bending his Sword
To his great Master, who, Threat-enrag'd,
Flew on him and amongst them fell'd him dead,
But not without that harmful Stroke which since
Hath pluck'd him after.

ALBANY – This shews you are above,
You Justices, that these our nether Crimes
So speedily can venge. – But O, poor Gloucester,
Lost he his other Eye?

MESSENGER Both, both, my Lord.
– This Letter, Madam, craves a speedy Answer:
'Tis from your Sister.

GONERIL – One way I like this well;
But being Widow, and my Gloucester with her,
May all the Building in my Fancy pluck
Upon my hateful Life. Another way
The News is not so Tart. – I'll read, and answer.

ALBANY Where was his Son when they did take his
Eyes?

MESSENGER Come with my Lady hither.

ALBANY He is not here.

MESSENGER No, my good Lord, I met him back again.

ALBANY Knows he the Wickedness?

MESSENGER Ay, my good Lord:
'Twas he inform'd against him, and quit the House

92 **I . . . thee** I hereby dedicate my life to thanking you.

IV.iii This scene, which takes place at the French camp near Dover, appears only in the Quarto text.

3 **Imperfect** in need of further attention.

4 **State** government of France.

5–6 **which . . . Danger** which portends so much urgent danger to the French kingdom. Shakespeare evidently decided not to compromise his positive portrayal of the King of France by having him reappear as the military leader of an invasion of Britain.

9 **Monsier** Monsieur.

13 **trill'd** trickled. This word echoes 'thrill'd with Remorse' (IV.ii.70) and reinforces the parallel between Cordelia's piercing 'Demonstration of Grief' (lines 10–11) and the courage of the Servant who was so moved by Gloucester's pain that he 'oppos'd against the Act' (IV.ii.71) at the cost of his own life.

15 **Passion** intense emotion.

17 **Patience . . . 'streme** Restraint and extreme sorrow. Another possibility is that the Quarto's *streme* is to be interpreted as *stream* (here meaning 'streamed'). Most editions emend *streme* to *strove*. The premise of this edition is that 'Sun shine and Rain at once' in line 19 is an appositional paraphrase of lines 17–18. According to this reading, the Gentleman is saying that 'if you have seen sunshine and rain occur simultaneously, you have seen the equivalent of Cordelia's extremities of "Patience and sorrow" '.

18 **goodliest** best; most fully. Cordelia's emotional conflict recalls the psychomachias (soul-struggles) described in such previous passages as I.i.63. 77–79; II.ii.454–68; III.i.4–11, 16–17; III.iv.6–11; III.vi.104–11; IV.i.51–52.

20 **a Better Way** a more exalted instance of that same striving for dominance. But this phrase can also mean 'a higher course'.
Smilets delicate little smiles.

21 **seem** seemed.

On purpose, that their Punishment might have
The Freer Course.

ALBANY – Gloucester, I live to thank thee for the Love
Thou shew'dst the King, and to revenge thine Eyes.
– Come hither, Friend; tell me what more thou
know'st. *Exeunt.*

Scene 3

Enter Kent and a Gentleman.

KENT Why the King of France is so suddenly gone back, know you no Reason?

GENTLEMAN Something he left Imperfect in the State, which since his coming forth is thought of, which imports to the Kingdom so much Fear and Danger that his personal Return was most required and necessary.

KENT Who hath he left behind him General?

GENTLEMAN The Marshal of France, Monsier La Far.

KENT Did your Letters pierce the Queen to any Demonstration of Grief?

GENTLEMAN I say she took them, read them in my
Presence,
And now and then an ample Tear trill'd down
Her delicate Cheek. It seemed she was a Queen
Over her Passion, who, most Rebel-like,
Sought to be King o'er her.

KENT O then it moved her.

GENTLEMAN Not to a Rage. Patience and Sorrow 'streme,
Who should express her goodliest, you have seen,
Sun shine and Rain at once; her Smiles and Tears
Were like a Better Way; those happy Smilets
That play'd on her ripe Lip seem not to know
What Guests were in her Eyes, which parted thence

24 **Rarity** precious gem. Compare I.i.58, 245, 255–64.

25 **become** befit, adorn.

27 **Faith** in faith.
heav'd struggled to emit. Lines 27–28 echo I.i.92–93, where Cordelia cannot heave her heart into her mouth. Compare II.ii.354–55.

28 **prest** both (a) pressed down upon (as with an instrument of torture to force a prisoner to confess or enter a plea of guilt or innocence), and (b) pressed into service. Compare *The Merchant of Venice*, I.i.160. *Prest* echoes *oppress'd*; II.ii.291, III.vi.99, and anticipates *Press-money* IV.vi.87.

31 **beleeft** either (a) left, abandoned, or (b) believed [in].

32 **Holy Water** a metaphor for Cordelia's tears. Compare III.ii.10–11.

33 **Clamour** the throes of emotion; an echo of I.i.168, II.ii.18–20.

35 **Conditions** dispositions, characters. This line recalls I.i.208, 303, and I.ii.134–46.

36 **self . . . Make** same husband and wife.

37 **Issues** offspring. This word recalls I.i.17–18, I.ii.8–9, and I.iv.2–4.

41 **sometime . . . Tune** at times when his wits are ordered.

44 **A sovereign Shame** both (a) a ruling sense of shame, and (b) the kind of shame that only a noble monarch can feel.
elbows him shoves him [out of the path that might lead him to reconciliation with Cordelia], urges him.

45 **stripp'd . . . Benediction** both (a) tore her away from his good graces, and (b) stripped her of his blessing (both her inheritance and her father's favour). See the notes to I.i.285, III.iv.85, IV.i.66, IV.ii.61.

46 **Foreign Casualties** the 'Chance' (I.i.261) of France; the fortunes of the world at large.
dear both (a) precious, and (b) loving.

48 **venomously** like the venom of a poisonous snake.

50 **Powers** armed forces.

51 **a foot** on foot; marching.

52 **Maister** master (from the Latin *magister*).

53 **dear Cause** important case (business). See the note to II.ii.375.

As Pearls from Diamonds dropp'd. In brief,
Sorrow would be a Rarity most beloved
If all could so become it.
KENT Made she no verbal Question?
GENTLEMAN Faith once or twice she heav'd the name of
'Father'
Pantingly forth as if it prest her Heart;
Cried 'Sisters, Sisters, Shame of Ladies, Sisters;
Kent, Father, Sisters; what i'th' Storm, i'th' Night?
Let Pity not be beleeft.' There she shook
The Holy Water from her Heavenly Eyes,
And Clamour moistened her; then away she started
To deal with Grief alone.
KENT It is the Stars,
The Stars above us, govern our Conditions;
Else one self Mate and Make could not beget
Such different Issues. You spoke not with her since.
GENTLEMAN No.
KENT Was this before the King return'd?
GENTLEMAN No, since.
KENT Well Sir, the poor distressed Lear's i'th' Town,
Who sometime in his Better Tune remembers
What we are come about, and by no means
Will yield to see his Daughter.
GENTLEMAN Why, good Sir?
KENT A sovereign Shame so elbows him, his own
Unkindness,
That stripp'd her from his Benediction, turn'd her
To Foreign Casualties, gave her dear Rights
To his Dog-hearted Daughters, these things sting
His Mind so venomously that burning Shame
Detains him from Cordelia.
GENTLEMAN Alack, poor Gentleman.
KENT Of Albany's and Cornwall's Powers you heard
not.
GENTLEMAN 'Tis so, they are a foot.
KENT Well Sir, I'll bring you to our Maister Lear,
And leave you to attend him. Some dear Cause

54 **wrap me up** both (a) consume me, and (b) clothe me.

55 **known aright** disclosed in my true identity.

IV.iv This scene occurs at the camp of the French forces.

3 **rank Fenitar** unkempt fumitory (a herb used to treat hypochondria).

Furrow Weeds weeds that grow in the furrows made by ploughs. Lines 1–6 echo Matthew 27:27–31, where we are told that the Roman soldiers stripped Jesus and 'put on him a scarlet robe. And when they had platted a crown of thorns, they put it upon his head, and a reed in his right hand: and they bowed the knee before him, and mocked him, saying, Hail, King of the Jews!'

4 **Hardokes** probably either (a) hard oaks, or (b) docks (weeds).

Hemlock a plant frequently used as a poison (as with Socrates).

5 **Darnel** tares, a grassy weed.

6 **our sustaining Corn** the wheat we cultivate to sustain our lives.

Centery century, a 100-soldier troop. Compare *Coriolanus*, IV.iii.47–49. Most likely one or more soldiers are to exit after Cordelia speaks this sentence.

8–10 **What . . . Worth** I'll give all I own to anyone who can employ the best medical knowledge available to Man to restore him to the sanity he's now deprived of. Here *bereaved* can mean both (a) bereft, and (b) distressed.

12 **Our . . . Repose** the nurse Nature provides for us is rest.

13–14 **to . . . operative** to prompt him to that, there are many effectual herbs. *Simples* (as distinguished from compounds) are remedies extracted from single plant species.

15 **blest Secrets** benign remedies. Compare I.iv.109–11.

16 **unpublish'd Virtues** unpublicized (secret) powers (medicinal herbs).

17 **aidant and remediate** helpful and curative (remediating).

18 **Desires** wishes. Most editions adopt the Quarto's *distress*. The Folio phrasing could be construed to yield much the same implication; meanwhile it reinforces the notion that what Lear needs most is an antidote to his 'sovereign Shame' (IV.iii.40–49), one that will restore him to what he most deeply desires.

19 **Least** lest. Compare II.ii.256–57, III.vii.8.1.

Will in Concealment wrap me up awhile.
When I am known aright you shall not grieve
Lending me this Acquaintance. I pray you go
Along with me. *Exeunt.*

Scene 4

Enter with Drum and Colours Cordelia, Gentlemen, and Soldiers.

CORDELIA Alack, 'tis he; why he was met even now
As Mad as the vex'd Sea, singing aloud,
Crown'd with rank Fenitar and Furrow Weeds,
With Hardokes, Hemlock, Nettles, Cuckoo Flow'rs,
Darnel, and all the idle Weeds that grow
In our sustaining Corn. A Centery send forth;
Search every Acre in the high-grown Field
And bring him to our Eye. What can Man's Wisdom
In the Restoring his bereaved Sense,
He that helps him take all my outward Worth.
GENTLEMAN There is Means, Madam.
Our Foster Nurse of Nature is Repose,
The which he lacks; that to provoke in him
Are many Simples operative, whose Power
Will close the Eye of Anguish.
CORDELIA All blest Secrets,
All you unpublish'd Virtues of the Earth,
Spring with my Tears; be aidant and remediate
In the good Man's Desires. Seek, seek for him,
Least his ungovern'd Rage dissolve the Life

20 **wants . . . it** lacks the wherewithal to guide it properly. *Means* recalls IV.i.20–21.

22 **'Tis known before** We were already aware of that.

23–24 **O . . . about** Cordelia's point is that she is leading a French invasion of Britain not for personal gain but for the rescue of her father. Her words echo Luke 2:49, where the youthful Jesus asks his anxious parents 'knewe ye not that I must go about my fathers business?' (1560 Geneva Bible).

26 **importun'd** both (a) solicited (by letters from Kent and others), and (b) importunate (urging the King of France to come to her father's aid). Compare III.iv.166, IV.iii.5.

27 **blown** full-blooming; puffed up, proud. Cordelia's phrasing echoes 1 Corinthians 13:4, where the Apostle Paul says that love 'suffereth long' and is 'not puffed up'.

28 **Rite** right. The rhymed spelling reminds us of the monarchical rituals that have been denied Lear since his abdication.

IV.v This scene returns us to Gloucester's castle for a look at a daughter whose arms *are* incited by 'blown Ambition'.

2 **with much ado** only after a great deal of persuasion.

4 **Lord . . . Home?** Regan's question reflects her suspicion that Goneril has tried to keep her husband from becoming aware of the kind of time she has been spending with the Bastard.

6 **import** mean, signify. Compare IV.iii.5–7.

9 **Ignorance** both (a) foolishness, and (b) neglect (ignoring a matter that should have been dealt with).

12 **In . . . Misery** out of compassion for his suffering. Regan's phrasing offers a telling contrast between the kind of 'pity' she and Edmund embody and the kind that Edgar is exhibiting as he leads his blind father towards Dover. Compare II.ii.162–63.

13 **nighted** both (a) cast into the darkness of night, and (b) benighted, made wretched. Compare II.i.120 and III.vii.94.
descry spy out (a poignant reminder that Edmund's father must now use other means to discern the 'Strength o'th' Enemy').

That wants the Means to lead it.

Enter Messenger.

MESSENGERS News, Madam:
The British Powres are marching hitherward.
CORDELIA 'Tis known before. Our Preparation stands
In Expectation of them. – O dear Father,
It is thy Business that I go about.
Therefore great France
My mourning and importun'd Tears hath pitied.
No blown Ambition doth our Arms incite,
But Love, dear Love, and our ag'd Father's Rite.
– Soon may I hear and see him. *Exeunt.*

Scene 5

Enter Regan and Steward.

REGAN But are my Brother's Powres set forth?
STEWARD Ay, Madam.
REGAN Himself in person there?
STEWARD Madam, with much ado:
Your Sister is the better Soldier.
REGAN Lord Edmund spake not with your Lord at Home?
STEWARD No, Madam.
REGAN What might import my Sister's Letter to him?
STEWARD I know not, Lady.
REGAN Faith he is posted hence on serious Matter.
It was great Ignorance, Gloucester's Eyes being out,
To let him live. Where he arrives he moves
All Hearts against us. Edmund, I think, is gone
In pity of his Misery, to dispatch
His nighted Life: moreover to descry
The Strength o'th' Enemy.

17 **Ways** roadways. See the note to IV.i.18, and compare I.i.214; II.i.43; III.i.52; III.iv.21; III.vii.91–92; IV.ii.1–2, 14–15. The word 'Madam' appears only in the Folio.

18 **charg'd . . . Business** commanded me to conduct 'this Business'. *Business* frequently carries erotic overtones in Shakespeare (see *Hamlet*, I.v.126, and *Troilus and Cressida*, V.i.88), and in this instance the word reinforces Regan's inferences. Compare II.i.125–29.

20 **Belike** likely, probably.

25 **Eliads** oeillades (French for suggestively 'speaking Looks'). *Looks* recalls II.ii.415.

28 **in Understanding** with knowledge.
y'are you are.

29 **take this Note** both (a) take note of what I am telling you now (that 'I'll love thee much', line 21, and reward you handsomely if you'll come over to my side), and (b) carry this message from me to Edmund.

31 **Convenient** fitting (with an echo of *cunnus*, the Latin word for the female genitalia). See the notes to I.i.20–21, III.vi.101–2, and IV.ii.24.

32 **gather more** both (a) infer more, and (b) collect more for your own hand [if you cooperate with me].

35 **call . . . her** remind her to let her good judgement control her unruly passion [remembering that she is a married woman, whereas I am now a widow and hence eligible to give 'my Hand' to Edmund]. *Wisdom* echoes IV.iv.8–10, where Cordelia uses the word with a very different implication.

38 **Preferment** advancement; a major promotion in status. The phrase *cuts him off* echoes Luke 12:42–48 (see the note to I.v.55) and anticipates IV.vi.259–66.

40 **What . . . follow** whose side I'm on (what kind of servant I am). Oswald's comments about service recall I.iv.104–7; II.ii.8–18, 32–34, 71–83, 251–69. *Party* echoes II.i.27–28 and III.v.11–13. In line 39 'him' is here supplied from the Quarto text; it does not appear in the Folio.

STEWARD I must needs after him, Madam, with my
Letter.
REGAN Our Troops set forth to morrow, stay with us:
The Ways are Dangerous.
STEWARD I may not, Madam:
My Lady charg'd my Duty in this Business.
REGAN Why should she write to Edmund? Might not
you
Transport her Purposes by Word? Belike,
Some things, I know not what – I'll love thee much,
Let me unseal the Letter.
STEWARD Madam, I had rather –
REGAN I know your Lady does not love her Husband,
I am sure of that; and at her late being here
She gave strange Eliads and most speaking Looks
To Noble Edmund. I know you are of her Bosom.
STEWARD I, Madam?
REGAN I speak in Understanding: y'are, I know 't,
Therefore I do advise you take this Note.
My Lord is dead; Edmund and I have talk'd,
And more Convenient is he for my Hand
Than for your Lady's. You may gather more:
If you do find him, pray you give him this,
And when your Mistress hears thus much from you,
I pray desire her call her Wisdom to her.
So fare you well.
If you do chance to hear of that blind Traitor,
Preferment falls on him that cuts him off.
STEWARD Would I could meet him, Madam, I should
shew
What Party I do follow.
REGAN Fare thee well. *Exeunt.*

IV.vi This scene returns us to Gloucester and Edgar as they approach what the old Earl believes to be the cliffs of Dover.

3 **Even** level.

7 **thy . . . alter'd** your manner of speaking is improved. In lines 69–72 Edgar will tell Gloucester that the creature who led him to the precipice was 'some Fiend'.

10 **Garments** the 'Covering' provided in response to Gloucester's request to the Old Man in IV.i. Despite his new apparel, however, and despite a new manner that differs from 'Poor Tom', Edgar remains a 'Naked Soul' (IV.i.44) in his absolute (and life-threatening) devotion to his father. Whereas in the immediately preceding scenes he has generally spoken in prose, he now reverts to the blank verse to be expected of a nobleman.

12 **Dizzy** dizzying.

13 **Choughs** jackdaws; smaller members of the crow family.

14 **Shew . . . gross** appear scarcely so large.

15 **Sampire** samphire, a sweet-smelling herb that grew on cliffs and was harvested by men who were lowered and raised by ropes.
dreadful fearful.

18 **Anchoring Bark** ship at anchor in the harbour.

19 **Diminish'd . . . Cock** as tiny-looking as the small cockboat she carries along her side. Compare I.v.55, III.ii.3, and III.iv.78–79.

21 **unnumb'red idle Pebble** innumerable passive pebbles.

23 **Least . . . turn** lest my mind turn mad. *Least* echoes IV.iv.19.
deficient Sight impaired ('Imperfect', line 5) ability to recognize danger. Compare III.iv.95; III.vii.91–92, 94; IV.i.67–68; IV.ii.12–14, 49–58.

26 **extreme Verge** very edge of the cliff (as in II.ii.330–31). Gloucester is now an emblem of Man in extremity (compare III.iv.105–14), on the verge of yielding to the Fiend's counsel to despair and be damned. *Extreme* echoes IV.iii.17–18.

Scene 6

Enter Gloucester and Edgar.

GLOUCESTER When shall I come to th' Top of that
same Hill?
EDGAR You do climb up it now. Look how we labour.
GLOUCESTER Me thinks the Ground is Even.
EDGAR Horrible Steep.
Hark, do you hear the Sea?
GLOUCESTER No, truly.
EDGAR Why then your other Senses grow Imperfect
By your Eyes' Anguish.
GLOUCESTER So may it be indeed.
Me thinks thy Voice is alter'd, and thou speak'st
In better Phrase and Matter than thou didst.
EDGAR Y'are much deceiv'd: in nothing am I chang'd
But in my Garments.
GLOUCESTER Me thinks y'are better spoken.
EDGAR Come on, Sir, here's the Place. Stand still: how
Fearful
And Dizzy 'tis to cast one's Eyes so low.
The Crows and Choughs that wing the Midway Air
Shew scarce so gross as Beetles. Half way down
Hangs one that gathers Sampire: dreadful Trade.
Me thinks he seems no bigger than his Head.
The Fishermen that walk'd upon the Beach
Appear like Mice; and yond tall Anchoring Bark,
Diminish'd to her Cock; her Cock, a Buoy
Almost too small for Sight. The murmuring Surge,
That on th' unnumb'red idle Pebble chafes,
Cannot be heard so high. I'll look no more,
Least my Brain turn, and the deficient Sight
Topple down headlong.
GLOUCESTER Set me where you stand.
EDGAR Give me your Hand: you are now within a Foot
Of th' extreme Verge. For all beneath the Moon
Would I not leap upright.

29–30 **Fairies . . . thee** May the Fairies (spirits) and Gods (higher divinities) help you prosper. Compare III.iv.38.

33–34 **Why . . . it** The reason I play with his suicidal hopelessness (compare IV.i.36–37) is to heal it and replace it with faith. The stage directions about Gloucester's kneeling and falling (lines 34, 41) are supplied from the Quarto. They do not appear in the Folio.

35 **renounce** both (a) give up, and (b) throw off, reject. Compare Edgar's remarks in IV.i.10–12.

36 **Shake . . . off** discard my sufferings [without defying you or allowing my doubts to become full-fledged quarrels]. *Shake* recalls such previous passages as I.i.39–40 and III.vii.74–75.

38 **To . . . Wills** to oppose 'Wills' that are not to be opposed.

39 **Snuff** burnt-down, smoking wick.

42–44 **And . . . Theft** And yet I worry that his state of mind ('Conceit', thought, imagination) may itself steal away his 'Life' when that 'Treasury' is all too willing to be robbed. While Edgar soliloquizes, Gloucester leaps upright (line 27), thinking that he is thereby throwing himself to his death on the pebbled beach below. Then Edgar speaks to his father again, now pretending to be a fisherman who has just come upon a man who has fallen from above. *Rob* recalls III.vi.38.

49 **ought but Gozemore** anything heavier than gossamer (cobwebs). The Folio spelling may involve wordplay on 'goes more'.

50 **So . . . precipitating** falling so many fathoms (lengths of six feet). *Fathom* echoes III.iv.37.

51 **shiver'd** shattered into slivers. *Egg* recalls I.iv.165–69.

52 **heavy Substance** far more weight than gossamer or an egg. Here *heavy* is a reminder of the heavy (melancholy) mood that precipitated what has turned out to be a fortunate fall (not *from* but *into* Grace).
Sound whole, healthy. Compare II.ii.294–95.

53 **at . . . Altitude** atop one another do not equal the height.

55 **Thy . . . Miracle** both (a) it's a miracle you survived, and (b) you are yourself a living miracle. Compare II.ii.162–63.

GLOUCESTER Let go my Hand.
Here, Friend, 's another Purse: in it a Jewel
Well worth a Poor Man's taking. Fairies and Gods
Prosper it with thee. Go thou further off,
Bid me Farewell, and let me hear thee Going.

EDGAR Now fare ye well, good Sir.

GLOUCESTER With all my Heart.

EDGAR – Why I do trifle thus with his Despair
Is done to cure it.

GLOUCESTER O you mighty Gods! *He kneels.*
This World I do renounce, and in your Sights
Shake patiently my great Affliction off;
If I could bear it longer and not fall
To Quarrel with your great opposeless Wills,
My Snuff and loathed Part of Nature should
Burn it self out. If Edgar live, O bless him.
– Now Fellow, fare thee well. *He falls.*

EDGAR Gone, Sir, farewell.
– And yet I know not how Conceit may rob
The Treasury of Life when Life it self
Yields to the Theft. Had he been where he thought,
By this had Thought been past. – Alive or Dead?
Ho, you Sir: Friend, hear you, Sir? Speak.
– Thus might he pass indeed; yet he revives.
– What are you, Sir?

GLOUCESTER Away, and let me die.

EDGAR Hadst thou been ought but Gozemore, Feathers,
Air
(So many Fathom down precipitating),
Thou'dst shiver'd like an Egg; but thou dost breath,
Hast heavy Substance, bleed'st not, speak'st, art Sound.
Ten Masts at each make not the Altitude
Which thou hast perpendicularly fell:
Thy Life's a Miracle. Speak yet again.

57 **dread . . . Bourn** fearful summit of this chalky boundary (white ridge). *Bourn* (spelled *borne* in the two Quartos) echoes *born* to reinforce Edgar's message that a desperate old man has been theologically reborn. See John 3:3–8, where Jesus tells Nicodemus of the need to be 'born again', and compare Ephesians 2:1–10, 4:17–24, and Colossians 3:1–16, where the Apostle Paul speaks of putting off 'the old man with his deeds' and putting 'on the new man, which is renewed in knowledge' and comforted by 'the peace of God'.

58 **a Height** on high; to the heights above.
shrill-gorg'd high-pitched (shrill-throated).

59 **look up** This phrase carries spiritual implications, as in Psalm 121:1, 'I will lift up mine eyes unto the hills, from whence cometh my help.' In effect, Edgar is saying, 'Look to Heaven and be restored to your faith.' In V.iii.309 he will utter the same words to Lear.

66 **Strangeness** echoes II.i.87–88, III.iv.20–22.

71 **wealk'd and waved** whelk'd (twisted) and curled.

73–74 **Think . . . thee** believe that the purest Gods, who glory in doing in what seems impossible, have saved you. See Luke 18:27, where Jesus says that 'the things which are impossible with men are possible with God'. And compare *Timon of Athens*, IV.iii.26–27, and *All's Well That Ends Well*, I.i.241–43 and II.i.136–52, 177–78.

80 **Bear . . . Thoughts** Arm yourself with thoughts free of despair. Edgar reminds Gloucester that he was deceiving himself (line 35) when he thought it possible to shake off the burdens of mortality 'patiently'. *Bear* echoes lines 37, 75–76. Compare I.i.174, II.ii.234–35, III.iii.12–13, III.iv.105–14, and IV.i.75–76. In the stage direction that follows this line the word *mad* is supplied here from the Quarto text. Many editions add that Lear is crowned with weeds and flowers; see IV.iv.1–6 for the basis of that hypothesis.

81–82 **The . . . thus** Gloucester's 'Sense' (mind), which is now in a 'Safer' place, will never be able to bear the knowledge that the King has finally gone mad. *Accommodate* recalls III.iv.111–13; compare IV.i.7, 20–21.

83 **touch . . . Crying** accuse me of being a weaker vessel. Compare II.ii.454–68, where Lear resolves not to weep, and IV.iii.40–49, where we learn that his 'sovereign Shame' prevents him from yielding to see Cordelia. *Touch* recalls IV.i.23–24. Here the Quarto reads *coining*.

GLOUCESTER But have I fall'n or no?
EDGAR From the dread Somnet of this Chalky Bourn.
Look up a Height: the shrill-gorg'd Lark so far
Cannot be seen or heard. Do but look up.
GLOUCESTER Alack, I have no Eyes:
Is Wretchedness depriv'd that Benefit
To end it self by Death? 'Twas yet some Comfort
When Misery could beguile the Tyrant's Rage
And frustrate his proud Will.
EDGAR Give me your Arm.
Up, so. How is't? Feel you your Legs? You stand.
GLOUCESTER Too well, too well.
EDGAR This is above all Strangeness;
Upon the Crown o'th' Cliff, what thing was that
Which parted from you?
GLOUCESTER A poor unfortunate Beggar.
EDGAR As I stood here below, me thought his Eyes
Were two full Moons; he had a thousand Noses,
Horns wealk'd and waved like the enraged Sea.
It was some Fiend: therefore thou happy Father,
Think that the clearest Gods, who make them Honours
Of Men's Impossibilities, have preserved thee.
GLOUCESTER I do remember now: henceforth I'll bear
Affliction till it do cry out it self
'Enough, enough,' and die. The thing you speak of,
I took it for a Man: often 'twould say
'The Fiend, the Fiend'; he led me to that place.
EDGAR Bear Free and Patient Thoughts.

Enter Lear mad.

– But who comes here?
The Safer Sense will ne'er accommodate
His Master thus.
LEAR No, they cannot touch me for Crying: I am
the King himself.

85 **Side-piercing** Edgar's phrasing recalls John 19:34, where one of the Roman soldiers who had crucified Jesus 'pierced his side, and forthwith came there out blood and water'.

86 **Nature's above Art** natural strength is superior to skill.

87 **Press-money** the money paid to a man who has just been pressed (conscripted, drafted) into military service.

88 **Crow-keeper** living scarecrow (inept at archery).
draw . . . Yard draw your bow back a full cloth-yard for me (the length of an arrow of a longbow).

91 **Gauntlet** steel-plated glove (thrown down to issue a challenge).

92 **Brown Bills** officers carrying brown-coloured pikes (weapons).
Bird arrow. It has hit the 'Clout' (centre of the target).

94 **Marjorum** marjoram, a herb to treat mental illness; here Edgar's password, as Lear notes when he says 'Pass' (line 95, echoing III.iv.64, III.vii.24, IV.ii.19, and IV.vi.47).

100 **I** ay (yea, as in Matthew 5:37). The Folio spelling is a reminder that 'I and No' can also be translated 'one and zero', 'something and nothing'. As Lear goes on to observe, by flattering his belief that he was an 'everything', an omnipotent 'Figure' (see I.iv.201), his daughters encouraged him in a 'Divinity' (theology) that was 'a Lie' (line 107).

105 **smelt** sniffed, detected. But since Lear is now thinking of a 'Sulphurous Pit' (line 126), *smelt* may also be intended to allude to the smelting process used to purify metals. This word recalls III.vii.91–92.
Men Lear's word keeps us aware that his daughters have assumed male prerogatives; see the notes to II.ii.206, 234.

107 **Ague-proof** armoured against fever (shaking).

108 **Trick** characteristic 'Phrase and Matter' (line 8).

109 **I** both 'I' and 'Ay'. Compare line 100.

111 **Cause** offence, case (see the notes to II.ii.375 and I.v.33). Here *Cause* hints at 'Corruption' (III.vi.55), and it foreshadows the anatomizing of female cases that follows.

112 **Die for Adultery?** In Leviticus 20:10 (alluded to by Jesus in John 8:4–5) adultery is defined as a crime punishable by death.

EDGAR O thou Side-piercing Sight!
LEAR Nature's above Art in that respect. There's your Press-money. That Fellow handles his Bow like a Crow-keeper: draw me a Clothier's Yard. Look, look, a Mouse: peace, this piece of toasted Cheese will do't. There's my Gauntlet, I'll prove it on a Giant. Bring up the Brown Bills. O well flown, Bird: i'th' Clout, i'th' Clout. Hewgh. Give the Word.
EDGAR Sweet Marjorum.
LEAR Pass.
GLOUCESTER I know that Voice.
LEAR Ha! Goneril with a White Beard? They flatter'd me like a Dog, and told me I had the White Hairs in my Beard ere the Black ones were there. To say I and No to every thing that I said: I and No too was no good Divinity. When the Rain came to wet me once, and the Wind to make me chatter, when the Thunder would not peace at my Bidding, there I found 'em, there I smelt 'em out. Go to, they are not Men o' their Words. They told me I was every thing: 'tis a Lie, I am not Ague-proof.
GLOUCESTER The Trick of that Voice I do well remember:
Is't not the King?
LEAR I, every Inch a King.
When I do stare, see how the Subject quakes.
I pardon that Man's Life. – What was thy Cause?
Adultery? Thou shalt not die. Die for Adultery?

117 **Luxury** lechery. Compare *Hamlet*, I.v.82.
pell mell with complete abandon. Lear's reference to his 'lack' of 'Soldiers' is a reminder of how far he has come since I.iv.254, when he enjoyed the services of 'a hundred Knights and Squires'.

118–19 **whose . . . Snow** whose genital 'Face' coyly pretends to be as chaste as ice even though it is sending 'Eliads' (IV.v.25) that forecast the ejaculatory 'Snow' to come. See the note to I.v.24–25. *Shake* (nod) recalls lines 35–36.

121 **The . . . to't** neither the polecat nor the lusty horse indulges.

123 **Waste** waist ('Girdle'), but with a reminder of the 'Waste of Shame' (Sonnet 129) associated with Centaurs (half-humans whose 'riotous' lower parts have horse-like features and appetites). See the note to I.iv.283. In Book III of the *Aeneid* Virgil describes Scylla as a virgin from the waist up and a sea-monster from the waist down.

125 **Fiends** (a) fiend's or (b) fiends' or (c) fiends.

126 **Sulphurous Pit** burning 'Lake of Darkness' (III.vi.8), here one Lear associates with foul, hot 'nether Crimes' (IV.ii.76, III.iv.89–90).

128 **Civet** musky perfume, from the anal glands of a civet cat.

131 **it smells of Mortality** Lear imagines that his hand is defiled by the 'Filths' (IV.ii.38) it has just 'smelt' out (line 105). For him *Mortality* (humanity) is nothing but the 'Stench' (line 127) of rank lust. Compare I.i.16.

135 **squiny** squint. Compare III.iv.122, IV.v.13, and V.iii.72.
blind Cupid the blindfolded god who prompts erotic love. According to *Much Ado About Nothing*, I.i.262–63, 'the Sign of Blind Cupid' could serve as an advertisement for 'a Brothel-house'.

139 **take . . . Report** believe this if it were merely told to me. *It is* recalls *is not* in IV.i.27.

142 **the Case of Eyes** empty eye-sockets. Gloucester's imagery links his blindness with the other instances in which genital cases (female 'eyes') have rendered male *I*'s incapable of 'Penning' (producing sons). See the note to III.iv.101. Gloucester's eyes are bloody O's (I.iv.207) without figures ('Letters', line 138) to make them function. *Suns* (here a reminder of Gloucester's sons) recalls II.ii.157–62. *Case* echoes line 111.

145 **Heavy Case** lamentable condition. Compare line 52.

No, the Wren goes to't, and the small gilded Fly
Does lecher in my Sight. Let Copulation thrive:
For Gloucester's Bastard Son was kinder to his Father
Than my Daughters got 'tween the Lawful Sheets.
To't, Luxury, pell mell, for I lack Soldiers.
Behold yond simp'ring Dame, whose Face between
Her Forks presages Snow; that minces Virtue and
Does shake the Head to hear of Pleasure's Name.
The Fitchew, nor the soiled Horse goes to't
With a more riotous Appetite. Down from
The Waste they are Centaurs, though Women all above.
But to the Girdle do the Gods inherit;
Beneath is all the Fiends. There's Hell, there's Darkness,
There is the Sulphurous Pit: burning, scalding,
Stench, Consumption. Fie, fie, fie; pah, pah.
Give me an Ounce of Civet; good Apothecary,
Sweeten my Imagination.
There's Money for thee.

GLOUCESTER O let me kiss that Hand.

LEAR Let me wipe it first: it smells of Mortality.

GLOUCESTER O ruin'd Piece of Nature: this great World
Shall so wear out to Naught. Dost thou know me?

LEAR I remember thine Eyes well enough. Dost thou
squiny at me? No, do thy Worst, blind Cupid,
I'll not love. Read thou this Challenge: mark
but the Penning of it.

GLOUCESTER Were all thy Letters Suns, I could not see.

EDGAR – I would not take this from Report. It is,
And my Heart breaks at it.

LEAR Read.

GLOUCESTER What with the Case of Eyes?

LEAR Oh ho, are you there with me? No Eyes in your
Head, nor no Money in your Purse? Your Eyes
are in a Heavy Case, your Purse in a Light;
yet you see how this World goes.

147 **feelingly** (a) deeply, intensely, and (b) by perceiving with senses other than sight. Compare IV.i.17–21.

148–49 **how . . . Eyes** both (a) the way the world stumbles blindly, and (b) the way of the world, even without eyes to view it. See the notes to I.iv.316, III.iv.162, III.vii.94, and IV.i.18–21.

151–52 **handy-dandy** choose whichever hand you please. Lear alludes to a childish game. The phrase 'change Places, and' appears only in the Folio.

155 **I** both 'ay' and 'I' (a reminder that Gloucester is now a 'Beggar'). Compare line 100 and IV.i.71.

158 **a . . . Office** even a dog has the power to rule others when he is put in a position of 'Authority'.

159 **Beadle** parish officer who whips prostitutes and other petty offenders. Lines 159–60 echo John 8:4–11, where Jesus rebukes the hypocrisy of the Pharisees who bring him 'a woman taken in adultery'. They also recall Romans 2:1, where Paul says that 'thou art inexcusable, O man, whosoever thou art, that judgest: for wherein thou judgest another, thou condemnest thyself: for thou that judgest doest the same things'.

162 **The . . . Cozener** The rich cheater (the man whose loan practices get people condemned for debt) sits in judgement on the small-time swindler. Lear's point is that it's 'handy-dandy' (purely a matter of guesswork) who the real 'Thief' is (lines 151–53).

164 **Place . . . Gold** (a) put the sinful rich in powerful places, (b) allow them to buy off judges and jurors with gold, and (c) fortify (surround) or replace sins with gold armour. Most editions emend the Folio's *Place Sins* to *Plate Sin*. This sentence and the two that follow it (that is, lines 164–69, from 'Place' to 'Lips') appear only in the Folio.

165 **hurtless breaks** breaks on impact, inflicting no pain (penalty).

166 **Arm . . . it** shield Sin in 'Tatter'd Clothes' (line 163), and it is just as vulnerable to 'Justice' as 'Unaccommodated Man' is to the 'Extremity of the Skies' (III.iv.111, 106–7).

167 **able 'em** assert 'every Inch' of my potency as a king and set them free to do as they wish. Compare lines 109–17 and II.i.85–86.

173 **Matter . . . mix'd** wisdom and irrelevance jumbled up together. Compare *Hamlet*, II.ii.212–13.

GLOUCESTER I see it feelingly.
LEAR What, art Mad? A Man may see how this World goes with no Eyes. Look with thine Ears: see how yond Justice rails upon yond simple Thief. Hark in thine Ear: change Places, and handy-dandy, which is the Justice, which is the Thief? Thou hast seen a Farmer's Dog bark at a Beggar?
GLOUCESTER I, Sir.
LEAR And the Creature run from the Cur. There thou might'st behold the Great Image of Authority: a Dog's obey'd in Office.
Thou Rascal Beadle, hold thy bloody Hand.
Why dost thou lash that Whore? Strip thy own Back:
Thou hotly lusts to use her in that kind
For which thou whip'st her. The Usurer hangs the Cozener.
Through Tatter'd Clothes great Vices do appear;
Robes and Furr'd Gowns hide all. Place Sins with Gold,
And the strong Lance of Justice hurtless breaks;
Arm it in Rags, a Pigmy's Straw does pierce it.
None does offend, none, I say, none; I'll able 'em.
Take that of me, my Friend, who have the Power
To seal th' Accuser's Lips. Get thee Glass-Eyes,
And like a scurvy Politician seem
To see the things thou dost not. Now, now, now, now.
Pull off my Boots: harder, harder, so.
EDGAR – O Matter and Impertinency mix'd;
Reason in Madness.

175 **take my Eyes** help yourself to my eyes [since I refuse to allow myself to 'weep']. Compare lines 83, 100, 142, 147.

177 **We . . . hither** we entered this world (and this 'Open Air', III.vi.1) as wailing infants.

179 **Mark** Some editions insert a stage direction at this point to indicate that Lear removes his crown and flowers. See the note to line 80.

181 **borne** born (borne into this world).

182 **this . . . Fools** human life. But Lear's phrasing also applies to 'the great Globe' (*The Tempest*, IV.i.153) in which Shakespeare's tragedy was first performed for the public. Compare II.ii.160.

This' . . . Block It is not clear whether Lear means a block of wood or a stump (to throw, to use for mounting a horse, to use as a blacksmith's anvil, to use as an executioner's block), a head (such as his own), a hat, a hat-block, a boot (see line 172), or a 'Stratagem' (plot) to block the way of his enemies.

183 **shoo** either (a) shoo away, or more likely (b) shoe (with the 'Felt' horseshoes making a sneak attack easier). Compare *The Merchant of Venice*, I.ii.44–47.

188 **No Rescue?** What, no supporters (line 192) to prevent my capture?

191 **cut** this word recalls IV.v.38.

193 **a Man of Salt** a man comprised solely of salt water (tears).

194 **ay . . . Dust** yes, and for wetting down the dry dust of autumn. This half-line occurs only in the Quarto.

195 **I . . . Bridegroom** both (a) I will die in my most trim attire, like a proud groom, and (b) I will be as courageous as a young groom. *Die* plays on the sense that relates to sexual potency. See the note to IV.ii.25. The word 'smug' appears only in the Folio.

196 **Jovial** both (a) happy, and (b) Jove-like (as in line 109). Compare *Macbeth*, III.ii.29.

199 **Life in't** still some hope; some 'Material Sap' (IV.ii.35) in this 'ruin'd Piece of Nature' (line 132). Here *and* means 'if'. In line 197 the word 'my' appears only in the Quarto text.

200 **Sa . . . sa** Lear exits with a rallying cry for hunting dogs. He is probably pursued by one or two of the Gentleman's attendants. These words appear only in the Folio.

LEAR If thou wilt weep my Fortunes, take my Eyes.
I know thee well enough, thy name is Gloucester:
Thou must be Patient. We came crying hither:
Thou know'st the first time that we smell the Air
We wawl and cry. I will preach to thee. Mark.
GLOUCESTER Alack, alack, the Day.
LEAR When we are borne, we cry that we are come
To this great Stage of Fools. This' a good Block.
It were a delicate Stratagem to shoo
A Troop of Horse with Felt: I'll put 't in Proof,
And when I have stol'n upon these Son-in-Laws,
Then kill, kill, kill, kill, kill, kill.

Enter a Gentleman [*attended*].

GENTLEMAN O here he is: lay hand upon him, Sir.
– Your most dear Daughter –
LEAR No Rescue? What, a Prisoner?
I am even the Natural Fool of Fortune. Use
Me well, you shall have Ransom. Let me have
Surgeons,
I am cut to th' Brains.
GENTLEMAN You shall have any thing.
LEAR No Seconds? All my self? Why, this would make
A Man a Man of Salt to use his Eyes
For Garden Water-pots, ay, and laying Autumn's Dust.
I will die bravely, like a smug Bridegroom. What?
I will be Jovial. Come, come, I am
A King, my Masters, know you that?
GENTLEMAN You are a Royal one, and we obey you.
LEAR Then there's Life in't. Come, and you get it,
you shall get it by running. Sa, sa, sa sa. *Exit.*

201 **meanest Wretch** basest beggar.

203–4 **Who . . . to** who ransoms a Nature that would otherwise be subjected to wholesale condemnation because of the evil Lear's two fallen Eves have brought into the world. The Gentleman's comment is another reminder of the play's implicit parallel between the degenerate Britain of *King Lear* and a human race so corrupt that God had to destroy all but a remnant of it in the Great Flood; see Genesis 6–8, and compare III.iv.37, 115–16, 187. Also see the note to I.v.16.

205 **speed** [may God] prosper. Here *ought* means 'anything'.

206 **Battell** army, battalion; one that will soon be engaged in battle.
toward in preparation.
Most . . . vulgar Most certainly, and everyone is talking of it. *Vulgar* here refers to that which is common knowledge.

208 **by your favour** if you'll pardon my asking.

209–10 **the . . . Thought** we hourly expect to see the largest portion of 'the other Army' (line 208).

211 **on special Cause** on an individual mission of great importance to her [to rescue her father]. Compare IV.iv.24–25. *Cause* echoes lines 111, 142, 145.

214 **Worser Spirit** bad angel; the part of my nature that is susceptible to despair. Gloucester's words justify the fear Edgar has expressed in lines 80–82. *Worser* recalls IV.i.1–28.

216 **what** who. Edgar's reply in line 215 probably makes Gloucester wonder if he has met this 'Sir' before their encounter on what the old man thought to be Dover Beach. 'Father' is a term of respect for an old man.

217 **tame . . . Blows** submissive to the buffetings of Fortune. Edgar's words echo IV.ii.45–48 (*tame*) and IV.ii.31, 49 (*Blows*). Compare IV.i.63–64.

218–19 **by . . . Pity** through the instruction provided by the 'Sorrows' I have witnessed and experienced am filled to the breaking point with compassion. *Art* recalls line 86 and I.i.228–29, III.ii.70–71; *feeling* echoes line 147.

220 **Biding** lodging; place to rest.

221 **Benizon** benison; benediction, blessing. Compare I.i.270, II.ii.158–59, IV.iii.45. *To boot* means 'in addition', 'as a bonus'.

GENTLEMAN A Sight most pitiful in the meanest Wretch,
Past speaking of in a King. – Thou hast a Daughter
Who redeems Nature from the general Curse
Which twain have brought her to.
EDGAR Hail, gentle Sir.
GENTLEMAN Sir, speed you. What's your Will?
EDGAR Do you hear ought,
Sir, of a Battell toward?
GENTLEMAN Most sure, and vulgar:
Every one hears that which can distinguish Sound.
EDGAR But by your favour, how near's the other Army?
GENTLEMAN Near, and on speedy Foot: the Main Descry
Stands on the Hourly Thought.
EDGAR I thank you, Sir, that's all.
GENTLEMAN Though that the Queen on special Cause is here,
Her Army is mov'd on.
EDGAR I thank you, Sir.
Exit [*Gentleman*].
GLOUCESTER You ever gentle Gods, take my Breath from me;
Let not my Worser Spirit tempt me again
To die before you please.
EDGAR Well pray you, Father.
GLOUCESTER Now good Sir, what are you?
EDGAR A most poor Man, made tame to Fortune's Blows,
Who by the Art of known and feeling Sorrows
Am pregnant to good Pity. Give me your Hand,
I'll lead you to some Biding.
GLOUCESTER Hearty Thanks;
The Bounty and the Benizon of Heaven
To boot, and boot.

Enter Steward.

223 **fram'd Flesh** conceived.

225 **Briefly . . . remember** quickly prepare your soul for death.

227 **Wherefore** why. Edgar defends his father.

228 **publish'd** 'proclaimed' (line 222). Compare IV.iv.16.

229 **Least** lest, as in line 23.

231 **Chill** I'll. Edgar has adopted the dialect of a 'Peasant'.
Zir Sir.
vurther further.
'Casion occasion (persuasion).

233 **go your Gate** proceed on your ways (take your gait to the next gate). Compare IV.i.54. The word 'and' appears only in the Folio.

234 **Volk** folk. *Pass* (proceed) recalls line 47 (where it means 'die').

234–36 **And . . . Vortnight** If I could have been swaggered out of my life [intimidated to death by a boaster], it would not have been as long as it is by a fortnight.

237 **che vor' ye** I warn you.
ice try whither I'll see whether.

239 **Costard** head.
Ballow cudgel.

241–42 **no . . . Foins** I'm not bothered by the thrusts of your sword. The stage directions following lines 242 and 248 appear only in the Quarto text.

244 **If . . . thrive** if you hope to prosper (be blessed as one who reveres Heaven's laws).

247 **Upon . . . Party** on the English side. *Party* recalls IV.v.39–40.

249 **serviceable** pliable, unprincipled. Edgar's remarks echo II.ii.13. Compare I.i.30; I.ii.1–2, 199; I.iii.10–11; I.iv.14–15, 26–46, 94–95, 101; II.i.117–18; II.ii.126–27; III.vii.71–73; IV.ii.6–7, 26–27.

254 **onely** only, solely. See the note to I.i.73.

STEWARD A proclaim'd Prize. Most happy
That Eyeless Head of thine was first fram'd Flesh
To raise my Fortunes. Thou old, unhappy Traitor,
Briefly thy self remember: the Sword is out
That must destroy thee.
GLOUCESTER Now let thy Friendly Hand
Put Strength enough to't.
STEWARD Wherefore, bold Peasant,
Dar'st thou support a publish'd Traitor? Hence,
Least that th' Infection of his Fortune take
Like hold on thee. Let go his Arm.
EDGAR Chill not let go, Zir, without vurther 'Casion.
STEWARD Let go, Slave, or thou di'st.
EDGAR Good Gentleman, go your Gate and let Poor
Volk pass. And 'chud ha' been zwagger'd out of
my Life, 'twould not ha' been zo long as 'tis
by a Vortnight. Nay, come not near th' Old Man.
Keep out, che vor' ye, or ice try whither your
Costard or my Ballow be the harder; chill be
plain with you.
STEWARD Out, Dunghill.
EDGAR Chill pick your Teeth, Zir. Come, no matter vor
your Foins. *They fight.*
STEWARD Slave, thou hast slain me. Villain, take my
Purse.
If ever thou wilt thrive, bury my Body,
And give the Letters which thou find'st about me
To Edmund, Earl of Gloucester: seek him out
Upon the English Party.
– Oh untimely Death, Death. *He dies.*
EDGAR I know thee well: a serviceable Villain,
As duteous to the Vices of thy Mistress
As Badness would desire.
GLOUCESTER What, is he dead?
EDGAR Sit you down, Father: rest you.
Let's see these Pockets: the Letters that he speaks of
May be my Friends. He's dead: I am onely sorry
He had no other Deathsman. Let us see.

256 **Leave** pardon.

258 **Their . . . Lawful** ripping open their letters is less sinful. Lines 257–58 recall I.ii.122–23; II.i.91; II.ii.466–68; III.ii.1–9, 57–59; III.iv.4–5; and IV.vi.139–40.

259 **reciprocal Vows** pledges of devotion to each other.

260–62 **if . . . offer'd** if you are not lacking in will to do it [both kill Albany and replace him in my bed], the occasion will be abundantly available to you. *Will* refers to more than one kind of male resolve, and *Will* and *Place* here carry genital implications. The Quarto prints *wit* rather than *will*. See the notes to line 111 and III.vi.55. The phrase 'cut him off' echoes Luke 12:42–48; see the note to I.v.55, and compare IV.v.38.

264 **Gaol** jail.

266 **supply . . . Labour** make my 'Place' the field for your 'Labour'. See the note to III.vi.55, and compare V.i.10–11.

268 **Servant** After this word the Quarto contains an additional phrase: 'and for you her owne for *Venter*'. Compare IV.ii.20.

269 **O . . . Will** O the undiscriminating boundlessness of female lust! *Space* recalls I.i.75, 82.

271 **Exchange** both (a) replacement [she seeks], and (b) currency (means of obtaining what she wants). Compare IV.ii.3, 17, 61.

272 **Post unsanctified** unholy ('ungracious', line 274) messenger; with *Post* as a reminder of the position Goneril is offering the post ('Will') whose 'Warmth' she seeks for her deliverance (line 265).

274–75 **strike . . . Duke** astonish the eyes of the Duke whose death is plotted.

277–79 **how . . . Sorrows?** How stubbornly upright is my worthless mind and sensibility, that I continue to withstand the agony imposed upon me by my weighty 'Griefs' (line 280).

279 **Distract** mad, schizophrenic, with my 'Thoughts' loosed (both released and lost) from the excruciating 'Knowledge' of my 'Woes'. See Lear's remarks in III.iv.6–14, 24–25.

– Leave, gentle Wax, and Manners: blame us not
To know our Enemies' Minds; we rip their Hearts,
Their Papers is more Lawful. *Reads the Letter.*
'Let our reciprocal Vows be rememb'red. You have many Opportunities to cut him off; if your Will want not, Time and Place will be fruitfully offer'd. There is nothing done. If he return the Conqueror, then I am the Prisoner, and his Bed my Gaol, from the loathed Warmth whereof deliver me, and supply the Place for your Labour.
Your (Wife, so I would say)
affectionate Servant, Goneril.'
Oh indistinguish'd Space of Woman's Will:
A Plot upon her virtuous Husband's Life,
And the Exchange my Brother. Here in the Sands
Thee I'll rake up, the Post unsanctified
Of murtherous Lechers; and in the mature Time
With this ungracious Paper strike the Sight
Of the Death-practis'd Duke. For him 'tis well
That of thy Death and Business I can tell.

GLOUCESTER The King is Mad: how Stiff is my vild
Sense,
That I stand up, and have ingenious Feeling
Of my huge Sorrows? Better I were Distract:
So should my Thoughts be sever'd from my
Griefs, *Drum afar off.*
And Woes by wrong Imaginations loose
The Knowledge of themselves.

EDGAR Give me your Hand:
Far off methinks I hear the beaten Drum.
Come, Father, I'll bestow you with a Friend.
Exeunt.

IV.vii This scene takes place at Cordelia's camp.

2 **match** equal, reciprocate [adding one 'Measure' after another]. In lines 1–3 Cordelia speaks more truly than she realizes.

3 **short** both (a) brief, and (b) inadequate, incommensurate.

6 **Nor . . . so** neither too much nor too little, but just so. Kent's phrasing recalls IV.vi.139–40; and *clipt* ('cut shorter', I.v.55, a phrase echoed in IV.vi.191, 260) is another reminder of the scars (IV.i.55) their 'Worser Hours' have inflicted on Kent, Edgar, Gloucester, and Lear. Compare IV.vi.214–15. *Clipt* ('clipp'd') can also mean 'clept' (called, named).
better Suited dressed in 'fresh Garments' (line 21, echoing IV.vi.9–10).

7 **Weeds are Memories** ragged clothes are reminders (as in I.iv.71–72).

9 **Yet . . . Intent** to have my identity disclosed at this point would be to give up my disguise sooner than I'd intended. *Made* ('created and maintained') can also mean 'enforced' (compare I.i.144); here it recalls the 'Maid' for whom Kent sacrificed his 'Freedom' (I.i.185, 184).

10–11 **My . . . meet** I'll consider it a great favour if you will not show that you know me until the time is right. Evidently Kent's identity is withheld from the Gentleman in this scene (see lines 87–91, where the Gentleman makes it clear that he is unaware that he is speaking to Kent). In all likelihood the Gentleman is not drawn into the conversation between Kent and Cordelia until she addresses him in line 12. It may be that the Gentleman enters with Cordelia and Kent but then exits momentarily to ascertain Lear's condition.

13 **Breach** fault, crack (like the 'wrong Imaginations', the 'sever'd' sensibility, desired by Gloucester in IV.vi.279–82). See the note to I.iv.186 and compare I.iv.165–74, IV.vi.191.

15 **wind up** re-tighten, restore to firm, harmonious balance. Compare the musical metaphor in IV.iii.40–42.

18 **i'th' Sway** under the rule. *Knowledge* (expertise) recalls IV.iv.8–10.

20 **in . . . Sleep** while he slept soundly. See IV.iv.11–15.

Scene 7

Enter Cordelia, Kent, and Gentleman.

CORDELIA O thou good Kent, how shall
I live and work to match thy Goodness? My Life
Will be too short, and every Measure fail me.
KENT To be acknowledg'd, Madam, is o'er-paid:
All my Reports go with the modest Truth,
Nor more, nor clipt, but so.
CORDELIA Be better Suited:
These Weeds are Memories of those Worser Hours.
I prythee put them off.
KENT Pardon, dear Madam,
Yet to be known shortens my made Intent;
My Boon I make it that you know me not
Till Time and I think meet.
CORDELIA Then be 't so, my
Good Lord. – How does the King?
GENTLEMAN Madam, sleeps still.
CORDELIA – O you kind Gods! Cure this great Breach in his
Abused Nature; th' untun'd and jarring Senses,
O wind up, of this Child-changed Father.
GENTLEMAN So please your Majesty that we may wake
The King? He hath slept long.
CORDELIA Be govern'd by
Your Knowledge, and proceed i'th' Sway of your
Own Will. Is he array'd?
GENTLEMAN Ay, Madam, in the Heaviness of Sleep
We put fresh Garments on him.

Enter Lear in a Chair carried by Servants.

Be by, good Madam, when we do awake him:

23 **I . . . Temperance** I worry about his balance and self-control. The Gentleman (identified as 'Doctor' in the Quarto) may be worried that Lear will try to flee or rebel (see IV.vi.199–200); *Temperance* recalls I.iv.315–18, I.v.50. Most editions insert the Quarto's *not* after *doubt*; that gives the Gentleman's words a more reassuring cast, with the implication that it is all right for Cordelia to 'Be by' because she need fear no ill effects either to or from her father. Here again (compare IV.i.10), the Folio reading makes good sense, so there is no reason to alter it.

24 **Music** Music was thought to be a means of harmonizing the 'jarring [discordant] Senses' of the mentally infirm. Compare *Pericles*, V.ii.65–70, where Marina employs 'Song' in an attempt to soothe her depressed father as he revives. Lines 23–24 ('CORDELIA . . . there') appear only in the Quarto.

25 **Restauration** restoration, here spelled in a French manner that befits the Queen of France and suggests play on *star* (see IV.iii.34–35) and on *stauros*, the Greek word for 'cross' (which means both 'zigzagging' and 'angry' in line 34).

27 **Repair** mend (compare I.i.95), heal. Compare IV.ii.22–24, where Goneril proffers a kiss that would 'stretch' Edmund's 'Spirits up into the Air'.

28 **Kind** Compare I.i.265, I.iv.64, II.ii.232–35, III.ii.16, III.iv.72–73. Here a father who does *not* 'bear Bags' will see at least one of his 'Children Kind' (II.ii.234–25).

29 **White Flakes** white hairs (both Lear's beard and his head).

30 **challenge Pity** demand a piteous response.

34 **Per du** lost, ruined one (from French); here, a lonely sentinel. This phrase echoes 'no Knave perdie' in II.ii.269.

35 **Helm** helmet (Lear's thin, white hair). Lines 32–35 ('To . . . Helm?') occur only in the Quarto text.

37–38 **And . . . Straw?** This sentence echoes Luke 2:7, where we read that Jesus' mother 'brought forth her firstborn son, and wrapped him in swaddling clothes, and laid him in a manger; because there was no room for them in the inn'. It also recalls Philippians 2:5–8, where the Apostle Paul says that 'Christ Jesus . . . made himself of no reputation, and took upon him the form of a servant, and . . . humbled himself, and became obedient unto death, even the death of the cross.' Meanwhile it echoes the story of the Prodigal Son in Luke 15:11–32.

I doubt of his Temperance.
CORDELIA Very well.
GENTLEMAN Please you draw near. – Louder the Music there.
CORDELIA O my dear Father, Restauration hang
Thy Medicine on my Lips, and let this Kiss
Repair those violent Harms that my two Sisters
Have in thy Reverence made.
KENT Kind and dear Princess.
CORDELIA Had you not been their Father, these White Flakes
Did challenge Pity of them. Was this a Face
To be oppos'd against the jarring Winds?
To stand against the deep dread bolted Thunder
In thc most terrible and nimble Stroke
Of quick cross Lightning? To watch, poor *Per du*, with this
Thin Helm? Mine Enemy's Dog, though he had bit me,
Should have stood that Night against my Fire.
– And wast thou fain, poor Father, to hovel thee
With Swine and Rogues forlorn in short and musty Straw?

38 **Rogues forlorn** forsaken vagabonds.
musty dank, mildewed, dirty.

40 **at once** both (a) simultaneously, and (b) immediately.

44 **Bliss** blessedness; Heaven. Compare III.iv.58, where Poor Tom says 'Bliss thy five Wits.'

44–45 **bound . . . Fire** Lear imagines himself to be suffering the punishment inflicted on Ixion (see the notes to I.iv.283, IV.vi.123). His situation also recalls that of the rich man who denied succour to the beggar Lazarus, and who then went to Hell and sought relief from the 'Soul in Bliss' who now rested in 'Abraham's bosom'. According to Luke 16:19–25, the rich man 'cried and said, Father Abraham have mercy on me, and send Lazarus, that he may dip the tip of his finger in water, and cool my tongue: for I am tormented in this flame'. Lear's belief that he has died and gone to Hell is another manifestation of the guilty despair that has led him, like Gloucester, to the 'extreme Verge' (IV.vi.26).

47 **Spirit** here an angelic one.

48 **far wide** way off target. Cordelia addresses the Gentleman, telling him that Lear is still in a hallucinatory state.

51 **abus'd** both (a) deceived, misled, and (b) mistreated. Compare lines 13–14. *Pity* recalls lines 35–36.

54–55 **assur'd . . . Condition** sure of what my true state is (whether dead or alive, dreaming or awake). See IV.iii.35.

56 **Benediction** blessing. Compare IV.vi.221. Cordelia seeks the 'Benizon' denied her in I.i.269–70. See III.ii.12.

57 **No Sir** These words appear only in the Quarto.
me This word appears only in the Folio.

58 **fond** doting, senile. Compare I.ii.53–56 and I.iv.315.

60 **deal plainly** speak directly; deal out my cards openly and honestly. Compare I.i.130, 150–51; I.iv.36–37; II.ii.89, 95–97, 107–11; IV.vi.238–39. The phrase 'not . . . less' (lines 59–60) appears only in the Folio text; so also with the second 'I am' in line 68.

63 **mainly** mostly.

64 **Skill** mental ability, memory.

Alack, alack, 'tis Wonder that thy Life
And Wits at once had not concluded all.
– He wakes, speak to him.

GENTLEMAN Madam, do you, 'tis Fittest.

CORDELIA How does my Royal Lord? How fares your Majesty?

LEAR You do me wrong to take me out o'th' Grave:
Thou art a Soul in Bliss, but I am bound
Upon a Wheel of Fire, that mine own Tears
Do scald like molten Lead.

CORDELIA Sir, do you know me?

LEAR You are a Spirit I know, where did you die?

CORDELIA – Still, still, far wide.

GENTLEMAN He's scarce awake: let him alone awhile.

LEAR Where have I been? Where am I? Fair Day Light?
I am mightily abus'd. I should ev'n die with Pity
To see another thus. I know not what to say.
I will not swear these are my Hands: let's see,
I feel this Pin prick. Would I were assur'd
Of my Condition.

CORDELIA O look upon me, Sir,
And hold your Hand in Benediction o'er me.
No Sir, you must not kneel.

LEAR Pray do not mock me.
I am a very foolish fond Old Man,
Fourscore and upward, not an Hour more
Nor less; and to deal plainly,
I fear I am not in my perfect Mind.
Me thinks I should know you, and know this Man,
Yet I am doubtful: for I am mainly ignorant
What Place this is, and all the Skill I have
Remembers not these Garments. Nor I know not
Where I did lodge last Night. Do not laugh at me,
For as I am a Man, I think this Lady
To be my Child Cordelia.

CORDELIA And so I am: I am.

LEAR Be your Tears wet? Yes faith: I pray weep not,
If you have Poison for me, I will drink it.

73 **Cause** both (a) reason to want to punish me, and (b) case against me. Compare IV.vi.111, 211. Cordelia's reply recalls I.i.93–94, where she tells her father that she loves him in accordance with her 'Bond, no more nor less'.

75 **abuse me** toy with me; deceive me. Compare line 51.

76 **Rage** both (a) fury, anger, and (b) madness. Compare IV.iv.18–20.

77–78 **And . . . lost** And yet it is risky to ask him to re-traverse (balance the accounts for) the time during which he has not been himself. This sentence occurs only in the Quarto.

79 **Desire** urge. Compare I.iv.260.

80 **Settling** calming; restoring to rational control.

S.D. **Manent** remain. From here to the end of the scene, the Quarto provides the only authoritative text.

86 **Conductor of his People** in charge of his attendants and soldiers. *Conductor* recalls IV.ii.15–16.

89 **changeable** fickle, varying from one rumour to the next.

90 **look about** be on the lookout; take precautions.
Powers armed forces.

91 **Arbiterment** arbitration; battle to decide the outcome.

92 **like** likely.

93–94 **My . . . fought** The height I reach, and the conclusion of my career [and my life] will be completely worked out, either to the good or to the bad, as today's battle determines. *Point and Period* can also refer to the punctuation at the end of a sentence. Compare V.iii.155, 204; and for a sampling of parallel instances see *Othello*, V.ii.351, *The Two Gentlemen of Verona*, II.i.116, 2 *Henry IV*, IV.v.226, *Richard III*, I.iii.237, and *Henry VIII*, I.ii.209.

I know you do not love me, for your Sisters
Have, as I do remember, done me wrong;
You have some Cause, they have not.

CORDELIA No Cause, no Cause.

LEAR Am I in France?

KENT In your own Kingdom, Sir.

LEAR Do not abuse me.

GENTLEMAN Be comforted, good Madam: the great Rage,
You see, is kill'd in him. And yet it is Danger
To make him even o'er the Time he has lost.
Desire him to go in; trouble him no more
Till further Settling.

CORDELIA Will't please your Highness walk?

LEAR You must bear with me.
Pray you now forget and forgive. I am Old
And Foolish. *Exeunt.*

Manent Kent and Gentleman.

GENTLEMAN Holds it true, Sir, that the Duke of Cornwall
Was so slain?

KENT Most certain, Sir.

GENTLEMAN Who is
Conductor of his People?

KENT As 'tis said,
The Bastard Son of Gloucester.

GENTLEMAN They say Edgar,
His banish'd Son, is with the Earl of Kent
In Germany.

KENT Report is changeable;
'Tis Time to look about. The Powers of
The Kingdom approach apace.

GENTLEMAN The Arbiterment
Is like to be Bloody: fare you well, Sir. [*Exit.*]

KENT My Point and Period will be throughly wrought,
Or Well or Ill, as this Day's Battle's fought. *Exit.*

V.i This scene takes place among the British forces near Dover.

1–3 **Know . . . Course** Go to the Duke of Albany and find out if he still plans to join us in battle against the French invaders, or whether in the meantime anything has persuaded him to alter his intentions. Edmund appears to be addressing one of his officers, who probably exits as soon as the Bastard finishes giving him his instructions.

4 **Self-reproving** self-rebuke [for making war against Cordelia and her allies].
his constant Pleasure what he firmly resolves to do.

5 **Our . . . miscarried** Goneril's messenger has suffered some mishap. Regan's verb is apt: because Oswald 'miscarried' (perverted the proper role of a servant by functioning as a corrupt carrier of treacherous messages), he has come to a well-deserved end. See the notes to IV.vi.249, 272.

6 **doubted** feared, suspected. Compare IV.vii.23.

7 **the . . . you** the good things I intend to do for you.

8 **then** therefore.

9 **honour'd** honourable, chaste.

10 **found . . . Way** sought out and discovered my brother-in-law's path and manner. *Way* recalls I.i.214; II.ii.14–15, 479; III.iv.21; III.v.3–5; III.vi.5–6; III.vii.91–92; IV.i.17–18, 53; IV.ii.1–2, 14–15, 80–84; IV.iii.19–20.

11 **Forefended** Regan means *forfended*, 'forbidden', sanctified by the vows of matrimony, but the Folio spelling also means 'previously defended'. The original meaning of *forfended* was 'staunchly defended'; Goneril has done anything but fend off a would-be invasion of the 'Place' in question. Compare IV.vi.259–62.
abuses dishonours. Compare III.vi.114, IV.vii.75. This reply and Regan's response (lines 12–13) occur only in the Quarto. So also with lines 17–18 and lines 22–27 ('Where . . . Nobly').

12 **doubtful** suspicious, fearful. Compare line 6.
conjunct conjoined (with the first syllable playing on the Latin word *cunnus*), intimately 'bosom'd' (line 13). Compare IV.v.31.

13 **as far . . . hers** to the full extent of her 'most precious Square of Sense' (I.i.75).

ACT V

Scene 1

Enter, with Drum and Colours, Edmund, Regan, Gentlemen, and Soldiers.

BASTARD Know of the Duke if his last Purpose hold,
Or whether since he is advis'd by ought
To change the Course. He's full of Alteration
And Self-reproving: bring his constant
Pleasure. [*Exit Gentleman.*]
REGAN Our Sister's Man is certainly miscarried.
BASTARD 'Tis to be doubted, Madam.
REGAN Now, sweet Lord,
You know the Goodness I intend upon you.
Tell me but truly, but then speak the Truth:
Do you not love my Sister?
BASTARD In honour'd Love.
REGAN But have you never found my Brother's Way
To the Forefended Place?
BASTARD That Thought abuses you.
REGAN I am doubtful that you have been conjunct
And bosom'd with her as far as we call hers.
BASTARD No, by mine Honour, Madam.
REGAN I never shall
Endure her: dear my Lord, be not Familiar
With her.
BASTARD Fear not. She and the Duke her Husband.

Enter, with Drum and Colours, Albany, Goneril, Soldiers.

17 **loose** both (a) lose, and (b) loose (forfeit, forgo).
Battaile both (a) battalion, army, and (b) battle.
then Goneril means 'than', but here as elsewhere (see I.i.215, I.iv.74, 136, V.iii.68) 'then' proves pertinent too.

19 **well bemet** I am pleased to see you.

21 **Rigour . . . State** extreme sternness (tyranny) of our regime.

23–26 **For . . . oppose** As for this situation, it concerns me because a foreign power invades Britain; the King is not being bold (unruly, as had been implied in I.iv.255), nor are his supporters, who, I fear, are motivated by just and serious grievances against those who oppress them. Compare II.i.55, where Edmund describes himself as 'Bold in the Quarrel's Right'. The honourable Albany is distancing himself from his fellow rulers.

28–30 **Combine . . . here** Let us set aside our internal differences ('domestic and particurlar Broils') which are not at issue here, and combine forces against France. The Folio spelling of *particurlar*, usually assumed to be a misprint, may involve puns on *party* (see the note to IV.v.40) and on *cur* (see the note to II.ii.362).

30–31 **Let's . . . Proceeding** Let us then gather our experienced officers and lay out our battle plan.

32 **presently** straight away. This line, which is probably addressed to Albany, appears only in the Quarto.

34 **Convenient** fitting. Regan's surface implication is that the strategy council should be attended only by men (a suggestion to be scorned by Goneril, who regards herself as 'the better Soldier', IV.v.3, echoing IV.ii.17–18); but Regan's underlying motive (the meaning of her 'Riddle', line 35, her indirect discourse) is to keep Goneril away from the man the widowed sister regards as more 'Convenient' (IV.v.31) for herself. It soon emerges that Goneril has a 'Riddle' for Regan too. Many editions mark line 35 as an aside; that is one way to interpret it, but not the only way. In this line 'you' appears only in the Quarto text of the play.

36 **had . . . Poor** condescended to listen to a man so beggarly as I. Edgar remains disguised as a peasant.

37 **overtake** catch up (as we walk forward).

40 **wretched** ragged, downcast in my fortunes.

GONERIL – I had rather loose the Battaile, then that Sister
Should loosen him and me.
ALBANY Our very loving Sister, well bemet.
– Sir, this I heard: the King is come to his Daughter,
With others whom the Rigour of our State
Forc'd to cry out. Where I could not be Honest
I never yet was Valiant. For this Business,
It touches us as France invades our Land;
Not bold's the King, with others whom, I fear,
Most just and heavy Causes make oppose.
BASTARD Sir, you speak Nobly.
REGAN Why is this reason'd?
GONERIL Combine together 'gainst the Enemy:
For these domestic and particurlar Broils
Are not the Question here.
ALBANY Let's then determine
With th' Ancient of War on our Proceeding.
BASTARD I shall attend you presently at your Tent.
REGAN Sister, you'll go with us?
GONERIL No.
REGAN 'Tis most Convenient, pray you go with us.
GONERIL Oh ho, I know the Riddle: I will go.
Exeunt both the Armies.

Enter Edgar.

EDGAR If ere your Grace had Speech with Man so Poor,
Hear me one Word.
ALBANY I'll overtake you, speak.
EDGAR Before you fight the Battle, ope this Letter.
If you have Victory, let the Trumpet sound
For him that brought it: wretched though I seem,

41 **Champion** knight.
prove prove true (by winning a trial by combat). Compare IV.vi.91.

42 **avouched** avowed; asserted as fact. Compare I.i.223.
miscarry fall in defeat. Compare line 5.

43–44 **Your . . . ceases** your concern with matters of this world comes to an end along with your earthly life, and all plotting [against you] ceases likewise. Compare IV.vii.93–94.

46 **let . . . cry** only allow your herald (spokesman) to call for me.

49 **draw . . . Powers** assemble your troops.

51 **By diligent Discovery** as determined by thorough reconnoitreing.

52 **greet the Time** be equal to the demands of the occasion.

55 **Adder** a small poisonous snake, here a symbol of the venomous lust that focuses on Edmund's own 'Adder'. Compare *Hamlet*, III.iv.199.

59 **hardly** only with the greatest difficulty. Edmund's word carries more than a hint of the tumescent condition that will be required of him to 'carry out' his 'Side' of the transaction if he does choose Regan.

60–61 **use / His Countenance** take advantage of the good face he gives our cause. Compare *Julius Caesar*, I.iii.157–60. *Countenance* often means 'authority', a sense that is pertinent here. It sometimes refers to a willingness to countenance (overlook, put the best face on) corruption or vice, a sense that Edmund may also have in mind, given his awareness of Albany's reservations about the policies of his allies (lines 22–26). But Edmund probably also uses the word to imply that Albany is an effeminate nothing (see the notes to II.ii.87, I.iv.201), to be used and then discarded.

66 **Shall** they shall.

66–67 **my . . . debate** my situation requires me to do everything I can to consolidate my power, not to trouble my conscience with a moral 'debate' over matters of justice, particularly when that would involve 'Mercy' to those (Lear and Cordelia) whose lives represent a threat to my own ambitions. *State* recalls IV.ii.55–58.

V.ii This scene takes place on a field near Dover. The initial stage direction indicates a battle 'Alarum' (trumpet call to arms), to be sounded from behind the theatre façade, followed by a march across the stage by Cordelia's army.

I can produce a Champion that will prove
What is avouched there. If you miscarry,
Your Business of the World hath so an End
And Machination ceases. Fortune loves you.

ALBANY Stay till I have read the Letter.

EDGAR I was forbid it:
When Time shall serve, let but the Herald cry
And I'll appear again.

ALBANY Why fare thee well.
I will o'er-look thy Paper. *Exit* [*Edgar*].

Enter Edmund.

BASTARD The Enemy's in view: draw up your Powers.
Here is the Guess of their true Strength and Forces,
By diligent Discovery; but your Haste
Is now urg'd on you.

ALBANY We will greet the Time. *Exit.*

BASTARD To both these Sisters have I sworn my Love,
Each Jealous of the other, as the Stung
Are of the Adder. Which of them shall I take?
Both? One? Or Neither? Neither can be enjoy'd
If both remain alive. To take the Widow
Exasperates, makes Mad, her Sister Goneril;
And hardly shall I carry out my Side,
Her Husband being alive. Now then we'll use
His Countenance for the Battle, which being done,
Let her who would be rid of him devise
His speedy Taking-off. As for the Mercy
Which he intends to Lear and to Cordelia,
The Battle done, and they within our Power,
Shall never see his Pardon: for my State
Stands on me to defend, not to debate. *Exit.*

Scene 2

Alarum within. Enter, with Drum and Colours, Lear, Cordelia, and Soldiers over the Stage, and Exeunt.

Enter Edgar and Gloucester.

1 **Father** a term of affection and reverence for an old man (as in IV.vi.215). Edgar has yet to reveal his identity to Gloucester.

2 **Host** sustaining shelter.

4 **Grace** Providence.

8 **rot even here** rot away here as well as anywhere else. Gloucester compares himself to an overripe, if not corrupt, fruit that has fallen from a tree (line 1). See the note to I.v.16.

9 **Ill** both (a) unhealthy, and (b) evil (because they smack of despair).

9–10 **Men . . . hither** Men must be patient (submitting their wills to Heaven) in their final hours even as in the 'crying' with which they entered this troubled world. Compare IV.vi.177–79.

11 **Ripeness . . . on** The key to everything is to allow our spirits to attain their full maturity, trusting in the Gods to take us 'hence' when our souls are ready for the passage, and for you that 'Ripeness' has now 'come on'. Most editions follow Nicholas Rowe (1709) and insert a stop before 'come on' (compare line 7); but the line appears without punctuation in all the seventeenth-century printings of the play. What Edgar says in V.iii.192–99 suggests that the old man is now ready to 'Burst smilingly'. Edmund's figure of speech relates to the fruit imagery of I.v.15–17, 47–48, and to the solar imagery of II.ii.157–62, with the implication that Gloucester is a fruit who has allowed the 'warm Sun' to mellow him completely before he receives 'Heaven's Benediction' to be harvested. Compare 'the Readiness is all' (*Hamlet*, V.ii.235), and see Matthew 7:18–20 (a passage that also relates to IV.ii.31–36). Gloucester's final speech (line 11) appears only in the Folio text; compare III.vi.87.

V.iii This scene takes place at the British camp near Dover.

1–3 **good . . . them** keep them under close watch until those of highest rank have made their judgement ('censure') known. *Censure* recalls III.v.3.

4 **Best Meaning** the purest of intentions. But Cordelia's phrase can also refer to what her life and her father's mean (signify) to those who will interpret them. Compare I.ii.193–95.

Worst Compare II.ii.440–41; IV.i.2–9, 25–28; IV.vi.135–36, 214.

EDGAR Here, Father, take the Shadow of this Tree
For your good Host. Pray that the Right may thrive.
If ever I return to you again,
I'll bring you Comfort.
GLOUCESTER Grace go with you, Sir. *Exit* [*Edgar*].
Alarum and Retreat within.

Enter Edgar.

EDGAR Away, Old Man, give me thy Hand, away:
King Lear hath lost, he and his Daughter ta'en.
Give me thy Hand: come on.
GLOUCESTER No further, Sir.
A Man may rot even here.
EDGAR What, in Ill Thoughts again? Men must endure
Their going hence even as their coming hither:
Ripeness is all come on.
GLOUCESTER And that's true too. *Exeunt.*

Scene 3

Enter, in Conquest with Drum and Colours, Edmund, Lear and Cordelia as Prisoners, Soldiers, Captain.

BASTARD Some Officers take them away: good Guard,
Until their greater Pleasures first be known
That are to censure them.
CORDELIA We are not the First
Who with Best Meaning have incurr'd the Worst.

5 **cast down** downcast, sorrowful; wagered. But Cordelia's words are also a reminder of what she said in IV.iv.24–28; she is thrown once more to Fortune's 'Chance' because she has refused to forsake the father who 'cast away' his fairest daughter at the beginning (I.i.261, 258). *Oppressed* recalls III.vi.99 and IV.iii.28.

6 **out-frown . . . Frown** outface fickle Fortune's disfavour; compare II.ii.180–81. *Frown* recalls I.iv.203–7. For previous references to Fortune, see I.i.95–96, 253–54, 282–83; I.ii.52–53, 134–46; II.i.20; II.ii.168–69, 236–37; III.ii.74–77; III.v.10–11; IV.i.2–12; IV.vi.175, 189, 217–19, 223–24, 228–30; V.i.44.

12 **and sing** this phrase appears only in the Folio; so also with the third and fourth 'no' in line 8.

13 **gilded Butterflies** gold-coated, richly arrayed court favourites. Lines 10–11 recall IV.vii.55–57. *Hear* derives from the Quarto; the Folio prints *here*.

15 **looses** Lear's primary meaning is 'loses'. But his verb can also mean (a) sets loose, releases (a sense that will soon apply to several characters), and (b) forfeits, forgoes. Compare V.i.17–18.

16 **take . . . Things** be the custodians of 'blest Secrets' (IV.iv.15).

17 **Gods Spies** intelligence officers of either (a) the gods, or (b) God. Because they do not employ the modern apostrophe to indicate possession, the early texts are often ambiguous. Compare *Love's Labour's Lost*, V.ii.422.
wear out outlive. Compare IV.vi.132–33, V.ii.11.

18 **Packs . . . Ones** factions and parties of the nobility. *Packs* recalls II.ii.262–65 and III.i.25–26.

20–21 **Upon . . . Incense** The gods themselves attend the sacrificial altar of such devoted priests as we now are. Lear's words echo Hebrews 13:16, 'To do good, & to distribute forget not: for with suche sacrifices God is pleased' (Geneva Bible).

22–23 **He . . . Foxes** Lear alludes to a device whereby hunters smoked out foxes. But his phrasing suggests the foxes to whose tails Samson attached firebrands to ignite the 'standing corn of the Philistines' (see Judges 15:3–8). It also hints at the 'brimstone and fire' (Genesis 19:24) with which God destroyed Sodom and delivered Lot and his family from its iniquity. *He that parts us* can mean both (a) the one who separates us from each other, and (b) the one who parts (fires) us from our 'Prison'. Compare I.v.54–55.

– For thee, oppressed King, I am cast down;
My self could else out-frown false Fortune's Frown.
– Shall we not see these Daughters and these Sisters?

LEAR No, no, no, no: come let's away to Prison,
We two alone will sing like Birds i'th' Cage.
When thou dost ask me Blessing, I'll kneel down
And ask of thee Forgiveness. So we'll live,
And pray, and sing, and tell Old Tales, and laugh
At gilded Butterflies, and hear poor Rogues
Talk of Court News; and we'll talk with them too –
Who looses and who wins, who's in, who's out –
And take upon's the Mystery of Things,
As if we were Gods Spies. And we'll wear out,
In a wall'd Prison, Packs and Sects of Great Ones
That ebb and flow by th' Moon.

BASTARD Take them away.

LEAR Upon such Sacrifices, my Cordelia,
The Gods themselves throw Incense. Have I caught thee?
He that parts us shall bring a Brand from Heaven
And fire us hence, like Foxes: wipe thine Eyes,
The Good Years shall devour them, Flesh and Fell,

24 **The . . . them** Compare Genesis 41, where the Pharaoh dreams that seven good ears of corn are followed, and devoured, by seven thin ears. As one of 'God's spies', Joseph interpreted the ears as years, predicting that a period of plenty would give way to a period of famine. For Lear the 'Good Years' are the devourers. Since *Good Year* was also a term for the syphilitic plague (from the French *goujères*, 'pox'), Lear's image is a warning that the gods will 'find out their Enemies now' (III.ii.51).

them . . . Fell our adversaries, flesh, skin, and all.

33 **bear Question** be subjected to 'debate' (V.i.67). As Edmund speaks line 27, he hands the Captain a written order ('this Note').

37–39 **I . . . do't** I'm above eating the provender and doing the drudgery of a horse; but if you have work that requires a real man, I'm yours. This speech occurs only in the Quarto.

40 **Strain** lineage; vein, disposition. Compare I.ii.6–22, II.ii.92–95.

42 **Opposites** opposition; opponents.

43 **require** request; here a tactful way of saying 'demand'.

44–45 **As . . . determine** as in our judgement their deservings and our security may dictate. Here *find* carries the legal sense of a court's determinations (findings). Compare V.i.63–67.

46 **miserable** wretched. See II.ii.162–63, III.vi.104–5, IV.v.11–12, IV.vi.60–64.

47 **Retention** confinement. The phrase that follows occurs only in the Quarto; so also with lines 54–59 ('At . . . Place').

48 **Charms** means of persuasion. Lines 48–49 echo IV.v.10–11.

49 **To . . . Side** to win the populace over to his side.

50 **our impress Launces** the lance-bearers we have 'levied', drafted into service (line 103). Compare IV.vi.86–87. *Eyes* recalls IV.vi.23, 142, 148–49, 175.

Ere they shall make us weep. We'll see 'em starv'd first.
Come. *Exeunt [under Guard].*

BASTARD Come hither, Captain, hark.
Take thou this Note, go follow them to Prison.
One Step I have advanc'd thee; if thou dost
As this instructs thee, thou dost make thy way
To Noble Fortunes. Know thou this, that Men
Are as the Time is: to be Tender-minded
Does not become a Sword. Thy great Employment
Will not bear Question: either say thou'lt do't
Or thrive by other Means.

CAPTAIN I'll do't, my Lord.

BASTARD About it, and write Happy when th' hast
done.
Mark, I say instantly, and carry it so
As I have set it down.

CAPTAIN I cannot draw
A Cart, nor eat dried Oats; if it be Man's Work,
I'll do't. *Exit Captain.*

Flourish. Enter Albany, Goneril, Regan, Soldiers.

ALBANY Sir, you have shew'd to day your Valiant
Strain,
And Fortune led you well. You have the Captives
Who were the Opposites of this day's Strife:
I do require them of you, so to use them
As we shall find their Merits and our Safety
May equally determine.

BASTARD Sir, I thought
It fit to send the old and miserable King
To some Retention and appointed Guard,
Whose Age had Charms in it, whose Title more,
To pluck the Common Bosom on his Side,
And turn our imprest Launces in our Eyes
Which do command them. With him I sent the Queen,
My Reason all the same, and they are Ready
To morrow or at further Space t' appear

56–57 **And . . . Sharpness** and even the causes that seem most just stir resentment in those who 'sweat and bleed' (line 55) and lose friends in the heat of battle.

58–59 **The . . . Place** Deciding what to do with 'the Queen' and her father is best left for a better time and place. *Place* echoes III.vi.55 and V.i.10–11.

59–61 **by . . . Brother** if you'll pardon my saying so, I regard you solely as one of my subjects, one whom I found it necessary to employ to win this battle, not as a permanent colleague. Compare Edmund's sentiments about Albany in V.i.60–63.

61 **as . . . him** to be decided by how I choose to recognize him.

62 **our . . . demanded** my wishes might have been consulted.

64 **Bore . . . Person** carried the authority 'invested' in him by my position ('Rights') and personal choice (lines 69, 68).

65 **Immediacy** close association, intimate relatedness.
stand up be counted (see the notes to I.i.20–21 and I.iv.201). This phrase echoes III.vii.78 and IV.vi.277–79. Compare I.i.200, 242–44; I.ii.2–3, 22; I.iv.5, 120–22; I.v.20–21; II.i.40–41, 68–69, 114; II.ii.38, 330–31, 440–41; III.ii.19; III.vi.95–97; III.vii.52; IV.iv.22–23; IV.vi.209–10; V.i.66–67.

68 **your Addition** the titles and powers you have added to the stature Nature graced (endowed) him with. Compare II.ii.20.

69 **compeers** both (a) compares, and (b) counts as a peer (equal). In context with 'by me invested' ('wrapped'), this word carries copulative innuendo; see V.i.12.

70 **husband you** (a) marry you, and (b) succeed in managing you and your affairs (see the note to *Measure for Measure*, III.i.359). Compare IV.ii.17–18. The Quarto assigns this line to Goneril.

72 **look'd but asquint** saw with impaired vision. Compare IV.vi.134–35.

74 **Stomach** seat of courage and proud defiance.

76 **the . . . thine** I yield my citadel (my self) to you. This line is unique to the Folio text; compare III.vi.87.

81 **Let . . . thine** In the Quarto the Bastard speaks here; he says, 'Let the drum strike, and prove my title good.'

82 **thee** Albany resorts to the familiar form (normally reserved for intimates or for social inferiors) to express his contempt for Edmund.

Where you shall hold your Session. At this Time
We sweat and bleed: the Friend hath lost his Friend,
And the best Quarrels in the Heat are curs'd
By those that feel their Sharpness.
The Question of Cordelia and her Father
Requires a Fitter Place.

ALBANY Sir, by your patience,
I hold you but a Subject of this War,
Not as a Brother.

REGAN That's as we list to grace him.
Methinks our Pleasure might have been demanded
Ere you had spoke so far. He led our Powers,
Bore the Commission of my Place and Person,
The which Immediacy may well stand up
And call it self your Brother.

GONERIL Not so Hot:
In his own Grace he doth exalt himself,
More then in your Addition.

REGAN In my Rights,
By me invested, he compeers the best.

ALBANY That were the most, if he should husband you.

REGAN Jesters do oft prove Prophets.

GONERIL Hola, hola,
That Eye that told you so look'd but asquint.

REGAN Lady, I am not well, else I should answer
From a full flowing Stomach. – General,
Take thou my Soldiers, Prisoners, Patrimony;
Dispose of them, of me; the Walls is thine.
Witness the World, that I create thee here
My Lord and Master.

GONERIL Mean you to enjoy him?

ALBANY The Let-alone lies not in your Good Will.

BASTARD Nor in thine, Lord.

ALBANY Half-blooded Fellow, yes.

REGAN Let the Drum strike, and prove my Title thine.

ALBANY Stay yet, hear Reason. – Edmund, I arrest thee

83 **capital** against the state's head, *caput*. Most editions substitute the Quarto's *attaint* for the Folio's *arrest* here.

84 **guilded** gilded (gold-plated, as in line 13). Albany's adjective recalls Lear's reference to the lecherous 'gilded Fly' in IV.vi.113. The Folio spelling, which plays on *guile*, is a reminder of the seductive 'Serpent' of Genesis 3:1–5, 14.

85 **bare** expose, strip bare; nullify. But *bare* can also mean 'bore' (the past tense of 'bear'). Most editors emend to *bar*.

87 **And . . . Banes** and I, as the master who husbands (oversees) her household speak against your banns (an announcement of a proposed marriage, to elicit any possible objections to it). See the note to line 70. *Banes* can also be 'poisons' (III.iv.54), an implication highly pertinent to Goneril at this moment, and 'Bans', curses (II.ii.188).

88 **make . . . me** make suit to me. Albany is announcing that he is no longer Goneril's husband in the matrimonial sense.

89 **bespoke** spoken for, reserved; already committed (to Edmund). **Interlude** farce; a brief playlet as part of a set of festivities. This speech and the first line of Albany's following speech appear only in the Folio.

93 **my Pledge** my commitment [to prove my accusation true by defeating you in a trial by combat]. Albany probably throws down a gauntlet, a steel-plated glove. Edmund replies with an 'Exchange' (line 97, echoing IV.vi.271) in kind.

94 **ere . . . Bread** before my next meal (with a strong hint of 'before I next take the Sacrament', partake of Communion bread).

100 **who not** whoever (anyone who is not yet designated).

102 **Single Virtue** individual prowess (strength, skill, and valour), because I've dismissed 'thy' army. In the Quarto, line 102 is preceded by a line in which the Bastard cries, 'A Herald ho, a Herald.' Many of today's editions insert that line; because there is some doubt about whether its omission from the Folio text is deliberate or accidental, the *Everyman* edition does not include the line. In the Folio version of this passage, with Albany being the only one to issue calls for the Herald, Edmund's adversary seems more completely in command of the situation.

106 **Come . . . Herald** Most of today's editions delay the Herald's entry (placed after line 101 in the Folio, which is followed here by the *Everyman* edition) until just prior to this line.

On capital Treason, and in thy Arrest
This guilded Serpent. – For your Claim, fair Sister,
I bare it in the Interest of my Wife:
'Tis she is sub-contracted to this Lord,
And I her Husband contradict your Banes.
If you will marry, make your Loves to me;
My Lady is bespoke.

GONERIL An Interlude.

ALBANY Thou art armed, Gloucester. Let the Trumpet sound:
If none appear to prove upon thy Person
Thy heinous, manifest, and many Treasons,
There is my Pledge. I'll make it on thy Heart
Ere I taste Bread, thou art in nothing less
Than I have here proclaim'd thee.

REGAN Sick, O Sick.

GONERIL – If not, I'll ne'er trust Medicine.

BASTARD There's my Exchange. What in the World he is
That names me Traitor, Villain-like he lies.
– Call by the Trumpet: he that dares approach,
On him, on you, who not, I will maintain
My Truth and Honour firmly.

Enter a Herald.

ALBANY – A Herald, ho.
– Trust to thy Single Virtue, for thy Soldiers,
All levied in my Name, have in my Name
Took their Discharge.

REGAN My Sickness grows upon me.

ALBANY She is not well: convey her to my Tent.
[*Exit Regan, attended.*]
– Come hither, Herald. Let the Trumpet sound,
And read out this.

108 CAPTAIN . . . **Trumpet!** This speech appears only in the Quarto; so also with Edmund's in line 115.

109 **of . . . Degree** of gentleman's rank or higher.

110 **Lists** both (a) files, membership, and (b) limits.

112 **manifold** both (a) many-fold (multiple), and (b) manifest, open. Compare II.i.48. Albany's phrasing is a reminder that 'Time shall unfold what plighted Cunning hides' (I.i.285).

S.D. **Enter . . . him** Here the phrases 'at the Third Sound' and 'a Trumpet before him' appear only in the Quarto text. Meanwhile the calls for trumpet flourishes in lines 108 and 115–17 occur only in the Folio, along with the word 'reads' in line 109.

119 **What are you?** What is your identity?

120 **Quality** degree; position in the social hierarchy.

121 **Know** know that.

122 **Treason's Tooth** the tooth of treachery. *Tooth* echoes I.iv.302–3.

Bare-gnawn chewed bare (like a dog's bone). *Bare* echoes line 85. Compare the allusions to dogs in lines 187–88, 303–4, and I.iv.87, 120; II.ii.79, 133–34, 196–97, 362; III.ii.67; III.iv.97; III.vi.61–72; III.vii.73; IV.iii.46–47; IV.vi.97–98, 153–58; IV.vii.35.

Canker-bit eaten away, either by a cankerworm (a caterpillar proverbial for devouring the heart of a rosebud before it could bloom) or by a cancer.

124 **cope** cope with; encounter.

127 **offend . . . Heart** wrong (slander) a valiant soldier's honour. Here *Noble* can refer either to rank or to integrity. In both senses Edmund is a bastard (an illegitimate pretender).

128 **do thee Justice** both (a) justify you (by putting down the challenge to your good name), and (b) be equal to the situation you face.

129 **it . . . Privilege** it is something I have a right to brandish [since I have taken my oath and been dubbed a true knight]. Compare II.ii.68–72.

132 **Despight** despite, a synonym for *maugre* (notwithstanding). This word, from the Quarto, is here substituted for *Despise*, the word to be found in the Folio printing.

thy . . . Fortune the victorious sword you carry and your fortune [which is like a sword hot off the forge].

CAPTAIN Sound, Trumpet! *A Trumpet sounds.*
HERALD *reads* 'If any Man of Quality or Degree within the Lists of the Army will maintain upon Edmund, supposed Earl of Gloucester, that he is a manifold Traitor, let him appear by the Third Sound of the Trumpet: he is bold in his Defence.'
BASTARD Sound. *1 Trumpet.*
HERALD Again. *2 Trumpet.*
Again. *3 Trumpet.*
Trumpet answers within.

Enter Edgar at the Third Sound, armed, a Trumpet before him.

ALBANY Ask him his Purposes, why he appears
Upon this Call o'th' Trumpet.
HERALD What are you?
Your Name, your Quality, and why you answer
This present Summons?
EDGAR Know my Name is lost
By Treason's Tooth: Bare-gnawn and Canker-bit.
Yet am I Noble as the Adversary
I come to cope.
ALBANY Which is that Adversary?
EDGAR What's he that speaks for Edmund, Earl of Gloucester?
BASTARD Himself: what sayst thou to him?
EDGAR Draw thy Sword,
That if my Speech offend a Noble Heart
Thy Arm may do thee Justice. Here is mine:
Behold it is my Privilege, the Privilege of
Mine Honours, my Oath, and my Profession. I
Protest, maugre thy Strength, Place, Youth, and Eminence,
Despight thy Victor-sword and Fire-new Fortune,
Thy Valour and thy Heart, thou art a Traitor:

134 **False** both (a) dishonest, and (b) unfaithful.

135 **Conspirant** conspiring, plotting. The Folio's *illustirous* may be a misprint; but it may also be an authorial variation on the usual spelling for purposes of euphony.

136 **extremest Upward** topmost point. *Extremest* recalls IV.iii.17.

137 **Descent** ground (here suggesting the nether world).

138 **Toad-spotted** Toads were thought to be cunning, venomous, and lecherous, and *spotted* was a biblical term for 'sinful'; see Jeremiah 13:23 ('Can the Ethiopian change his skin, or the leopard his spots? then may ye also do good, that are accustomed to evil'), Hebrews 9:14, and 2 Peter 3:14. Compare *Othello*, IV.ii.59–60 and III.iii.424.

143 **say** report. In the Quarto, which lacks the brackets supplied by the Folio, *say* appears to function as an aphetic form of *assay* ('proof'), with the meaning 'touch, trace'. Most of today's editions (even those that claim to be based on a Shakespeare-revised Folio version of the play) retain the Quarto reading. Since the Folio reading is not manifestly erroneous, however, there is no reason to alter it. Compare IV.vii.23.

144 **safe and nicely** if I were to adhere prudently and fastidiously to the rules of knightly combat (as explained in lines 152–53). Line 144 appears only in the Folio text.

148 **Which . . . bruise** which, because they ['these Treasons', line 146, which I have thrown back to you] are as yet only glancing blows that do you little harm. Compare IV.vi.165. *Scarely* is another Folio word that may be a compositorial error; but it may also be a sardonic pun, with Edmund satirizing his adversary and implying that his 'Lie' can 'bruise' only to the extent that it sounds 'scarely'.

149 **give . . . Way** immediately open up a pathway for them [to your heart]. *Way* recalls V.i.10.

151 **Save him** attend the fallen Edmund before he expires.
Practice a piece of treachery. Compare II.ii.296–98.

152 **answer** acknowledge and respond to. See line 73 and IV.ii.13–14.

154 **cozen'd** tricked, cheated; 'beguil'd' (see line 84). Edmund will soon learn that he was 'cousined' (defeated by a blood relative, whom the Bastard himself had rendered 'Unknown'). Compare IV.vi.162.

False to thy Gods, thy Brother, and thy Father,
Conspirant 'gainst this high illustirous Prince,
And from th' extremest Upward of thy Head
To the Descent and Dust below thy Foot,
A most Toad-spotted Traitor. Say thou no,
This Sword, this Arm, and my best Spirits are bent
To prove upon thy Heart, whereto I speak,
Thou liest.

BASTARD In Wisdom I should ask thy Name,
But since thy Outside looks so Fair and Warlike,
And that thy Tongue (some say) of Breeding breathes,
What safe and nicely I might well delay
By Rule of Knighthood, I disdain and spurn:
Back do I toss these Treasons to thy Head,
With the Hell-hated Lie o'er-whelm thy Heart,
Which, for they yet glance by and scarely bruise,
This Sword of mine shall give them Instant Way
Where they shall rest for ever. – Trumpets,
speak. *Alarums. Fights.*

ALBANY Save him, save him.

GONERIL This is Practice, Gloucester:
By th' Law of War thou wast not bound to answer
An Unknown Opposite. Thou art not vanquish'd,
But cozen'd and beguil'd.

ALBANY Shut your Mouth, Dame,

155 **stop** both (a) stuff, block, and (b) silence. Albany may also be punning on 'full stop' (period, the terminal punctuation the 'Paper' both contains and embodies); see *1 Henry IV*, V.iv.80–85, and compare IV.vii.93–94. The command 'Hold, Sir', appears only in the Folio; so also with 'O' in line 159.

157 **Tearing** either (a) ripping the paper to shreds, or (b) weeping in feigned innocence like a 'weaker vessel'.

159 **arraign me** bring me to trial. Compare III.vi.22, 47. The *Exit* following this speech appears in both the Quarto and the Folio; most editors move it to line 160, based on the assumption that Albany's next question is directed to Goneril, to whom 'Ask me not what I know' is assigned in the Quarto.

161 **desperate** frenzied; suicidal. Compare II.ii.486.

166 **exchange Charity** forgive each other (as in *Hamlet*, V.ii.341). *Exchange* echoes line 97.

170 **our Pleasant Vices** our 'good Sport' (I.i.23). Edgar's words recall Jeremiah 2:19, 'Thine own wickedness shall correct thee.'

172–73 **The . . . Eyes** The place in which he committed the 'Act of Darkness' (III.iv.89–90) that made you resulted in his blindness. *Place* is both genital and topographical; compare lines 58–59 and see V.i.10–11. *Eyes* (which plays on *I*'s, as in IV.vi.142) recalls both (a) the spiritual and mental dullness that rendered Gloucester susceptible to being misled by Edmund, and (b) the physical blindness that made it necessary for the old man to be led to Dover by Edgar. See the notes to I.iv.316; IV.i.20–21; IV.vi.23, 148–49.

174 **The . . . here** Edmund applies Edgar's moral about Gloucester to himself. *Wheel* recalls IV.vii.44–45; see the references to Fortune in lines 6, 29–30, 40–41, 132, 164–65.

175 **Gate** gait; manner. Compare III.vii.91, IV.i.54, IV.vi.233–34.

180 **Miseries** sufferings. See line 46.

181 **List** listen to.

Or with this Paper shall I stop it. – Hold, Sir,
Thou Worse than any Name, read thine own Evil.
– No Tearing, Lady: I perceive you know it.

GONERIL Say if I do, the Laws are mine, not thine.
Who can arraign me for't? *Exit.*

ALBANY Most Monstrous! O,
Know'st thou this Paper?

BASTARD Ask me not what I know.

ALBANY – Go after her, she's desperate; govern her.
[*Exit at least one Attendant.*]

BASTARD What you have charg'd me with, that have I done,
And much, much more; the Time will bring it out.
'Tis past, and so am I; but what art thou
That hast this Fortune on me? If thou'rt Noble,
I do forgive thee.

EDGAR Let's exchange Charity.
I am no less in Blood than thou art, Edmund;
If more, the more th' hast wrong'd me.
My Name is Edgar, and thy Father's Son.
The Gods are Just, and of our Pleasant Vices
Make Instruments to plague us.
The Dark and Vicious Place where thee he got
Cost him his Eyes.

BASTARD Th' hast spoken Right, 'tis True:
The Wheel is come full Circle, I am here.

ALBANY Me thought thy very Gate did prophesy
A Royal Nobleness: I must embrace thee.
Let Sorrow split my Heart if ever I
Did hate thee or thy Father.

EDGAR Worthy Prince,
I know't.

ALBANY Where have you hid your self?
How have you known the Miseries of your Father?

EDGAR By nursing them, my Lord. List a Brief Tale,
And when 'tis told, O that my Heart would burst.
The Bloody Proclamation to escape
That follow'd me so near (O our Lives' Sweetness,

185 **That . . . die** that we would suffer hourly death agonies (fears). Compare IV.i.10–12, and *Julius Caesar*, II.ii.32–37 and III.i.104–6.

186 **shift** change; with wordplay on *shift* as a word for 'clothing'.

188 **Habit** costume, apparel; 'Semblance'.

189 **Rings** eye-sockets, here compared to ring-settings.

192 **Fault** sin. Compare I.iv.280–81, III.iv.69–70.

193 **arm'd** prepared for single combat. See the note to V.ii.11.

195 **ask'd his Blessing** Compare IV.vii.55–56, where Cordelia does likewise.

196 **Pilgrimage** travels. This word carries spiritual overtones, with reference to life on earth as a trying journey in preparation for the heavenly city that awaits the elect who stay the course. In Hebrews 11:13–16 we read that the pre-Christian patriarchs 'all died in faith, not having received the promises but having seen them afar off, and were persuaded of them, and embraced them, and confessed that they were strangers and pilgrims on the earth'.
flaw'd cracked. Compare II.ii.467, IV.vii.13–14.

197 **support** hold up under, bear (compare I.iv.277–80, IV.vi.80).

199 **smilingly** inclined towards 'Joy', with faith and hope intact. See the note to II.i.92.

201 **as** as if. So also in line 213.

203 **dissolve** become 'a Man of Salt' (IV.vi.192–94). Compare IV.iv.18–20.

204 **a Period** a full stop (see line 155); a conclusion. This speech and the two that follow ('This . . . Slave', lines 204–21) appear in the Quarto only.

207 **top Extremity** make the liquid boil over the top. See IV.vi.25–26.

207–8 **big / In Clamour** pregnant with grief. Compare IV.iii.33 and IV.vi.218–19.

210 **abhorr'd** abhorrent; to be avoided.

216 **puissant** powerful, overwhelming (as in line 147).

That we the Pain of Death would hourly die
Rather than die at once) taught me to shift
Into a Madman's Rags, t' assume a Semblance
That very Dogs disdain'd. And in this Habit
Met I my Father with his bleeding Rings,
Their precious Stones new lost; became his Guide,
Led him, begg'd for him, sav'd him from Despair.
Never (O Fault) reveal'd my self unto him
Until some Half Hour past, when I was arm'd;
Not sure, though hoping of this Good Success,
I ask'd his Blessing, and from first to last
Told him our Pilgrimage. But his flaw'd Heart
(Alack too weak the Conflict to support)
'Twixt two Extremes of Passion, Joy and Grief,
Burst smilingly.

BASTARD This Speech of yours hath mov'd me,
And shall perchance do good; but speak you on,
You look as you had something more to say.

ALBANY If there be more, more Woeful, hold it in,
For I am almost ready to dissolve,
Hearing of this.

EDGAR This would have seem'd a Period
To such as love not Sorrow; but another
To amplify too much would make much more,
And top Extremity. Whilst I was big
In Clamour, came there in a Man
Who, having seen me in my Worst Estate,
Shunn'd my abhorr'd Society; but then finding
Who 'twas that so endur'd, with his strong Arms
He fasten'd on my Neck and bellow'd out
As he'd burst Heaven, threw me on my Father,
Told the most piteous Tale of Lear and him
That ever Ear receiv'd, which in Recounting
His Grief grew puissant and the Strings of Life
Began to crack twice; then the Trumpets sounded,
And there I left him traunc'd.

ALBANY But who was this?

EDGAR Kent, Sir, the banish'd Kent, who in Disguise

220–21 **Service . . . Slave** the most demeaning service imaginable, worse than would be fitting for the lowest slave. See the note to IV.vi.249.

S.D. **with . . . Knife** This phrase occurs only in the Quarto text.

222 **O help** These words appear only in the Folio. The Folio also adds two speech headings (ALBANY, EDGAR, lines 222–23) in order to assign 'Speak, Man' to Albany rather than Edgar, who has an uninterrupted speech in the Quarto version of the play.

229 **marry . . . Instant** consummate their perversion of matrimonial bonds at the same moment. *Contracted* means that Edmund had pledged himself to marry; compare line 86. *Instant* carries the tumescent and copulative implications noted at II.i.114. It recalls lines 149–50 and I.ii.182–84; I.iv.259–60; II.i.128–29; II.ii.90–92. Compare lines 63–66.

231–32 **This . . . Pity** This proof that the 'Gods are Just' (line 170), which makes us shiver with fear [lest we should find ourselves in such a plight at some future time], leaves our sense of compassion unmoved. Albany's point is that Goneril and Regan have turned themselves into such monsters (line 159) that their fates are unable to prompt the human sympathy normal to a tragedy. *Touches* recalls II.ii.459, where Lear bids the gods to touch him with 'Noble Anger'; compare IV.i.23, IV.vi.83, and V.i.24.

232 **he** Kent, whom Albany has just noticed.

233 **Complement** welcome; complete display of courtesy (I.i.308–9).

234 **Which . . . urges** which even the most rudimentary etiquette would bid us to show.

235 **aye** for ever. As Edgar has noted in lines 212–18, Kent's heart is about to 'crack' in the way that Gloucester's has just done.

236 **Great** both (a) all-important, and (b) pregnant, ready to 'burst' (see lines 198–99, 207–8, and IV.vi.36, 218–19).

238 **Object** sight (the bodies of Goneril and Regan). This word echoes I.i.217, and it thereby reminds us that Lear and his 'best Object' are as yet unaccounted for. Compare II.ii.185. In the Quarto, it is here that we read '*The bodies of Goneril and Regan are brought in.*' Compare the Folio stage direction following line 230.

239 **Yet . . . belov'd** Edmund's words suggest a perverse, and somewhat pathetic, sense of satisfaction.

Follow'd his Enemy King and did him Service
Improper for a Slave.

Enter a Gentleman with a Bloody Knife.

GENTLEMAN Help, help: O help.
EDGAR What kind of Help?
ALBANY Speak, Man.
EDGAR What means this Bloody Knife?
GENTLEMAN 'Tis hot, it smokes:
It came even from the Heart of – O she's dead!
ALBANY Who dead? Speak, Man.
GENTLEMAN Your Lady, Sir, your Lady. And her Sister
By her is poison'd: she confesses it.
BASTARD I was contracted to them both: all three
Now marry in an Instant.
EDGAR Here comes Kent.

Enter Kent.

ALBANY Produce the Bodies, be they alive or dead.
Goneril and Regan's Bodies brought out.
– This Judgement of the Heavens, that makes us tremble,
Touches us not with Pity. O is this he?
The Time will not allow the Complement
Which very Manners urges.
KENT I am come
To bid my King and Master aye good night.
Is he not here?
ALBANY Great thing of us forgot.
– Speak, Edmund, where's the King? And where's Cordelia?
– Seest thou this Object, Kent?
KENT Alack, why thus?
BASTARD Yet Edmund was belov'd:

243 **Despight** in spite. *Nature* recalls I.i.1–2.

244 **brief** hasty.
Writ death warrant; writ of execution.

247 **Office** designated responsibility.

247–48 **thy . . . Reprieve** a symbol of your own office to assure the executioner that the countermand carries your authority. Some editions follow the example of Edmond Malone's text (1790) and indicate that it is Edgar who rushes to the Castle; accordingly they reassign line 249 to Albany, to whom it is assigned in the Quarto.

252 **To . . . Despair** Ironically, Edmund's pretext for the execution of Cordelia has just turned out to be the real reason for Goneril's death (lines 161, 240–41). In Christian theology despair (hopelessness, a conviction that redemption is impossible) is the unforgivable sin; hence Edgar's efforts to 'cure' Gloucester of his temptation to surrender to melancholy, his apparently successful campaign to instil in the old man the kind of patience that 'bears it out even to the edge of Doom' (Sonnet 116, line 12). See IV.vi.33–34, 80; V.ii.9–11; and V.iii.190–91.

253 **for-did** killed; did in; did away with. 'For' is an Anglo-Saxon prefix that means 'intensely' or 'completely'.

254 **Bear . . . awhile** In all likelihood Edmund is carried offstage in accordance with Albany's order; after line 291 a Messenger enters with word that the Bastard is dead.

255 **Men of Stones** men without feelings (an echo of III.vi.76–77). Compare *Julius Caesar*, I.i.41, III.ii.148, 226–27, and *Macbeth*, II.i.57. Behind Lear's image is Luke 19:37–40, where Jesus tells the Pharisees that if his disciples 'should hold their peace, the stones would immediately cry out'. The Fool echoes this New Testament passage in I.iv.198. So does the Duke in *Measure for Measure*, V.i.427–29. Lear says 'Howl' four times in the Quarto.

257 **Heaven's . . . crack** the crystalline sphere above the earth should shatter and end the world. Compare lines 177–78, 182, 196–99, 212–17, and IV.vi.257–58.

260 **Stone** reflecting surface. *Taint* recalls I.i.224.

261 **promis'd End** Doomsday. Compare I.i.185, 265–66.

262 **Image** foreshadowing. Compare I.ii.196–97, II.ii.273, IV.vi.156–58.
Fall and cease either (a) let us kneel down in grief and reverent silence, or (b) let 'Heaven's Vault' fall now.

The one the other poison'd for my sake,
And after slew her self.

ALBANY Even so: cover their Faces.

BASTARD I pant for Life: some Good I mean to do
Despight of mine own Nature. Quickly send
(Be brief in it) to th' Castle: for my Writ
Is on the Life of Lear, and on Cordelia.
Nay, send in time.

ALBANY Run, run, O run.

EDGAR To who,
My Lord? Who has the Office? Send thy Token
Of Reprieve.

BASTARD Well thought on: take my Sword,
Give it the Captain.

EDGAR Haste thee for thy Life.

[*Exit Gentleman.*]

BASTARD He hath Commission from thy Wife and me
To hang Cordelia in the Prison, and
To lay the Blame upon her own Despair,
That she for-did her self.

ALBANY The Gods defend her,
Bear him hence awhile.

Enter Lear with Cordelia in his Arms.

LEAR Howl, howl, howl: O you are Men of Stones.
Had I your Tongues and Eyes, I'd use them so
That Heaven's Vault should crack; she's gone for ever.
I know when one is dead, and when one lives:
She's dead as Earth. Lend me a Looking-glass;
If that her Breath will mist or stain the Stone,
Why then she lives.

KENT Is this the promis'd End?

EDGAR Or Image of that Horror.

ALBANY Fall and cease.

263 **This . . . lives** either (a) this feather moves, therefore she continues to breathe, or (b) if this feather moves, she remains alive.

264 **Chance** happening. See the note to line 5, and compare III.vii.77.
redeem ransom, purchase back. Compare IV.vi.202–4.

269 **stay** both (a) wait, and (b) stay here. Compare line 82 and I.iv.8, II.ii.266–67.

270–71 **Her . . . Woman** Lear is explaining why it is difficult to hear Cordelia. His remarks echo I.i.61–63, 77–79, 88–96, 154–56. Compare lines 303–4.

274 **biting Faulchion** sharp-toothed light sword.

276 **And . . . me** and because I am now spoiled (beyond 'Ripeness', V.ii.11), these challenges I once handled with ease make a 'spoil' (battle victim) of me. *Crosses* recalls IV.vii.25, 32–34; see the note to I.iv.44–45.

277 **best** This word recalls lines 4, 69, 139; compare IV.i.49.

278–79 **If . . . behold** If fickle Fortune wants to boast of two men she flattered with favour and then cast off with cruel hatred, we each see one before us. See the note to line 174. Lear's half of line 279 appears only in the Folio.

279 **This . . . Sight** either (a) This is a dismal 'Object' (line 238, with Lear referring to the daughter in his arms), or (b) what I now look at I can see only dully (Kent, whom Lear is viewing through tear-filled eyes that are fading rapidly). Compare lines 172–73.

281 **Caius** evidently the name Kent has assumed in disguise.

282 **strike** both (a) strike back, and (b) deliver a telling blow. The word 'you' appears only in the Folio.

283 **rotten** decayed. Compare line 276 and V.ii.7–11.

284 **see that straight** either (a) look into that matter right away, or (b) see that (see whether that is true) by looking with unimpaired, direct vision, not asquint (compare IV.vi.22–24, 135–49; IV.vii.60–65; V.iii.72). *Man* recalls I.iv.10–46.

285 **your . . . Decay** the beginning of your differences (disputes) with your daughters, the differences (alterations) those quarrels brought about in you, and the erosion of your mind and body that ensued. *Difference* recalls I.iv.96–97, 146–47; II.i.123–25; II.ii.49; IV.ii.26.

LEAR This Feather stirs, she lives: if it be so,
It is a Chance which does redeem all Sorrows
That ever I have felt.
KENT O my good Master.
LEAR Prythee away.
EDGAR 'Tis Noble Kent, your Friend.
LEAR A Plague upon you Murderers, Traitors all;
I might have sav'd her, now she's gone for ever.
– Cordelia, Cordelia, stay a little. Ha:
What is't thou sayst? – Her Voice was ever Soft,
Gentle, and Low, an excellent thing in Woman.
– I kill'd the Slave that was a hanging thee.
GENTLEMAN 'Tis true, my Lords, he did.
LEAR Did I not, Fellow?
I have seen the Day, with my good biting Faulchion
I would have made him skip. I am Old now,
And these same Crosses spoil me. – Who are you?
Mine Eyes are not o'th' best, I'll tell you straight.
KENT If Fortune brag of two she lov'd and hated,
One of them we behold.
LEAR This is a dull Sight,
Are you not Kent?
KENT The same: your Servant Kent,
Where is your Servant Caius?
LEAR He's a good Fellow,
I can tell you that, he'll strike and quickly too;
He's dead and rotten.
KENT No, my good Lord,
I am the very Man.
LEAR I'll see that straight.
KENT That from your first of Difference and Decay

286 **follow'd . . . Steps** (a) trailed after you no matter where you went, and (b) remained your servant through it all. Compare lines 219–21 and IV.v.39–40. See I.iv.44–45.

288 **fore-done themselves** 'for-done' (killed) themselves (see the note to line 253) just before (the meaning of *fore* here) you entered.

290 **vain** in vain; useless ('bootless', line 291).

294 **this great Decay** Albany refers to what remains of Lear and his mind and body (lines 285–86). The word 'great' appears only in the Folio.

297 **our absolute Power** my authority in its entirety. Albany is healing the breach with which the play began (compare line 174).

298 **Boot** additional rewards. Compare line 291 and IV.vi.172, 221–22. *Addition* recalls line 68.

299–300 **All . . . Virtue** everyone who has been faithful shall be rewarded. *Taste* recalls II.ii.471–72; *Wages* echoes I.i.158–59, II.ii.391–92.

301 **Cup . . . Deservings** bitterness they've earned. Compare Matthew 27:39.

302 **my poor Fool** probably (but not definitely) a term of endearment for Cordelia. If the same actor who played her role also played the Fool (who disappears after III.vi.87), Lear's line carries an additional theatrical implication. Lear says 'no' only twice in the Quarto.

306 **Pray . . . Button** It is not clear whether Lear refers to a button of his own (perhaps because he finds himself choking, as in II.ii.242) or to a button of Cordelia's (to allow her 'Breath' free passage), but the words he speaks immediately after this final divestiture suggest a sudden shift in mood. One possibility is that, like Gloucester, Lear bursts 'smilingly' (line 199), believing Cordelia to be alive. If so, he is granted a dying vision – even if in mortal terms it is a delusion – 'which does redeem all Sorrows' (line 264) and saves him from despair. Compare III.iv.113–14. The Quarto follows line 306 with 'O, o, o, o.' It does not contain the Folio lines marked here as lines 307–8 ('Do . . . there'). In the Quarto Lear's last words are the ones the Folio reassigns to Kent in line 309. The word 'you' appears only in the Folio.

Have follow'd your Sad Steps.

LEAR You're welcome hither.

KENT Nor no Man else. All's Cheerless, Dark, and Deadly:
Your eldest Daughters have fore-done themselves
And desperately are dead.

LEAR Ay, so I think.

ALBANY He knows not what he says, and vain is it
That we present us to him.

EDGAR Very bootless.

Enter a Messenger.

MESSENGER Edmund is dead, my Lord.

ALBANY That's but a Trifle here.
You Lords and Noble Friends, know our Intent:
What Comfort to this great Decay may come
Shall be appli'd. For us, we will resign,
During the Life of this old Majesty,
To him our absolute Power, you to your Rights,
With Boot and such Addition as your Honours
Have more than merited. All Friends shall taste
The Wages of their Virtue, and all Foes
The Cup of their Deservings. O see, see.

LEAR And my poor Fool is hang'd. No, no, no Life?
– Why should a Dog, a Horse, a Rat have Life,
And thou no Breath at all? Thou'lt come no more,
Never, never, never, never, never.
– Pray you undo this Button. Thank you, Sir.
Do you see this? Look on her? Look her Lips,
Look there, look there. *He dies.*

EDGAR He faints. – My Lord, my Lord.

KENT Break, Heart, I prythee break.

EDGAR Look up, my Lord.

KENT Vex not his Ghost. O let him pass: he hates him

311 **Wrack** both (a) rack (an instrument of torture), and (b) wreck, 'great Decay' (line 294), 'gor'd State' (line 317). The idea of a *Wrack* (shipwreck) anticipates Kent's reference to the 'journey' he must 'shortly' undertake (line 318). *Tough* recalls II.ii.380.

312 **Stretch him out** (a) torment his body, and (b) extend his life. *State* recalls V.i.66–67.

319 **My . . . me** the Lord I serve has summoned me. Kent's words can apply equally to (a) the King who has just exited 'this tough World', and (b) the King whom Lear now serves if in fact he has been fired hence with a 'Brand from Heaven' (lines 22–23). See the note to I.iv.44–45.

320 **Waight** weight; heavy sorrow; pressing torture. The Folio spelling hints at wordplay on *wait*. Compare I.i.5–7.

321 **Speak . . . feel** give honest expression to our griefs, fears, doubts, and other emotions.

what . . . say what is dictated by the decorum of our prescribed roles. Although Edgar is not the designated ruler of 'this Realm', the one whose new duty is to 'sustain' a 'State' that has been cut to the quick, he is the survivor best suited to speak for the 'Young' who must heal its wounds and direct its course in the future. In the Quarto, Albany is the character to whom the concluding speech is assigned.

322 **borne** both (a) carried, and (b) given birth to (with wordplay on *Young* as a term that can mean 'offspring' as well as 'youthful', as in I.iv.230), bequeathing to posterity a 'Sad Time' that is the product of all the play's broken hearts and bosoms (see the note to line 257). Fittingly, a tragedy that began with ribald jests about conception concludes with a sombre reference to a delivery of sorts – here one that leaves the survivors feeling anything but purged of the 'Waight' (including the corpses of Edmund, Lear, and the King's three daughters) that they in turn will bear as they leave 'this great Stage' (IV.vi.182) and bequeath it to their own heirs. For previous references to bearing, see I.i.173–74; II.ii.234–35; III.iii.12–13; III.vi.104–5; IV.i.75–76; IV.vi.37–40, 75–77, 80, 181–82

S.D. **Dead March** funeral procession, probably accompanied by solemn music.

That would upon the Wrack of this tough World
Stretch him out longer.

EDGAR He is gone indeed.

KENT The Wonder is, he hath endur'd so long;
He but usurp'd his Life.

ALBANY Bear them from hence:
Our present Business is general Woe.
– Friends of my Soul, you twain,
Rule in this Realm, and the gor'd State sustain.

KENT I have a Journey, Sir, shortly to go;
My Master calls me, I must not say no.

EDGAR The Waight of this Sad Time we must obey,
Speak what we feel, not what we ought to say.
The Oldest hath borne most; we that are Young
Shall never see so much, nor live so long.

Exeunt with a Dead March.

FINIS

PERSPECTIVES ON *King Lear*

More, perhaps, than any other Shakespearean work, *King Lear* disturbed the sensibilities of post-Restoration readers and theatre audiences. One difficulty was the grotesque foolery the dramatist had introduced into a tragic action. A more serious concern was the play's denouement: the death of the innocent Cordelia seemed to violate the neoclassical requirement that a drama should provide 'poetic justice', a distribution of rewards and punishments that evinced an orderly cosmos in the hands of a righteous God.

In 1681, in the most notorious of the adaptations Shakespeare's works were to undergo between 1660 and 1800, Nahum Tate addressed the problem by transforming *King Lear* into a tragicomedy. Tate eliminated two of the play's characters, the Fool and the King of France. He turned Edgar and Cordelia into a romantic couple. And at the end of the drama he sent a restored Lear off to peaceful retirement with Kent and Gloucester while the King's youngest daughter, whom her father had saved from death by slaying her would-be executioners, reigned with her new husband over their portion of a reunited Britain.

For a hundred and fifty years Tate's *History of King Lear* commanded the English stage – and not surprisingly, given the way most eighteenth-century critics felt about the tragedy Shakespeare had bequeathed to posterity. According to Joseph Warton, writing in *The Adventurer* (London, 1754), *King Lear*

> is chargeable with considerable imperfections. The plot of Edmund against his brother, which distracts the attention, and destroys the unity of the fable; the cruel and horrid extinction of Glo'ster's eyes, which ought not to be exhibited on the stage; the utter improbability of Gloster's imagining, though blind, that he had leaped down Dover cliff; and some passages that are too turgid and full of strained metaphors, are faults which the warmest admirers of Shakespeare will find it difficult to excuse. I know not, also, whether the cruelty of the

> daughters is not painted with circumstances too savage and unnatural . . .

A contemporary of Warton's, Charlotte Lennox (*Shakespear Illustrated*, London, 1754), was troubled by 'the absurd Trial Scene' that opens *King Lear*, in part because

> The Lover who is made to Marry the disinherited Cordelia on account of her Virtue, is very injudiciously contrived to be Absent when she gave so glorious a Testimony of it, and is touch'd by a cold Justification of her Fame, and that from herself, when he might have been charm'd with a shining Instance of her Greatness of Soul, and inviolable Regard to Truth.
>
> So unartfully has the Poet managed this Incident, that Cordelia's noble Disinterestedness is apparent to all but him who was to be the most influenced by it. In the Eyes of her Lover she is debased, not exalted; reduced to the abject Necessity of defending her own Character, and seeking rather to free herself from the Suspicion of Guilt, than modestly enjoying the conscious Sense of Superior Virtue.

A few years later, in the 'Notes on the Plays' that accompanied his edition of Shakespeare's works (London, 1765), Samuel Johnson pointed to a similar improbability in the playwright's portrayal of Oswald.

> I know not well why Shakespeare gives the Steward, who is a mere factor of wickedness, so much fidelity. He now refuses the letter [IV.v.15–40], and afterwards, when he is dying [IV.vi.243–47], thinks only how it may be safely delivered.

Johnson went on to confess that he was troubled by such things as

> the extrusion of Gloucester's eyes, which seems an act too horrid to be endured in dramatick exhibition, and such as must always compel the mind to relieve its distress by incredulity. Yet let it be remembered that our authour well knew what would please the audience for which he wrote.
>
> The injury done by Edmund to the simplicity of the action is abundantly recompensed by the addition of variety, by the art with which he is made to co-operate with the chief design, and the opportunity which he gives the poet of combining perfidy with perfidy, and connecting the wicked son with the wicked daughters, to impress this important moral, that villainy is never at a stop, that crimes lead to crimes, and at last terminate in ruin.
>
> But though this moral be incidentally enforced, Shakespeare has suffered the virtue of Cordelia to perish in a just cause, contrary to the

natural ideas of justice, to the hope of the reader, and what is yet more strange, to the faith of chronicles [since Cordelia survives her father in all the versions of the story prior to Shakespeare's drama]. Yet this conduct is justified by the Spectator [a contemporary periodical, and specifically an article by its editor, Joseph Addison, author of the drama *Cato*], who blames Tate for giving Cordelia success and happiness in his alteration, and declares that, in his opinion, the tragedy has lost half its beauty. [John] Dennis has remarked, whether justly or not, that, to secure the favourable reception of Cato, the town was poisoned with much false and abominable criticism, and that endeavours had been used to discredit and decry poetical justice [the doctrine that in the end virtue must always be rewarded and vice punished]. A play in which the wicked prosper, and the virtuous miscarry, may doubtless be good, because it is a just representation of the common events of human life: but since all reasonable beings naturally love justice, I cannot easily be persuaded, that the observation of justice makes a play worse; or, if other excellencies are equal, the audience will not always rise better pleased for the final triumph of persecuted virtue.

In the present case the publick has decided. Cordelia, from the time of Tate, has always retired with victory and felicity. And, if my sensations could add any thing to the general suffrage [the vote in favour of Tate's adaptation of *King Lear*], I might relate, that I was many years ago so shocked by Cordelia's death, that I know not whether I ever endured to read again the last scenes of the play till I undertook to revise them as an editor.

As the eighteenth century drew to an end, however, the critical climate was beginning to shift. In an essay that appeared in *The Mirror* (London, 1780) fifteen years after the publication of Johnson's Shakespeare, Henry Mackenzie proclaimed that

Shakespeare's genius attended him in all his extravagancies. In the licence he took of departing from the regularity of the drama [the 'unities' of time, place, and action], or in his ignorance of those critical rules which might have restrained him within it, there is this advantage, that it gives him an opportunity of delineating the passions and affections of the human mind, as they exist in reality, with all the various colourings which they receive in the mixed scenes of life; not as they are accommodated by the hands of more artificial poets, to one great undivided impression, or an uninterrupted chain of congenial events. It seems therefore preposterous, to endeavour to regularize his plays at the expence of depriving them of this peculiar excellence, especially as the alteration can only produce a very partial and limited improvement, and can never bring his pieces to the standard of

> criticism, or the form of the Aristotelian drama. Within the bounds of a pleasure-garden, we may be allowed to smooth our terraces and trim our hedge-rows; but it were equally absurd as impracticable, to apply the minute labours of the roller and the pruning-knife, to the noble irregularity of trackless mountains and impenetrable forests.

Three decades later, in his essay 'On Shakespeare's Tragedies' (London, 1808), Charles Lamb carried Mackenzie's observations a step further. Lamb argued that, because of its untamed wildness, its extraordinary appeals to the imagination,

> the Lear of Shakespeare cannot be acted. The contemptible machinery by which [theatre professionals] mimic the storm which he goes out in, is not more inadequate to represent the horrors of the real elements, than any actor can be to represent Lear: they might more easily propose to personate the Satan of Milton upon a stage, or one of Michael Angelo's terrible figures. The greatness of Lear is not in corporal dimension, but in intellectual: the explosions of his passion are terrible as a volcano: they are storms turning up and disclosing to the bottom that sea his mind, with all its vast riches. It is his mind which is laid bare. This case of flesh and blood seems too insignificant to be thought on; even as he himself neglects it. On the stage we see nothing but corporal infirmities and weakness, the impotence of rage; while we read it, we see not Lear, but we are Lear, – we are in his mind, we are sustained by a grandeur which baffles the malice of daughters and storms; in the aberrations of his reason, we discover a mighty irregular power of reasoning, immethodized from the ordinary purposes of life, but exerting its powers, as the wind blows where it listeth, at will upon the corruptions and abuses of mankind. What have looks, or tones, to do with that sublime identification of his age with that of the heavens themselves, when in his reproaches to them for conniving at the injustice of his children, he reminds them that 'they themselves are old'? What gesture shall we appropriate to this? What has the voice or the eye to do with such things? But the play is beyond all art, as the tamperings with it show: it is too hard and stony; it must have love-scenes and a happy ending. It is not enough that Cordelia is a daughter, she must shine as a lover too. Tate has put his hook in the nostrils of this Leviathan, for Garrick and his followers, the showmen of the scene, to draw the mighty beast about more easily. A happy ending! – as if the living martyrdom that Lear had gone through – the flaying of his feelings alive, did not make a fair dismissal from the stage of life the only decorous thing for him. If he is to live and be happy after, if he could sustain this world's burden after, why all this pudder and preparation, – why torment us with all this unnecessary sympathy? As if the childish pleasure of getting his gilt

> robes and sceptre again could tempt him to act over again his misused station, – as if at his years, and with his experience, anything was left but to die.

A contemporary, William Hazlitt, shared Lamb's admiration for *King Lear*. In *Characters of Shakespear's Plays* (London, 1817), Hazlitt admitted that

> ... To attempt to give a description of the play itself or of its effect upon the mind, is mere impertinence: yet we must say something. – It is then the best of all Shakespear's plays, for it is the one in which he was the most in earnest. He was here fairly caught in the web of his own imagination. The passion which he has taken as his subject is that which strikes its root deepest into the human heart; of which the bond is the hardest to be unloosed; and the cancelling and tearing to pieces of which gives the greatest revulsion to the frame. This depth of nature, this force of passion, this tug and war of the elements of our being, this firm faith in filial piety, and the giddy anarchy and whirling tumult of the thoughts at finding this prop failing it, the contrast between the fixed, immoveable basis of natural affection, and the rapid, irregular starts of imagination, suddenly wrenched from all its accustomed holds and resting-places in the soul, this is what Shakespear has given, and what nobody else but he could give ...

In the same year John Keats expressed similar sentiments in a letter to two of his relatives: 'The excellence of every Art is its intensity, capable of making all disagreeables evaporate, from their being in close relationship with Beauty & Truth – Examine King Lear – you will find this exemplified throughout.'

Shortly thereafter (in 1818) Keats wrote a sonnet 'On Sitting Down to Read *King Lear* Once Again':

> O golden tongued Romance, with serene Lute!
>   Fair plumed Syren, Queen of far-away!
>   Leave us melodizing on this wintry day,
> Shut up thine olden pages, and be mute:
> Adieu! for, once again, the fierce dispute
>   Betwixt damnation and impassion'd clay
>   Must I burn through; once more humbly assay
> The bitter-sweet of this Shakespearian fruit:
> Chief Poet! and ye clouds of Albion,
>   Begetters of our deep eternal theme!
> When through the old oak Forest I am gone,
>   Let me not wander in a barren dream,
> But, when I am consumed in the fire
> Give me new Phoenix wings to fly at my desire.

The greatest of the Romantic critics was Samuel Taylor Coleridge. In his *Lectures and Notes on Shakspere* (London, 1818), the author of 'The Ancient Mariner' observed that

> It was not without forethought, nor is it without its due significance, that the division of Lear's kingdom is in the first six lines of the play stated as a thing already determined in all its particulars, previously to the trial of professions . . . The strange, yet by no means unnatural, mixture of selfishness, sensibility, and habit of feeling derived from, and fostered by, the particular rank and usages of the individual; – the intense desire of being intensely beloved, – selfish, and yet characteristic of the selfishness of a loving and kindly nature alone; – the self-supportless leaning for all pleasures on another's breast; – the cravings after sympathy with a prodigal disinterestedness, frustrated by its own ostentation, and the mode and nature of its claims; – the anxiety, the distrust, the jealousy, which more or less accompany all selfish affections, and are amongst the surest contradistinctions of mere fondness from true love, and which originate Lear's eager wish to enjoy his daughter's violent professions, whilst the inveterate habits of sovereignty convert the wish into claim and positive right, and an incompliance with it into crime and treason; – these facts, these passions, these moral verities, on which the whole tragedy is founded, are all prepared for, and will to the retrospect be found implied, in these first four or five lines of the play. They let us know that the trial is but a trick; and that the grossness of the old king's rage is in part the natural result of a silly trick suddenly and most unexpectedly baffled and disappointed.

Coleridge asserted that

> In Lear old age is itself a character, – its natural imperfections being increased by life-long habits of receiving a prompt obedience. Any addition of individuality would have been unnecessary and painful; for the relations of others to him, of wondrous fidelity and of frightful ingratitude, alone sufficiently distinguish him. Thus Lear becomes the open and ample play-room of nature's passions.

But Coleridge saved his most eloquent praise for the storm scenes and their aftermath.

> O, what a world's convention of agonies is here! All external nature in a storm, all moral nature convulsed, – the real madness of Lear, the feigned madness of Edgar, the babbling of the Fool, the desperate fidelity of Kent – surely such a scene was never conceived before or since! Take it but as a picture for the eye only, it is more terrific than

> any which a Michel Angelo, inspired by a Dante, could have conceived, and which none but a Michel Angelo could have executed. Or let it have been uttered to the blind, the howlings of nature would seem converted into the voice of conscious humanity. This scene ends with the first symptoms of positive derangement; and the intervention of the fifth scene is particularly judicious, – the interruption allowing an interval for Lear to appear in full madness in the sixth scene.
>
> How beautifully the affecting return of Lear to reason, and the mild pathos of these speeches prepare the mind for the last sad, yet sweet, consolation of the aged sufferer's death!

Across the Atlantic, an American editor, H. N. Hudson, focused on the ethical patterns in *King Lear*. In his *Lectures on Shakespeare* (New York, 1848), Hudson noted that

> As, in actual life, men in the exercise of present virtues often incur the evils consequent upon their former vices; so, in Lear, the perverse self-willed habit of preferring lip-service and glib-tongued flattery to silent obedience, as a test of love, is visited upon him in the hypocrisy and ingratitude of his daughters; and, in Gloster, the vices of his youth and his criminal levity in talking about them, are visited upon him in the light-hearted, gamesome treachery and subtlety of his natural son. Yet both the sufferers are justly represented as men 'more sinned against than sinning.' For here again, as in actual life, the vices of some are the occasion of still greater vices in others; while, as if to cut off all excuse from the more vicious, the same occasion is seen ministering to the noblest and loveliest virtue; the goodness of Cordelia and Edgar being only tried and purified by the self-same causes that operate to deprave Goneril, Regan, and Edmund . . .
>
> There is no accounting for the conduct of Goneril and Regan but by supposing a thorough fiendishness of nature, a very instinct and impulse of malignity . . . Selfishness reigns in them to such an extent as to make all objects seem equidistant from self; and Edmund is the only person in the play who is wicked enough and energetic enough in his wickedness, to interest their feelings. It is difficult to think of them otherwise than merely as instruments of the plot; not so much ungrateful persons as personifications of ingratitude.

For Edward Dowden, however, Cordelia's older sisters were 'distinguishable'. In *Shakspere: A Critical Study of His Mind and Art* (London, 1875), Dowden observed that

> Regan is a smaller, shriller, fiercer, more eager piece of malice. The tyranny of the elder sister is a cold, persistent pressure, as little affected by tenderness or scruple as the action of some crushing hammer; Regan's ferocity is more unmeasured, and less abnormal or

monstrous. Regan would avoid her father, and, while she confronts him alone, quails a little as she hears the old man's curse pronounced against her sister:

> O the blest gods! so will you wish on me
> When the rash mood is on.

Writing in the same year as Dowden, Francis Jacox pointed to an interesting connection between Lear's initial and final moments. In *Shakespeare Diversions* (New York, 1875) Jacox asked:

> Has any one ever observed, I wonder, – or did Shakespeare himself consciously intend, – a painful analogy, but by contrast, between this Never of Lear's in the last scene of the last act, and another (quite other) Never of his, in the first of the first? When, in his turbulent wrath at her lack of demonstrative affection, and her resolute abstinence from her sisters' hyperbole of adulation, Lear dismisses Cordelia to a foreign home, it is in these resentfully implacable words:
>
> Thou hast got her, France: let her be thine; for we
> Have no such daughter, nor shall ever see
> That face of hers again.
>
> So raged the exasperated father in his pride of power. But he was to see that face of hers again. It was to be the first face he should see, and know, on recovering from delirium – when all else that were near of kin to him, had proved themselves less than kind, and, having stripped him of all, were banded together against him . . .

For Algernon Charles Swinburne, any search for a tragedy to compare with *King Lear* required a return to the Athens of classical antiquity. In *A Study of Shakespeare* (London, 1876), Swinburne said that

> Of all Shakespeare's plays, *King Lear* is unquestionably that in which he has come nearest to the height and to the likeness of the one tragic poet on any side greater than himself whom the world in all its ages has ever seen born of time. It is by far the most Aeschylean of his works; the most elemental and primaeval, the most oceanic and Titanic in conception . . .
>
> . . . in this the most terrible work of human genius it is with the very springs and sources of nature that her student has set himself to deal. The veil of the temple of our humanity is rent in twain. Nature herself, we might say, is revealed – and revealed as unnatural. In face of such a world as this a man might be forgiven who should pray that chaos might come again.

To Bernhard ten Brink, however, 'the most profound' of

Shakespeare's tragedies, the one that confronts us with the most 'remorseless truth', was not a work that denied the existence of 'a Providence'. In his *Five Lectures on Shakespeare* (translated into English by Julia Franklin and published in London in 1895), ten Brink says that the 'miracle' of *King Lear*

> consists in this: that in misery human fortitude is best developed, that virtue, like a lovely lily, springs forth out of the common slough of depravity. Gloucester only learns to know in his wretchedness the true worth of man and of life, and Lear then first experiences what love means. The optimism which the poet does not renounce even in 'Lear' is of a purely ethical nature; he appeals to our conscience. In loud tones he preaches the duty of resigned endurance, of manly steadfastness, of strenuous moral conduct; he makes us feel how the good, totally regardless of any outward success, is in itself a thing most real, to be striven for above all other things. He strengthens our faith in virtue and incites us to it in figures like that of Kent, and, above all, in the gracious and lofty figure of Cordelia; he animates us with hope in the eventual triumph of the good in this world in the fortunes of Edgar.
>
> The picture of the world which Shakespeare presents to us is illuminated in one way in his tragedy, and in another in his comedy; the deeply religious spirit of the artist is apparent in both – a religiousness whose root and essence lie in his moral sense, and which, therefore, does not need to shut its eyes to unpleasant facts. Shakespeare loves life and is penetrated with a sense of its high worth, but yet, like Schiller, he is convinced that life is not the highest good, and he knows that no one can be pronounced happy before his death. To him the best thing on earth is love – self-sacrificing, active; and he feels that it is infinite love which pervades and animates the universe.

In his great study *Shakespearean Tragedy* (London, 1904), A. C. Bradley acknowledged that

> . . . *King Lear*, as a whole, is imperfectly dramatic, and there is something in its very essence which is at war with the senses, and demands a purely imaginative realisation. It is therefore Shakespeare's greatest work, but it is not what Hazlitt called it, the best of his plays; and its comparative unpopularity is due, not merely to the extreme painfulness of the catastrophe, but in part to its dramatic defects, and in part to a failure in many readers to catch the peculiar effects to which I have referred, – a failure which is natural because the appeal is made not so much to dramatic perception as to a rarer and more strictly poetic kind of imagination . . .
>
> . . . The very first words of the drama, as Coleridge pointed out, tell

us that the division of the kingdom is already settled in all its details, so that only the public announcement of it remains. Later we find that the lines of division have already been drawn on the map of Britain (l. 38), and again that Cordelia's share, which is her dowry, is perfectly well known to Burgundy, if not to France (ll. 197, 245). That then which is censured as absurd, the dependence of the division on the speeches of the daughters, was in Lear's intention a mere form, devised as a childish scheme to gratify his love of absolute power and his hunger for assurances of devotion. And this scheme is perfectly in character. We may even say that the main cause of its failure was not that Goneril and Regan were exceptionally hypocritical, but that Cordelia was exceptionally sincere and unbending . . .

There is a further point, which seems to have escaped the attention of Coleridge and others. Part of the absurdity of Lear's plan is taken to be his idea of living with his three daughters in turn. But he never meant to do this. He meant to live with Cordelia, and with her alone. The scheme of his alternate monthly stay with Goneril and Regan is forced on him at the moment by what he thinks the undutifulness of his favourite child . . .

Having illustrated that 'The improbabilities in *King Lear* . . . far surpass those of the other great tragedies in number and in grossness', Bradley then asked:

How is it . . . that this defective drama so overpowers us that we are either unconscious of its blemishes or regard them as almost irrelevant? As soon as we turn to this question we recognise, not merely that *King Lear* possesses purely dramatic qualities which far outweigh its defects, but that its greatness consists partly in imaginative effects of a wider kind. And, looking for the sources of these effects, we find among them some of those very things which appeared to us dramatically faulty or injurious. Thus, to take at once two of the simplest examples of this, that very vagueness in the sense of locality which we have just considered, and again that excess in the bulk of the material and the number of figures, events and movements, while they interfere with the clearness of vision, have at the same time a positive value for imagination. They give the feeling of vastness, the feeling not of a scene or particular place, but of a world; or, to speak more accurately, of a particular place which is also a world.

But it was the tragedy's ethical and spiritual resonance that engaged Bradley's attention most fully.

. . . There is nothing more noble and beautiful in literature than Shakespeare's exposition of the effect of suffering in reviving the greatness and eliciting the sweetness of Lear's nature . . . Should we not be at least as near the truth if we called this poem *The Redemption of King Lear*, and declared that the business of 'the gods' with him was neither to torment him, nor to teach him a 'noble anger', but to lead him to attain through apparently hopeless failure the very end and aim of life? One can believe that Shakespeare had been tempted at times to feel misanthropy and despair, but it is quite impossible that he can have been mastered by such feelings at the time when he produced this conception.

... The parallel between Lear and Gloster ... is, up to a certain point, so marked that it cannot possibly be accidental. Both are old white-haired men (III.vii.37); both, it would seem, widowers, with children comparatively young. Like Lear, Gloster is tormented, and his life is sought, by the child whom he favours; he is tended and healed by the child whom he has wronged. His sufferings, like Lear's, are partly traceable to his own extreme folly and injustice, and, it may be added, to a selfish pursuit of his own pleasure. His sufferings, again like Lear's, purify and enlighten him; he dies a better and wiser man than he showed himself at first ... And finally, Gloster dies almost as Lear does.

Two years after Bradley pronounced *King Lear* 'Shakespeare's greatest work', the *Fortnightly Review* (1906) published an English translation of Russian novelist Leo Tolstoy's intemperate attack on what he referred to as 'the pompous, characterless language' of the tragedy. But Tolstoy didn't limit his criticism to the play's verbal texture; he also focused on the preposterousness of its plot.

For any man of our time – if he were not under the hypnotic suggestion that this drama is the height of perfection – it would be enough to read it to its end (were he to have sufficient patience for this) in order to be convinced that, far from being the height of perfection, it is a very bad, carelessly composed production, which, if it could have been of interest to a certain public at a certain time, cannot evoke amongst us anything but aversion and weariness. Every reader of our time who is free from the influence of suggestion will also receive exactly the same impression from all the other extolled dramas of Shakespeare, not to mention the senseless dramatised tales, *Pericles*, *Twelfth Night*, *The Tempest*, *Cymbeline*, *Troilus and Cressida*.

The most forceful reply to Tolstoy came from George Orwell. In *Shooting an Elephant and Other Essays* (London, 1945), Orwell suggested that one reason for Tolstoy's animus against Shakespeare, and against *King Lear* in particular, was that, in a way that painfully echoed Lear's story, the Count in old age had 'renounced his estate, his title and his copyrights, and made an attempt – a sincere attempt, though it was not successful – to escape from his privileged position and live the life of a peasant'. Unfortunately, again like Lear, Tolstoy 'acted on mistaken motives and failed to get the results he had hoped for'. According to Orwell:

> Shakespeare starts by assuming that to make yourself powerless is to invite an attack. This does not mean that *everyone* will turn against you (Kent and the Fool stand by Lear from first to last), but in all probability *someone* will. If you throw away your weapons, some less scrupulous person will pick them up. If you turn the other cheek, you will get a harder blow on it than you got on the first one. This does not always happen, but it is to be expected, and you ought not to complain if it does happen. The second blow is, so to speak, part of the act of turning the other cheek. First of all, therefore, there is the vulgar common-sense moral drawn by the Fool: 'don't relinquish power, don't give away your lands.' But there is also another moral. Shakespeare never utters it in so many words, and it does not very much matter whether he was fully aware of it. It is contained in the story, which after all, he made up, or altered to suit his purposes. It is: 'Give away your lands if you want to, but don't expect to gain happiness by doing so. Probably you won't gain happiness. If you live for others, you must live *for others*, and not as a roundabout way of getting an advantage for yourself.'

Another famous writer turned his attention to *King Lear* in 1913. In 'The Theme of the Three Caskets', later published in his *Complete Psychological Works* (London, 1958), Sigmund Freud suggested that the three daughters in *King Lear* correspond to the three caskets in *The Merchant of Venice*, and by extension to the three sisters in the Cinderella story and to the three goddesses Paris has to choose between when it falls to the shepherd on Mount Ida to award a golden apple 'To the Fairest'.

Freud observed that the 'paleness' that moves Bassanio to 'more than eloquence' and induces him to choose the dull, lead casket in III.ii of *The Merchant of Venice* is a dumbness (an undemonstrative quietude) like that of Cordelia in *King Lear*, 'who "loves and is silent"'. Freud then pointed out that in many fairy tales 'dumbness is to be understood as representing death'.

> These indications would lead us to conclude that the third one of the sisters between whom the choice is made is a dead woman. But she

may be something else as well – namely, Death itself, the Goddess of Death . . . But if the third of the sisters is the Goddess of Death, the sisters are known to us. They are the Fates, the Moerae, the Parcae or the Norns, the third of whom is called Atropos, the inexorable . . .

Lear is an old man. It is for this reason . . . that the three sisters appear as his daughters. The relationship of a father to his children, which might be a fruitful source of many dramatic situations, is not turned to further account in the play. But Lear is not only an old man: he is a dying man. In this way the extraordinary premiss of the division of his inheritance loses all its strangeness. But the doomed man is not willing to renounce the love of women; he insists on hearing how much he is loved. Let us now recall the moving final scene, one of the culminating points of tragedy in modern drama. Lear carries Cordelia's dead body on to the stage. Cordelia is Death. If we reverse the situation it becomes intelligible and familiar to us. She is the Death-goddess who, like the Valkyrie in German mythology, carries away the dead hero from the battlefield. Eternal wisdom, clothed in the primaeval myth, bids the old man renounce love, choose death and make friends with the necessity of dying . . .

. . . We might argue that what is represented here are the three inevitable relations that a man has with a woman – the woman who bears him, the woman who is his mate and the woman who destroys him; or that they are the three forms taken by the figure of the mother in the course of a man's life – the mother herself, the beloved one who is chosen after her pattern, and lastly the Mother Earth who receives him once more. But it is in vain that an old man yearns for the love of woman as he had it first from his mother; the third of the Fates alone, the silent Goddess of Death, will take him into her arms.

A few years later, in *Shakspere's Silences* (Cambridge, Mass., 1929), Alwin Thaler noted that

Professor Bradley complains that we are left 'in ignorance' as to the fate of the fool – that is to say, he objects to the fact that immediately after the storm the fool is allowed (according to his last words in the play) ' "to go to bed at noon" as though he felt he had taken his death,' without further or more explicit comment upon Shakspere's part. But to have made too much of the fool's death – if, indeed, he does die – would have been to ignore essential human as well as dramatic distinctions . . . The end must belong to Cordelia. The fool disappears long before, because he has done his work. He has outjested his master's heartstruck injuries in the storm, but he has been a bitter fool withal, a pestilent gall to Lear. Cordelia brings true healing, and so the fool, his occupation gone, disappears. So far as we know, he is faithful to the end – even though his last speech may be, after all, merely a jest to cap Lear's immediately preceding 'We'll go to supper i' the morning.' In any case, Shakspere probably remembered that he had on his hands not a second Mercutio but a much-loved fool slightly touched in the brain. Perhaps he purposely allowed the fool to drop quietly out of sight because he also remembered that there was another person of the play who *must* go to bed at noon – Cordelia, a daughter and a queen.

In 'The Occasion of *King Lear*' (*Studies in Philology*, 1937), John W. Draper directed attention back to the political implications of the tragedy. He observed that

On the accession of the King in 1603, the company for which Shakespeare was the chief playwright had become the 'King's Men'; and so Shakespeare, in effect, had commenced court dramatist; and only a short time later, in *Macbeth*, he had celebrated the patriotic fervor and the timely popularity of the King that followed on the discovery of the Gunpowder Plot. Years before, in the epilogue of *King Richard III*, he had emphasized the calamities that must arise from rival kings in England: surely, when this theme was paramount in the national consciousness, when the King himself had cited Chronicle history as evidence, a court dramatist, whose company must depend directly on the favor of their royal patron to protect them from the growing attacks of the Puritans – surely such a dramatist, endowed with the shrewdness and sagacity of William Shakespeare, might well develop this same theme in a play that showed the audience the miseries that such a division brought to the king, to the dynasty and so to the whole nation . . .

According to Holinshed, and obviously in Shakespeare, Lear is King of all Britain: the play refers to a 'British man,' the 'British powers' as opposed to France, and the quarto of 1608 to the 'British party.' The dividing of Lear's realm is the first action depicted on the stage, and has every appearance of theatrical significance . . .

. . . According to Shakespeare, Lear divided his kingdom into three, and then, after Cordelia's answer, he re-divided her share between the other two, thus leaving two parts in his final division of the realm. Since the island of Great Britain is long and rather narrow north and south, the lines of demarcation must have cut across it east and west, separating it, in the first division, into a southern, a middle, and a northern section. Cordelia's must have been the middle part; for it is later divided between the other two. Thus, in the final division, the two realms of Goneril and of Regan must roughly have corresponded to England and to Scotland. The titles of the respective husbands bear this out . . . Cornwall in ancient times was more extensive than the modern shire; and Lear seems appropriately to have given to this Duke the southern half of his dominions; for Cornwall's capital is the city of Gloucester in the south-central section of the island. Albany,

> then, apparently received the northern half of Britain; and his title at the opening of the play suggests that he was already duke of ancient 'Albany,' the region north of the Firths of Clyde and Forth, including all the Scottish Highlands. Surely the Elizabethans had enough sense of their historical geography to recognize these names. In more recent times, the Dukedom of Albany dates from 1398; and Mary Queen of Scots in the sixteenth century re-created it in the person of Henry Stuart, Lord Darnley, whom she married. Thus when Shakespeare wrote *King Lear*, there was a Duke of Albany, and that Duke was James I . . . Is it this glance at Shakespeare's royal patron that made the playwright change the Albany of Holinshed to a character consistently good and virtuous? Is this why, at the conclusion of the play, the distracted kingdom seems to be happily re-united under his sovereign power?

Two decades later Harry V. Jaffa returned to the same historical context in 'The Limits of Politics: An Interpretation of *King Lear*, Act I, Scene I' (*American Political Science Review*, 1957). Noting, like Draper, 'that Cornwall and Albany represent the geographical extremities of Britain', Jaffa pointed out that

> . . . The selection of sons-in-law from the remote portions of his kingdom indicates . . . that Lear's unification of the kingdom was in part due to his ability to secure the adhesion of the lords of these outlying districts through marriage with the royal house.

That being the case, in the opening scene Lear is seeking, not to abdicate the throne, but to assure the continued stability of the kingdom by means of marriages that will prevent 'future strife'.

> Lear's original plan, I think, called for precisely equal shares to go to Albany and Cornwall, husbands of the two older daughters. But Cordelia was to receive a third 'more opulent' than the other two . . . Cordelia was not only to be situated in the middle, but to have the richest portion of the realm . . . Living on as king with Cordelia, with Albany and Cornwall acting as his deputies in regions which he could not control without their loyalty anyway, does it seem that Lear was giving up anything that he could in any case have kept to himself much longer? . . .
>
> Concerning the marriage of Cordelia, I think the evidence is overwhelming in favor of the view that she was intended as the bride of Burgundy. First, because Lear offers her to Burgundy, although this is after her disinheritance. Second, because Burgundy has had previous knowledge of Cordelia's dowry . . . France and Burgundy were traditional enemies . . . [And] a French marriage would

> inevitably have given rise to the French claims to the British throne, such as actually led to the French invasion that occurs in the play ... On the other hand, however, Cordelia's dowry, added to Burgundy, might have aided the balance of power on the continent. And, conversely, Burgundy, added to Cordelia's part of Britain, would have neutralized any combination of the older sisters ... A Burgundian marriage, in short, would have made the succession of Cordelia to the throne a viable political arrangement. Lear's scheme of marrying Cordelia to Burgundy gave good promise of leading to a stable international system, and a peaceful acceptance of Lear's will and testament at home.

For Harley Granville-Barker, the eminent director, the essence of *King Lear* was not politics but dramatic conflict. In his *Prefaces to Shakespeare* (Princeton, 1946), Granville-Barker emphasized that for a producer of the tragedy

> It will be a fatal error to present Cordelia as a meek saint. She has more than a touch of her father in her. She is as proud as he is, and as obstinate, for all her sweetness and her youth. And, being young, she answers uncalculating with pride to his pride even as later she answers with pity to his misery. To miss this likeness between the two is to miss Shakespeare's first dramatic effect; the mighty old man and the frail child, confronted, and each unyielding ...
>
> ... Shakespeare has provided in this encounter ... that prime necessity of drama, clash of character; that sharpest clash, moreover, of like in opposition to like. He has added wonder and beauty by setting these twin spirits in noble and contrasted habitations. Pride unchecked in Lear has grown monstrous and diseased with his years. In her youth it shows unspoiled, it is in flower. But it is the same pride.

Robert B. Heilman reinforced Granville-Barker's observations in this book *This Great Stage: Image and Structure in 'King Lear'* (Baton Rouge, La., 1948).

> In some respects the relationship between Lear and Cordelia submits easily to definition: Cordelia is the side of Lear capable of tenderness, love, and insight. Yet in Cordelia is the best evidence that ... the children do not become mere allegorical equivalents for isolated parental qualities. For if Cordelia is chiefly the part of Lear which makes him capable of redemption, she also embodies some of his proneness to error ... Lear makes ... a whole series of desperate mistakes, in most of which Cordelia conspicuously does not share ... But Lear's abdication represents a flaw which *is* echoed in Cordelia. For the abdication is a kind of refusal of responsibility, a withdrawal from the necessary involvement in the world of action, and the effect

> of it is to turn the kingdom over to Goneril and Regan. Likewise Cordelia's rejection of Lear's distribution scheme – her nonjurancy, so to speak – is a withdrawal from the immediate world of action, and it leaves the world of action entirely to her sisters. Perhaps her motive is entirely honorable, and there is for her no practical way of mediating between two claims each with its own kind of validity; in that case her situation is roughly analogous to Antigone's. But perhaps in her refusal we are to see something of spiritual pride (of which Lear accuses her in I.i.131).

In his article 'On Shakespeare's Language' (*Sewanee Review*, 1947), John Crowe Ransom focused on a speech in III.iv.

> When Lear finds his Fool beside him in the storm, his thought suddenly turns from his own sufferings to the plight of the poor. It is a kingly thought, and leads him to apostrophize privilege everywhere:
>
> O, I have ta'en
> Too little thought of this. Take physic, pomp;
> Expose thyself to feel what wretches feel,
> That thou mayst shake the superflux to them
> And show the heavens more just.
>
> There is a slight flurry of latinity in the *physic*, *pomp*, *expose*. But the key to this passage is *superflux*, a word that nobody had used till now, and, to tell the truth, a word that even this usage did not fix securely in the language. It would mean overflow; in Schlegel the German is *das Überflüssige*. I judge that we are all reminded more or less consciously of Lazarus begging for the crumbs which fall – without being noticed because there is so much food – from the rich man's table. But I believe we should balk at speaking of them as an overflow. We are not prepared to accept a bolder metaphor in the Latin than we can take in the English. Especially striking is the collocation of *shake* and *superflux*. All we can think of really shaking to the poor in this connection would be the tablecloth holding the surplus crumbs; which would not exactly be flowing. The whole image receives more notice and not less from our having these literal difficulties with it.

O. J. Campbell extended Ransom's kind of exegesis to the entire play. In 'The Salvation of Lear' (*ELH: English Literary History*, 1948), he described *King Lear* as

> a sublime morality play, the action of which is set against a back-drop of eternity. Lear's problem and his career resemble those of the central figure in the typical morality play, who is variously called Genus Humanum, Mankind, or Everyman. And the action of Shakespeare's play is his greatly modified version of man's endless search for true and everlasting spiritual values, rewarded, in this case, by the final

discovery of them just before he must answer Death's awful summons. *The Tragedy of King Lear* differs however from the usual Morality first, in being cast in a much deeper tragic mould and second, in presenting the salvation of Mankind not in orthodox theological terms nor even in strictly Christian terms. For Lear is not so much an erring Christian as a completely unstoical man and he is converted to a state of mind which is a mixture of stoic insight and Christian humility . . .

. . . On his pilgrimage he is accompanied by two companions, and commentators, both of whom are creatures of Cynic-Stoic primitivism and introduced into Elizabethan literature by way of Roman satire. These two are Kent, the stoic plain man, and the Fool, or the wise innocent – each a child of Nature. Kent follows the rules for the proper Cynic behavior, as defined among others by Epictetus; that is, 'the exercise of the right and duty to rebuke evil in others' . . .

In 'The Clothing Motif in *King Lear*' (*Shakespeare Quarterly*, 1954), Thelma N. Greenfield related the allegorical aspects of the play to its imagery of garments and their absence. Citing Erwin Panofsky's *Studies in Iconology* (New York, 1939), Greenfield pointed out that 'in the Biblical and Roman traditions' nudity usually

represented something bad, such as poverty or shamelessness. However, it was also associated with truth – i.e., 'the naked truth' – and so had favorable symbolic meaning too. Medieval theological tradition likewise gave both favorable and unfavorable interpretations . . .

. . . In the Proto-Renaissance, nudity became the conventional representation of ecclesiastical virtues: temperance, fortitude, truth, chastity, etc. Clothing was used for personifications of vain, worldly, passing things. In the fifteenth century this symbolism was brought to a secular level, . . . [Thus Titian's] Profane Love, instead of being a naked Venus, is richly dressed and holds a vessel of jewels; Sacred Love, undraped, bears a vessel of fire. Shakespeare, with his fine eye for double meanings and ironic contrasts, exploited these complexities and contradictions of meaning in employing the motif in *King Lear* . . .

. . . Regan is finely dressed but at the same time partially unclothed, wearing what 'scarce keeps her warm.' Regan's partial nudity reminds us that one of the meanings of nakedness, symbolically, is 'lust, vanity, and absence of all virtues.' . . . The image of 'poor naked wretches' exposed to the storm suggests to Lear a whole world of pitiful suffering of which he heretofore had taken too little heed. This image, soon to be manifested on the stage in the figure of Tom, inspires Lear, through pity, to dissociate himself from the 'lendings' of royalty ... Finally, Tom's physical appearance leads Lear to consider the essence of man and to seek for self-knowledge through identification with the 'thing itself' ...

Lear at the depths of his disillusionment and wretchedness and with the first onset of madness deliberately assumes the symbolic state of the nude figure ... First bareheaded, now plucking off his garments, he achieves the symbolic condition which brings him self-recognition and the way to his salvation. The Christian analogy to Lear's psychological state and its relation to the use of the clothing motif provides familiar overtones. Man, in *Nature*, prepared for his heavenly salvation by casting off his garments.

... When Lear is restored to his senses and to his friends, his new status is accompanied by new garments: 'In the heaviness of sleep / We put fresh garments on him' (IV.vii.21–22); and he notices these clothes very quickly upon his awakening. At his death he reiterates on a quieter note but again physically and verbally the act of divesture: 'Pray you, undo this button' (V.iii.308).

Since the 1950s interpreters of *King Lear* have found it less simple to approach the tragedy as an allegory of redemption. In *'King Lear' and the Gods* (San Marino, Cal., 1966), for example, William R. Elton emphasizes that,

Living before the Christian revelation, as well as outside it, Lear could not know or accept the basic paradox of Creation, that God created the world out of nothing. Thus Shakespeare's ascription to him, expositionally twice mentioned, that nothing could come of nothing, could signify, ambiguously, that Lear was a pagan, although a skeptic from a Christian standpoint; and that, although a pagan, Lear expresses his belief in such terms as might serve to foreshadow disbelief to come.

At the end of the play, as Elton reads it, Lear's

laments against divine providence, his repeated 'why?', his sense of man's reduced place in the scheme of things beneath the lowly animals, his offering of violence to heaven's vault, are in large part motivated by a view that death, excluding Resurrection, ends all. The view of death, which is the premise of the play, implicit in its beginnings, and never contradicted, is by definition a skeptical-pagan, not a Christian, attitude. It thus explains the funereal chorus at the end of the play, which, syncretically, also invokes the Last Judgment (V.iii.263–264), while, at the same time, heathenishly, denies that immortality is possible; here syncretism intensifies Lear's despair, implying the disparity between pagan hopelessness and Christian

> possibility. The pagan attitude in the final scene also disposes of modern contentions that Lear is saved, or that the hope of salvation operates in the denouement. For we have the evidence of a Renaissance English bishop that Lear's attitude was the pagan attitude towards death, with the grief consequent upon an awareness that death ends all; Bishop Jewell admonishes that 'to mourn in such sort as the heathen did we are forbidden. They, as did neither believe in God nor in Christ, so had they no hope of life to come. When a father saw his son dead, he thought he had been *dead for ever*,' as Lear exclaims of his daughter, 'now she's *gone for ever*.'

For Elton, *King Lear* is a play about

> annihilation of faith in poetic justice and, within the confines of a grim, pagan universe, annihilation of faith in divine justice. In this dark world, the last choruses tell us, we find the promised end, or the image of that horror, in which man's chief joy is to be removed from the rack of this tough world and in which man's pathetic solace is – ultimate irony! – the *illusion* that that which he has lost still breathes: 'Look on her, look, her lips, / Look there, look there!' (V.iii.310–311). No redemption stirs at this world's end; only suffering, tears, pity, and loss – *and* illusion.

As Elton deciphers it, the ultimate message of *King Lear*, to borrow a phrase from J. Stampfer ('The Catharsis of *King Lear*', *Shakespeare Survey*, 1960), is 'that we inhabit an imbecile universe'.

Nicholas Brooke comes close to the same conclusion in his essay 'The Ending of *King Lear*' in *Shakespeare 1564–1964*, an anthology edited by Edward A. Bloom (Providence, R.I., 1964).

> My notion – I can do no more than hint it here – is that the play insists on our adjusting to a state of universal disorder, of looking hard at *that*. But while there is no order, nor any wish for one, there are *values*, good as well as evil; but they can have no reference beyond themselves, no ultimate sanctions – they are quite superfluous, in fact. It is the very superfluity which alone is encouraging: without superfluity there would be no hope, only clear sight which is, at once, both necessary and impossible: 'She's dead as earth.' That naked knowledge must be clothed, though to clothe it is to be deluded – 'no cause, no cause' was not true, it was superfluously loving. 'Look on her . . . there, look there' was to look and see what was not. Hope springs eternal: it had better. 'This,' as Swift said, 'is the sublime and refined point of felicity, called, the possession of being well deceived;

the serene peaceful state, of being a fool among knaves.' To recognize that, is to get about as close to *Lear* as most of us can manage.

For Frank Kermode, it is difficult even to affirm that 'All's Cheerless, Dark, and Deadly'. In *The Sense of an Ending* (New York, 1967), Kermode says that

> In *King Lear* everything tends toward a conclusion that does not occur; even personal death, for Lear, is terribly delayed. Beyond the apparent worst there is a worse suffering, and when the end comes it is not only more appalling than anybody expected, but a mere image of horror, not the thing itself. The end is now a matter of immanence; tragedy assumes the figuration of apocalypse, of death and judgment, heaven and hell; but the world goes forward in the hands of exhausted survivors. Edgar haplessly assumes the dignity; only the king's natural body is at rest. This is the tragedy of sempiternity; apocalypse is translated out of time into the *aevum*. The world may, as Gloucester supposes, exhibit all the symptoms of decay and change, all the terrors of an approaching end, but when the end comes it is not an end, and both suffering and the need for patience are perpetual.

Stephen Booth carries Kermode's insights even further. In his essay 'On the Greatness of *King Lear*' in *Twentieth Century Interpretations of 'King Lear'*, a collection edited by Janet Adelman (Englewood Cliffs, N.J., 1978), Booth notes that

> Not ending is a primary characteristic of *King Lear*. The last sixteen lines of the play provide a brief sample of the varieties of inconclusiveness in *Lear*; an audience's experience of them is emblematic of the experience of the whole. The play begins in doubt about who would rule; the three final speeches, a reprise of the division of the kingdom in I.i, leaves us in new doubt about who will rule: Albany? Albany, Kent, and Edgar? Kent and Edgar? Albany and Edgar? Edgar? Other varieties of inconclusiveness are exemplified in Kent's 'I have a journey, sir, shortly to go. / My master calls me; I must not say no.' It makes literally endless the endless succession of inconclusive journeys in *King Lear*; it echoes Kent's banishment in I.i, and that of Cordelia who said *no* . . .
>
> These final speeches are also inconclusive theatrically. After the last speech, the folios provide an urgently necessary stage direction: *Exeunt with a dead march*. This is the only one of the tragedies where the last lines do not point to an immediate off-stage destination and invite the remaining characters to repair to it. The last lines of *King Lear* leave the survivors just to walk off the stage . . .
>
> Even our evaluations of the play are unfixed. Whenever we find fault with something Shakespeare does in *King Lear*, the alternative

turns out to be in some way less acceptable. The plotting of *King Lear* invites adverse criticisms . . . The crowning example, of course, is the end of the play – where we wish events otherwise than they are and where remedy would give more discomfort than the disease. *King Lear* turns out to be faithless to the chronicle accounts of Lear, but its perfidy is sudden; the movement of the plot is toward a happy ending. I expect that every audience has felt the impulses that drove Nahum Tate to give *Lear* its promised end and led Dr Johnson to applaud the deed. But Tate made wholesale changes; after he had strung and polished the treasure he had seiz'd, he had a new 'heap of Jewels' altogether . . . To allow Lear and Cordelia to retire with victory and felicity would be to allow *more* to occur, would be to allow the range of our consideration and of our standards of evaluation to dilate infinitely. It would be a strong man whose natural ideas of justice and hopes for a happy ending could outweigh his more basic need – his simple need of an ending – if, instead of Tate, he had seen Shakespeare.

SUGGESTIONS FOR FURTHER READING

Many of the works quoted in the preceding survey, or excerpts from those works, can be found in modern collections of criticism. Of particular interest are four anthologies:

Adelman, Janet (ed.), *Twentieth Century Interpretations of 'King Lear'*, Englewood Cliffs, N.J., 1978 (17 entries, including the essays quoted above by Stephen Booth and Nicholas Brooke).

Bonheim, Helmut (ed.), *The 'King Lear' Perplex*, Belmont, Cal.: Wadsworth, 1960 (71 entries, including all the items quoted above except for those by Stephen Booth, Nicholas Brooke, and John Keats).

Colie, Rosalie L., and F. T. Flahiff (eds), *Some Facets of 'King Lear': Essays in Prismatic Criticism*, Toronto: University of Toronto Press, 1974.

Muir, Kenneth (ed.), *'King Lear': Critical Essays*, New York: Garland, 1984 (26 entries, including the items quoted above by Samuel Johnson, Charles Lamb, Samuel Taylor Coleridge, William Hazlitt, John Keats, A. C. Bradley, George Orwell, Robert B. Heilman, J. Stampfer, and Nicholas Brooke).

Other studies of Shakespeare that include valuable discussions of *King Lear*:

Battenhouse, Roy, *Shakespearean Tragedy: Its Art and Its Christian Premises*, Bloomington: Indiana University Press, 1969.

Blayney, Peter W. M., *The Texts of 'King Lear' and Their Origins*, Cambridge: Cambridge University Press, 1982.

Booth, Stephen, *'King Lear', 'Macbeth', Indefinition, and Tragedy*, New Haven: Yale University Press, 1983.

Calderwood, James L., *Shakespearean Metadrama*, Minneapolis: University of Minnesota Press, 1971.

Cartwright, Kent, *Shakespearean Tragedy and Its Double: The Rhythms of Audience Response*, University Park: Pennsylvania State University Press, 1991.

Dollimore, Jonathan, *Radical Tragedy: Religion, Ideology, and Power in the Drama of Shakespeare and his Contemporaries*, Brighton: Harvester, 1984.

Empson, William, *The Structure of Complex Words*, London: Chatto & Windus, 1951.

Fraser, Russell A., *Shakespeare's Poetics in Relation to 'King Lear'*, London: Routledge & Kegan Paul, 1962.

Gardner, Helen, *King Lear*, London: London University Press, 1967 (included in the Muir anthology cited above).

Goldberg, S. L., *An Essay on 'King Lear'*, Cambridge: Cambridge University Press, 1974.

Goldman, Michael, *Shakespeare and the Energies of Drama*, Princeton: Princeton University Press, 1972.

Holland, Norman N., *Pyschoanalysis and Shakespeare*, New York: McGraw-Hill, 1966.

Knight, G. Wilson, *The Wheel of Fire*, London: Oxford University Press, 1930.

Knights, L. C., *Some Shakespearean Themes*, London: Chatto & Windus, 1959.

Kott, Jan, *Shakespeare Our Contemporary*, Garden City, N.Y.: Doubleday, 1964.

Mack, Maynard, *'King Lear' in Our Time*, Berkeley: University of California Press, 1965.

Muir, Kenneth (ed.), *Shakespeare Survey*, 33 (1980).

Novy, Marianne, *Love's Argument: Gender Relations in Shakespeare*, Chapel Hill: University of North Carolina Press, 1984.

Ribner, Irving, *Patterns in Shakespearean Tragedy*, London: Methuen, 1960.

Snyder, Susan, '*King Lear* and the Psychology of Dying', *Shakespeare Quarterly*, 33 (1982), 449–60.

Taylor, Gary, and Michael Warren (eds), *The Division of the Kingdoms: Shakespeare's Two Versions of 'King Lear'*, Oxford: Clarendon Press, 1983.

Welsford, Enid, *The Fool: His Social and Literary History*, London: Faber & Faber, 1935.

Whitaker, Virgil K., *The Mirror Up to Nature: The Technique of Shakespeare's Tragedies*, San Marino, Cal.: Huntington Library, 1965.

Background studies and useful reference works:

Abbott, E. A., *A Shakespearian Grammar*, New York: Haskell House, 1972 (information on how Shakespeare's grammar differs from ours).

Allen, Michael J. B., and Kenneth Muir (eds), *Shakespeare's Plays in Quarto: A Facsimile Edition*, Berkeley: University of California Press, 1981.

Andrews, John F. (ed.), *William Shakespeare: His World, His Work, His Influence*, 3 vols, New York: Scribners, 1985 (articles on 60 topics).

Barroll, Leeds, *Politics, Plague, and Shakespeare's Theater*, Ithaca: Cornell University Press, 1992.

Bentley, G. E., *The Profession of Player in Shakespeare's Time, 1590–1642*, Princeton: Princeton University Press, 1984.

Blake, Norman, *Shakespeare's Language: An Introduction*, New York: St Martin's Press, 1983 (general introduction to all aspects of the playwright's language).

Bullough, Geoffrey (ed.), *Narrative and Dramatic Sources of Shakespeare*, 8 vols, New York: Columbia University Press, 1957–75 (printed sources, with helpful summaries and comments by the editor).

Campbell, O. J., and Edward G. Quinn (eds), *The Reader's Encyclopedia of Shakespeare*, New York: Crowell, 1966.

Cook, Ann Jennalie, *The Privileged Playgoers of Shakespeare's London*: Princeton: Princeton University Press, 1981 (argument that theatre audiences at the Globe and other public playhouses were relatively well-to-do).

De Grazia, Margreta, *Shakespeare Verbatim: The Reproduction of Authenticity and the Apparatus of 1790*, Oxford: Clarendon Press, 1991 (interesting material on eighteenth-century editorial practices).

Eastman, Arthur M., *A Short History of Shakespearean Criticism*, New York: Random House, 1968.

Gurr, Andrew, *Playgoing in Shakespeare's London*, Cambridge: Cambridge University Press, 1987 (argument for changing tastes, and for a more diverse group of audiences than Cook suggests).

—— *The Shakespearean Stage, 1574–1642*, 2nd edn, Cambridge: Cambridge University Press, 1981 (theatres, companies, audiences, and repertories).

Hinman, Charlton (ed.), *The Norton Facsimile: The First Folio of Shakespeare's Plays*, New York: Norton, 1968.

Muir, Kenneth, *The Sources of Shakespeare's Plays*, New Haven: Yale University Press, 1978 (a concise account of how Shakespeare used his sources).

Onions, C. T., *A Shakespeare Glossary*, 2nd edn, London: Oxford University Press, 1953.

Partridge, Eric, *Shakespeare's Bawdy*, London: Routledge & Kegan Paul, 1955 (indispensable guide to Shakespeare's direct and indirect ways of referring to 'indecent' subjects).

Schoenbaum, S., *Shakespeare: The Globe and the World*, New York: Oxford University Press, 1979 (lively illustrated book on Shakespeare's world).

—— *Shakespeare's Lives*, 2nd edn, Oxford: Oxford University Press, 1992 (readable, informative survey of the many biographers of Shakespeare, including those believing that someone else wrote the works).

—— *William Shakespeare: A Compact Documentary Life*, New York: Oxford University Press, 1977 (presentation of all the biographical documents, with assessments of what they tell us about the playwright).

Spevack, Marvin, *The Harvard Concordance to Shakespeare*, Cambridge, Mass.: Harvard University Press, 1973.

Wright, George T., *Shakespeare's Metrical Art*, Berkeley: University of California Press, 1988.

PLOT SUMMARY

1.1 In King Lear's palace, the Earls of Kent and Gloucester discuss Lear's division of his kingdom, Britain. Edmund, Gloucester's illegitimate son, is also present.

Lear enters, with his three daughters and the elder two's husbands – Goneril and the Duke of Albany, Regan and the Duke of Cornwall, and Cordelia. Lear asks his daughters to tell him which of them loves him most, so that he can decide what share of the kingdom each deserves. Goneril and Regan declare their unreserved love of their father, but Cordelia explains that while she loves her father, she will also love her husband. Lear, enraged, disinherits Cordelia, and divides the kingdom between her two sisters, granting their husbands the rule of the kingdom in all but title. Kent tries to dissuade him, and is exiled by the King.

The King of France and the Duke of Burgundy, Cordelia's suitors, enter. Burgundy no longer wants to marry her, but France does; he claims her for his wife. Goneril and Regan, left alone on stage, discuss how to manage their unpredictable father.

1.2 In Gloucester's castle, Edmund plans to usurp the place of his elder and legitimate brother, Edgar. Gloucester enters, and Edmund shows him a letter, apparently from Edgar, which asks for Edmund's aid in killing their father. Gloucester is upset and uncertain, wanting more proof of Edgar's treachery. He accepts Edmund's offer to provide it.

Alone, Edmund discusses the influence of the stars on men's actions. Edgar enters, and Edmund warns his elder half-brother that their father is dangerously displeased with him. Edgar leaves to hide in Edmund's room.

1.3 At Albany's residence, Goneril complains at her father's and his retainers' abuse of her hospitality and orders her Steward, Oswald, to show them little respect.

1.4 Elsewhere at Albany's residence, a disguised Kent meets Lear, who agrees to take him into his service. Oswald ignores Lear's command, prompting the King to send one of his men for his daughter.

Lear's fool jests with him. Goneril then arrives and rebukes her father for his retinue's behaviour. Albany enters and attempts to moderate between father and daughter. Lear angrily departs.

1.5 En route to Cornwall's residence, Lear sends Kent with letters to Gloucester.

2.1 At Gloucester's castle, Edmund discusses with a courtier the rumours of a possible war between Cornwall and Albany. When the courtier leaves, Edmund calls Edgar out of hiding and tells him that their father is coming – Edgar must fly. When his father arrives, Edmund describes how Edgar attacked him when he refused to help murder his father. Gloucester resolves to kill his elder son.

Cornwall and Regan arrive, and Gloucester tells them of Edgar's plot. Cornwall, impressed by Edmund's loyalty to his father, takes him into his service.

2.2 Outside Gloucester's castle, Kent, at Cornwall's and Regan's insistence, and against Gloucester's wishes, is put into stocks for trying to make Oswald fight.

Lear arrives later and is enraged to see his messenger in the stocks. He asks to speak to his daughter and son-in-law, who eventually come to see him. Kent is freed. Lear tells Regan of Goneril's behaviour towards him. Goneril arrives. Regan asks Lear to return to Goneril's care for the remaining part of his agreed time of stay. His daughters declare they will only accommodate him, not any of his followers. Lear refuses this offer and leaves the castle as a storm breaks out. Cornwall and Regan tell Gloucester to lock the doors.

3.1 On a barren heath, Kent learns from a gentleman that Lear is running mad in the storm.

3.2 Lear, accompanied by his fool, rages amidst the wind and rain. The Fool urges him to take shelter. Kent arrives, and leads them off towards a hovel.

3.3 Inside his castle, Gloucester tells Edmund that he intends to help Lear, although this has been forbidden. He asks Edmund to divert Cornwall so that his own actions are not noticed. Edmund immediately goes to tell Cornwall what his father intends to do.

3.4 Kent brings Lear, with the Fool, to the hovel. The Fool goes inside only to re-emerge followed by Edgar, disguised as the mad beggar Poor Tom. Gloucester arrives, but Lear will not go with him, wishing to stay with Poor Tom.

3.5 In Gloucester's castle, Edmund has betrayed his father to Cornwall. Cornwall promises to make Edmund Earl of Gloucester, and sends him to find his father.

3.6 Inside the hovel, Lear conducts a mock-trial of his daughters. Gloucester returns with news of a plot to kill the King. He tells Kent to take Lear to Dover.

3.7 In Gloucester's castle, Cornwall asks Goneril, accompanied by Edmund, to take a letter to her husband. After they have left, Gloucester is brought in as a prisoner and questioned by Cornwall and Regan. Cornwall blinds Gloucester, but one of Cornwall's servants – trying to stop his master – wounds him before he himself is slain by Regan. Regan orders that Gloucester be turned out of the castle.

4.1 On the heath, Edgar meets his father, led by an old man. Gloucester asks Poor Tom to lead him to a cliff at Dover.

4.2 Before Albany's residence, Goneril and Edmund are met by Oswald. He tells Goneril that Albany is not pleased with what has happened. Goneril declares her love for Edmund, before sending him to tell Cornwall to hurry his preparations for war. Albany enters, and upbraids Goneril. A messenger arrives with news of Cornwall's death.

4.3 In the camp of the French forces who have landed at Dover, Kent learns from a Gentleman of Cordelia's reaction to news of her father's treatment. Lear is too ashamed to see his daughter. The two men leave to go to the King.

4.4 Elsewhere in the camp, Cordelia orders a search for her father, who has been seen nearby. A messenger brings news of the British forces' approach.

4.5 At Gloucester's castle, Regan asks Oswald to show her Goneril's letter to Edmund, which she suspects may be a declaration of love. When he refuses to do this, she gives Oswald a note of her own to Edmund, whom she also desires to marry.

4.6 Edgar convinces Gloucester that he has jumped off a cliff and been miraculously saved. Lear enters and his voice is recognised by Gloucester. Lear discourses on justice and mortality. A gentleman with attendants arrives to bring Lear to Cordelia. Lear runs away.

Oswald enters, and in going to kill Gloucester is mortally wounded by Edgar. He asks Edgar to bury him and deliver the letters he carries to Edmund.

Edgar reads Goneril's letter. She asks Edmund to murder her husband, so that he can marry her. The drums of battle sound, and Edgar leads Gloucester off.

4.7 At the French camp, Cordelia thanks Kent for his care of her father. Lear, asleep in a chair, is brought in and woken. Cordelia speaks to him, and after a short while he recognises her and asks her forgiveness. Father and daughter walk off-stage.

5.1 Among the British forces near Dover, Edmund is in command of Cornwall's forces. He denies to Regan that he is Goneril's lover. Albany and Goneril enter. Albany declares that he fights against the French and not against Lear or his daughter.

Edgar, still disguised, arrives and speaks privately to Albany. He gives Albany Goneril's letter to Edmund, asking him to read it before the battle, and then leaves.

5.2 On the battlefield, Edgar, still leading Gloucester, learns that Lear's forces have lost.

5.3 At the British camp, Edmund orders Lear and Cordelia to be taken to a prison, and sends a Captain after them with orders to kill them.

Albany enters, with Goneril and Regan, and asks Edmund for Lear and Cordelia. Edmund replies that he has sent them to be guarded. Albany halts Regan's declaration of love for Edmund by charging him with being a traitor. Edmund denies the charge. (Regan, poisoned by Goneril, falls sick and is taken to Albany's tent.) Edgar steps forward to prove the charge against Edmund by combat. He fatally wounds Edmund. Albany confronts Goneril with her letter to Edmund and she leaves.

Edmund, dying, confesses his wrongdoings. Edgar identifies himself, and recounts how, when he finally told his father who he was, Gloucester, overcome by joy and grief, died of a heart attack.

A gentleman enters, bringing news that Regan has died and Goneril killed herself. Kent arrives and asks to be allowed to say farewell to Lear. Albany, recollecting Lear's and Cordelia's plight, asks Edmund exactly where they are. Edmund warns them that he ordered the Captain to hang both of them. They send a gentleman to try to prevent this.

Lear enters with Cordelia dead in his arms. He recognises Kent. Albany gives Lear back the rule of the kingdom. Lear dies, looking upon Cordelia. Albany orders their bodies taken away, and the living leave at a dead march.

ACKNOWLEDGEMENTS

The editor and publishers wish to thank the following for permission to use copyright material.

The University of North Carolina Press for material from John W. Draper, 'The Occasion of *King Lear*', *Studies in Philology*, 34, 2 (April 1937);

Shakespeare Quarterly for material from Thelma N. Greenfield, 'The Clothing Motif in *King Lear*', *Shakespeare Quarterly*, (1954);

Every effort has been made to trace all the copyright holders, but if any have been inadvertently overlooked the publishers will be pleased to make the necessary arrangement at the first opportunity.